WHITEWATER KAYAKING

THE ULTIMATE GUIDE
2nd Edition

by World Champion Ken Whiting
& Kevin Varette

WHITEWATER
KAYAKING THE ULTIMATE GUIDE
2nd Edition

Ken Whiting & Kevin Varette

Photos by Paul Villecourt, Mariann Saether and Tyler Curtis

THE HELICONIA PRESS

Written by: Ken Whiting and Kevin Varette
Photography by: Paul Villecourt, Mariann Saether and Tyler Curtis, except as noted
Design and Layout: Robyn Hader
Edited by: Tim Shuff

ISBN 978-1-896980-73-7

To learn more about the other great books from Fox Chapel Publishing, or to find a retailer near you, call toll-free 800-457-9112 or visit us at *www.FoxChapelPublishing.com*.

Note to Authors: We are always looking for talented authors to write new books. Please send a brief letter describing your idea to Acquisition Editor, 1970 Broad Street, East Petersburg, PA 17520.

Printed in China
First printing

Whitewater kayaking is an activity with inherent risks, and this book is designed as a general guide, not a substitute for formal, professional instruction. The publisher and the author do not take responsibility for the use of any of the materials or methods described in this book. By following any of the procedures described within, you do so at your own risk.

TABLE OF CONTENTS

INTRODUCTION TO KAYAKING

For newcomers to the sport, the first thing to know is that all you need to become a kayaker and to keep improving are a good attitude and a healthy appetite for fun. Contrary to what is commonly believed, this is not just a fringe activity reserved for adrenaline junkies, testosterone-laden extremists, and suicidal risk-takers with nothing to lose. If you're already doing it (in a controlled environment with relatively sane people), you'll probably agree. If not, then it's important that we dispel this myth of extremism at the outset, because it has kept far too many people (young and old) from experiencing the thrill of whitewater kayaking. Let the truth be known that kayaking is PURE FUN! The reality is that you can learn to do it

in a short period of time, and continue doing it safely for as long as you are mobile. Whether you're new to paddling or are already on your way, know that this is something you will enjoy for a long, long time!

For you paddlers, a few words about progression, conceptual understanding, and keeping it fun. One of the most wonderful things about paddling is that it doesn't let up; an endlessly rewarding learning process lies in store for paddlers of all kinds who are keen to take it on. We've dedicated much of our teaching careers to elevating paddlers (actually, to helping paddlers elevate themselves) out of their "intermediate ruts" and into the world of advanced techniques. The foundation is in discovering and truly understanding the concepts upon which the advanced skills are based. From here, it's a matter of practising the right exercises and staying focused on the basics as you push your own personal envelope. Most importantly, however, make your way through this process without expecting to conquer the world in a day! A lifetime of paddling awaits you, and the real measure of success after each paddle is how much fun you had!

The past decade has been full of exciting changes and growth for whitewater paddling. Paralleling its close cousins, skiing and snowboarding, this growth has fuelled technological advances in equipment design, which have made it much easier, more comfortable, and more fun to progress, regardless of your shape or size. While this has led to substantial leaps in terms of what can be done in a kayak, it has also made the sport much easier for beginners to learn. Alongside this progress we are quickly evolving in both the analysis and instruction of techniques and concepts. Kayaking is now an everyday component of phys-ed programs, summer camps, and outdoor clubs. More and more cities around the world are building paddling parks to accommodate the growing interest and demand. It also continues to branch out into increasingly specialized areas including playboating, creek boating, expedition paddling, competitive freestyle, slalom and downriver racing, c-boating, squirt boating, and surf kayaking—all of which we take a look at in this book.

Whitewater kayaking is much more than just a physical activity, though; any paddler you talk to will have their own version of why. However, most would agree that it's an ongoing journey with many incredible discoveries en route. It will in myriad ways challenge you, strengthen you, reward you, connect you, mystify you, and, most importantly, free you. In a shrinking world increasingly characterized by the pressures of industrialized chaos, there's much to be said for pure escapism! The act of kayaking demands 100% of you, so as you focus on your strokes, balance, edging, timing, and the constantly changing river, there is simply no space for intrusions—you are free. No cell phone, no e-mail, no "real world" stressors whatsoever—just you being with the water.

Oh, and the people you'll find yourself surrounded by—well, in our experience, they're okay, too. You may find yourself hanging out with a schoolteacher or a fourteen-year-old student, with a young doctor or a retired farmer, with a mother of three, or maybe someone just like you. The thing is, when you run into one of these people in the real world, whether they know you or not, you share something very special that industrialization can never touch.

So get out there and try it. You will inevitably find that the days that you paddle, the rest of your world seems a little brighter. But be warned—addiction rates are extremely high and we accept no liability for the ensuing consequences!

Ken Whiting

Through the '90s, Ken became one of the most recognized and respected whitewater athletes in the world and was recognized so by *Paddler Magazine* in 2000 as one of their "Paddlers of the Century." Ken was the 1997/98 World Freestyle Kayaking Champion, the 1998 Japan Open Champion, and a five-time National Champion. Since 1998, Ken has written and produced a best-selling and award-winning series of whitewater kayaking instructional books and videos, started an industry leading kayak school, founded the Canadian Freestyle Kayaking Association, Coached the Junior Freestyle Kayaking Team, and produced both the US and Canadian Freestyle Team Trials Events.

...During the summer of 1989, Ken picked up a kayak paddle for the first time. He was fourteen years old at the time, and was taking a five-day kayaking course on the Ottawa River. Little did Ken know that this week of paddling would set the course of his life. Four years later he postponed his plans for university to satisfy his need to pursue his addiction to whitewater kayaking.

In 1994, Ken's competitiveness broke through the surface as he began frequenting, and winning, freestyle competitions across the continent. Three years later, in 1997, he reached his ultimate goal by winning the World Freestyle Kayaking Championships. Winning the World's was a major turning point in Ken's life, as shortly afterwards he made the decision to develop a career within the whitewater industry that he loved so much.

In 1998, Ken wrote and published *The Playboater's Handbook*, a reference for freestyle kayaking technique. Following the great success of the book, Ken teamed up with Chris Emerick, a talented American videographer, and began producing instructional videos.

Since that time, Ken has been one of the most active whitewater professionals in the world. He has produced seven best-selling and award-winning instructional whitewater kayaking books and videos and he regularly appears on the covers and writes articles for virtually every paddling magazine in the world. He co-founded the world renowned Liquid Skills Kayak School in Canada, which led the new school movement of kayak instruction. He also co-founded Kayak Futaleufu, an adventure kayaking travel company with a base camp in Chile's Patagonia region. Ken's various whitewater projects have taken him to over 200 different rivers in fifteen different countries, including Japan, Honduras, Guatemala, Chile, Peru, Argentina, New Zealand, and Australia, as well as throughout Europe and North America.

Nowadays, Ken, his beloved wife Nicole, and their dog Jake live in the small, rural town of Beachburg only minutes from the put-in to the Ottawa River.

Kevin Varette

Originally from Ottawa, Ontario, Kevin Varette currently lives with his family just a short walk from the rapids of the Ottawa River, where he grew up paddling from the age of fourteen. He is one of Canada's foremost kayak instructors and a founding partner of both Liquid Skills Kayak School and the Kayak Futaleufu adventure travel company.

A five-time member of Canada's National Freestyle Team, with the top Canadian finish at the 2001 World Championships in Spain, Kevin combines a unique capacity for working with others with world-class skills and experience. He has paddled, competed, and guided around the globe, including the U.S., Central America, South America, Africa, New Zealand, and Australia.

Kevin initiated a coaching program for Canada's juniors in 2001, has sat as Freestyle Chair for Whitewater Ontario, has taught countless volunteer clinics, has written many instructional articles and has contributed to the sport in myriad ways throughout his career. Along with his fiancée, Tagget, and children, Noa, Lucie, and Finn, Kevin plans on remaining a fixture in the Ottawa River Valley for the foreseeable future.

Outside of kayaking, he has a degree in psychology, a diploma in Adventure Tourism, a certificate in Life Coaching, a master's degree in Physiotherapy and several certifications in mountain guiding. While he now practises a day job as a physiotherapist, kayaking has been a fundamental part of his life and his passion is to share everything the sport has to offer with as many people as he can.

CONTRIBUTORS

TYLER CURTIS

An Ottawa River local, Tyler sure knows how to throw down. As a four-time Canadian National Champion, he has been a major influence in the international freestyle scene for many years. He has been on the national freestyle team for ten years and has no intention of quitting anytime soon.

Not only a veteran playboater, he is also one of the best all-round kayakers in the world. Tyler spends as much time running Class 5, dropping waterfalls, and throwing himself into big water as anyone. He has spent the last three summers exploring and roaming the Norwegian rivers with Mariann as well as continuing to spend a few months on the Rio Futaleufu. He is the author of *Futaleufu Whitewater* and enjoys giving back by getting youngsters involved in the sport that has given him so much.

PHIL DERIEMER

Phil DeRiemer is a renowned whitewater professional, with over twenty years of experience teaching, guiding, and exploring from a kayak. For four of those years he lived between rivers, his truck and a storage shed. This itinerant lifestyle made him an obvious choice to write the section about self-contained trips. His knowledge and experience on the topic stems from numerous self-contained adventures including a traverse of Baffin Island, Peru's Paucartambo River, an early self-supported trip on the Grand Canyon of the Stikine, and explorations in the Sierra Nevada mountains near his home in California. He and his wife Mary are owners of DeRiemer Adventure Kayaking, offering kayaking trips in the US and abroad: www.adventurekayaking.com.

PAUL VILLECOURT

Paul Villecourt is a French photographer and whitewater paddler who is dedicated to capturing the sensations of adventure and outdoor sports. His passion for whitewater has taken him and his camera to all corners of the world. Paul is regarded as one of the finest whitewater photographers in the world and his work has been published in virtually every outdoor magazine in Europe and North America. For more info, visit www.outdoor-reporter.com

MARIANN SAETHER

Mariann has paddled since the age of seventeen and has since paddled on all continents and in more than thirty countries. As a five-time Norwegian National Champion she is an accomplished freestyle kayaker who has participated in three World Championships and places in top positions in competitions around the world.

Her heart and soul lies in running rivers, and you will see her enjoying a beautiful Class 3 river one day and picking lines on a Class 5 the next. Next to her home country of Norway she calls Chile home, where she and Tyler have built a cabin on the shore of the Futaleufu River.

DUNBAR HARDY

Dunbar Hardy is well-known freelance photographer and writer focused within the paddlesports industry with over fifteen years' worth of articles/photos published in national and international publications. He has also held the position of Senior Editor for and magazines. Dunbar is also recognized as one of the most experienced and accomplished expedition paddlers/leaders in the world. He has successfully completed first descents and paddling expeditions throughout Colorado and the United States, as well as in such exotic places as Bhutan, Russia, Morocco, China, Mexico, Honduras, Guatemala, Costa Rica, Panama, Venezuela, Ecuador, Peru, Chile, Argentina, New Zealand, Italy, France, Switzerland, and Canada. He is also a co-owner/lead instructor of Tarkio Kayak Adventures (www.teamtarkio.com) based in Missoula, Montana, which offers domestic and international multi-day instructional kayaking clinics. To catch up on Dunbar's latest adventures, or to view his writing/photography, go to www.dunbarhardy.com.

ANNA LEVESQUE

Anna Levesque, founder of Girls at Play LLC, has a passion for inspiring and teaching women through her Girls at Play workshops, instructional kayaking DVDs and books for women, her Girls at Play Summer Tour and her Girls at Play paddling and yoga vacations in Mexico. She is a World Kayak Freestyle Medalist and a five-time Canadian Kayak Freestyle Team member with female first descents in California and on the White Nile River in Uganda. She has worked in over ten countries as a professional kayaker and guide. Anna currently teaches most of her workshops at the Nantahala Outdoor Center in North Carolina. For more information on Anna and Girls at Play please visit www.whitewatergoddess.com

PAUL MASON

Paul Mason is the son and former paddling partner of the late Bill Mason. Paul is a die hard openboater and hopes his paddling buddies will still speak to him after drawing all these kayaks. As a freelance cartoonist, Paul has created artwork for a variety of applications including: educational posters, comic strips, editorial cartoons, murals, books and his popular personal commemorative cartoons. See more of Paul's work at www.redcanoes.ca

BRENDAN MARK

As the 2003 World Squirtboating Champion, and a long-time kayaking instructor, Brendan Mark was the obvious choice to write the squirtboating segment of this book. Brendan has also been an innovator of whitewater kayaking instructional techniques, introducing squirtboats as a highly effective means for teaching general paddling and playboating techniques. Although he still logs a large number of river days, Brendan recently settled down with his wife Lauren on the banks of the Ottawa River in Beachburg Ontario, where he works as the Sales and Marketing Director of The Heliconia Press. www.helipress.com

GETTING STARTED

Because whitewater kayaking is a technical sport with specialized equipment and some inherent risks, we highly recommend learning through a reputable kayak school or club. There are too many stories of people going out for their first time with friends and getting scared or frustrated when they should really be leaving that experience craving the next, and confident in their ability to succeed. This book provides you with the most cutting edge instructional techniques and concepts that will serve as invaluable references as you progress, but it's not a replacement for on-water instruction. There's no shortage of kayak schools, paddling clubs, associations, and organizations available to help get you started. By using the Internet, asking at retail stores, or even going to a local river, you should have no trouble getting going on the right path.

EQUIPMENT

1

Like many outdoor sports, kayaking requires an initial investment of specialized equipment, and there are retail stores, outfitters, and on-line forums packed with stuff to sell you. In terms of performance, your boat and paddle are the two key pieces of gear to make informed decisions about. The rest of the gear is to keep you safe, comfortable, and functional. In general, though, you are best off to try out whatever equipment you can before buying.

THE KAYAK

The days of long, skinny kayaks shaped like logs with a hole carved into the top of them are gone, and along with them the performance characteristics that a log offers! Boat design is now a sophisticated process that makes use of professional designers, athletes, flashy software packages with digital simulations, and multi-prototype trial runs. Today's boats are shorter (from 1.5 m to 3 m, or 5 ft to 9 ft), wider (about 40 cm, or 25 in), flat-hulled, and far more thoroughly outfitted than their predecessors. These fundamental changes have afforded the paddler substantially increased manoeuvrability, stability, and control.

Let's start by taking a quick look at the terminology used to describe the characteristics of a kayak.

Hull and deck: The bottom and top of the kayak.

Bow and stern: The front and back portions of the kayak.

Cockpit: The hole through which a paddler enters the kayak.

Grab loops: The loops at the bow and stern ends that are used for carrying the kayak and for towing swimmers.

Security bars: Metal bars that are permanently attached to the kayak just in front and just behind the cockpit. These are the strongest points on the kayak and get used for rescues, or when locking a kayak up.

Foot pegs/bulkhead: Adjustable foot support systems in the bow of the kayak.

Thigh hooks: Contoured pieces of plastic that support the upper leg and provide the leverage from which to rock the kayak back and forth.

Back band: An adjustable support for the lower back.

Support wall: A wall of foam that provides structural support, and runs vertically, separating the kayak into two equal halves.

Drain plug: A screwable plug that provides an easy way of letting water out of the kayak.

Sidewalls: The sides of the kayak, between the hull and the deck.

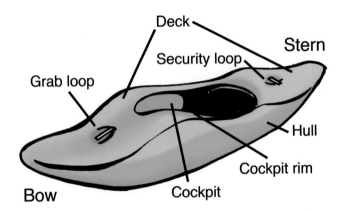

Rocker

Rocker is the curvature from bow to stern, as viewed from the side. As a general rule, the more rocker a kayak has, the more quickly it will turn. It will also travel through rapids more easily and surf waves with greater ease because the ends won't get caught by the incoming water.

A playboat's rocker is focused in the ends. This creates a long, flat section of the hull and allows the kayak to plane, and therefore spin the most effectively while surfing waves. River running boats have more consistent rocker from bow to stern, which makes them more forgiving and manoeuvrable in river running situations.

Hull Shapes

The shape of a kayak's hull as viewed from an end can be classified as either a planing hull or a displacement hull.

Planing hulls: These are flat hulls that create a wide footprint in the water. They are the most common form of kayak hull because they are the most stable, and surf waves incredibly well. The edges of the "planing" hull are bevelled up to the sidewalls at varying angles of aggressiveness; the more bevel, the "softer" the edge, and therefore the more forgiving and less tippy the boat will be when its side is exposed to the current.

Displacement hulls: These are rounded hulls. These were once the standard for whitewater kayaks, but

KAYAK CONSTRUCTION

For a long time, whitewater kayaks were made only of cloth and resin (commonly referred to as "composite" materials). Composite kayaks are made with layers of fibreglass, Kevlar or graphite cloth, glued together and stiffened by resin. These composite kayaks are very strong and light. The only downside is that if they were to hit a rock hard enough, they would crack. It was for this reason that there was much excitement when the first plastic kayak hit the market in 1970. Since that time, plastic has been the material of choice for recreational whitewater kayaks, although it is still possible to find some composite boats on the market. Plastic (polyethylene) kayaks are incredibly durable, long lasting, and relatively cheap to produce in comparison to composite boats. When they hit rocks hard, they may dent, but will seldom break. These dents will usually pop out after a little time spent in the sun.

have been largely replaced by the preferred planing hull. Displacement hulls track most effectively and are easily tilted on edge, but they aren't as stable or as manoeuvrable as planing hulls.

Choosing a Kayak

Boats designed specifically for playboating (surfing and performing various other acrobatics) will typically be shorter, have wider planing hulls, larger sidewalls, more aggressive edges, and the rocker focused in their ends in order to maximize performance and manoeuvrability. These boats will also tend to have less volume in the bow and stern to allow the ends of the boat to be forced underwater easily when desired. Boats designed for more all-around river running are typically a bit longer for increased speed. They also have narrower hulls that carve a better track in the water, more bevelled (and therefore forgiving) edges, more consistent rocker and more volume in the ends (to prevent them from submerging). As you can see, your intended use for the boat is important in making a choice.

One of the most remarkable areas of progress in design has been the inside of the boats. Specially contoured and adjustable seats, thigh hooks, foot braces, and lower back support systems have become the norm in all new models. It used to take us so long to outfit boats with mini-cell foam, a grater and soppy cement that we'd have a party and make an evening out of it! Today, you can unwrap your boat, make some minor adjustments, and paddle away—too easy!

In concept, the snugger you are, the more responsive the boat will be to your every movement and the better your posture will be. In reality, there's a comfort/control trade-off and each individual has his limits. You will figure out your own soon enough!

Now that you're aware of the basic design features, it's time to get out there and test-drive. If you're just starting, you'll want to take lessons; while you're there, ask your instructors for advice and, most importantly, try out different boats. Manufacturers now produce most models in a variety of sizes so you shouldn't have too much trouble getting relatively comfortable in one. The decision should be made based on the following factors: your intended use for

Playboats are shorter, have larger sidewalls,
and the rocker is focused in their ends.

River running boats tend to be longer, have more volume
in the ends, and more consistent rocker from bow to stern.

the boat, your size and weight, your comfort level in the boat, your budget, and any personal preferences. Remember that you will be improving fairly quickly, so pick a boat that has at least some features you will appreciate as your skill level progresses. New boats typically range from about US $850–$1200. Many retail stores or outfitters will allow you to rent a boat as a demo and then allocate the rental cost toward the purchase if you are still keen. By doing this, you maximize your trial time and will have made the most informed decision possible.

THE PADDLE

In whitewater kayaking, the paddle becomes an extension of your upper body, so the most logical choice is to use one that feels good to you. Designs vary slightly, but the general anatomy of paddles is the same. The two blades are attached to a shaft that can be straight or bent in various ways. The blades may be symmetrical or asymmetrical in shape, but all have a slightly concave power (front) face and a non-power (back) face.

Paddle blades are most commonly made from plastic, fibreglass, or carbon fibre (or a combination thereof). Although plastic blades are the most affordable, they

Paddle blades can be offset very differently. The offset, or "twist", of a paddle ranges between 0 and 90 degrees.

are heaviest and lack durability unless reinforced with fibreglass or carbon fibre. Fibreglass blades are lighter and stiffer than plastic blades, but cost significantly more. Carbon fibre yields the lightest weights and tremendous stiffness, but is also the most expensive material. Paddle blades made from a combination of plastic and fibreglass or carbon fibre offer a great blend of performance, durability, and affordability.

Paddle shafts are made from aluminium, fibreglass, or carbon fibre. We would recommend staying away from aluminium paddles for whitewater kayaking because they don't hold up well to abuse. Fibreglass or carbon fibre shafts are your best options.

You can expect to spend in the neighbourhood of US $150–$400 for a good quality paddle.

The most influential factor in choosing a paddle is your size. You need to consider the length of the paddle, the width of the shaft, and the size of the blades. Smaller paddlers should look for a paddle with slightly smaller blades and with a narrower shaft that makes it easier to grip. The stronger you are, the larger the paddle blades you will be able to control. Using a paddle that is too long or too large will cost you some control and could put an undue amount of stress on your body.

Paddles are conventionally measured in centimetres. In general, a paddle 194–200 cm in length is good for paddlers between 5'8" and 6'1". For paddlers between 5'3" and 5'8", a paddle 188–196 cm in length should work great.

Next, you will need to consider the offset of your blades. The offset, or "twist," refers to the difference in angles between the two blades. Traditional kayak paddles have blades that are offset at ninety degrees so that as one blade pulls through the water, the other slices efficiently through the air. For whitewater kayaking, a thirty- or forty-five-degree twist is most popular, although more and more people are using paddles with no offset at all! A lower offset means less repetitive twisting of the wrist, which can help prevent tendonitis and will facilitate some moves.

Something else you might see on the water are paddles with bent shafts. The goal of bent shaft paddles is to lessen wrist and muscle fatigue by placing the joints of the hand and wrist in a more natural position when taking a stroke. Because of the added complexity of manufacturing the shaft, these paddles are often quite costly. There's endless debate on how effective bent shafts really are—try one yourself and make up your own mind!

TIP

The lightness, strength and stiffness of carbon fibre paddles make them the highest performance paddles on the market, but they are not the best option for everyone. Although a stiff paddle provides additional power for each of your strokes, it will also be more jarring to your joints because the paddle absorbs less shock.

PERSONAL GEAR

When choosing your personal gear, safety and comfort should be the main considerations. Of course, in this day and age, style is always a factor, but that's okay, because gear manufacturers are pretty in tune with the times. You're likely to find yourself in a variety of paddling and weather conditions, so our general advice is to shop comparatively, but to buy good gear. It will go a long way towards making your paddling experiences safer and more enjoyable, particularly in cold conditions.

Helmets

Helmets are available in plastic and composite materials (such as fibreglass and Kevlar), and a variety of designs ranging from aesthetically plain to off-the-wall. You want to be sure that the helmet you buy is sturdy and shaped so that it protects your forehead and temples. Give it a good squeeze on its sides to gauge its sturdiness. It also needs to fit snugly enough so that it won't move around on your head, especially when upside- down in whitewater. Helmets often require a little fine-tuning of the inner foam lining to provide this comfortably snug fit, and will usually come with foam inserts that can be attached to do so. Another consideration is the sun protection factor that the helmet offers, as the river is a great place to get fried. Many helmets have brims that do a reasonable job of keeping your face safe. Cost: US $50–$200.

PFDs

Needless to say, your personal flotation device is an essential piece of safety equipment, so be sure to go for a quality product. Manufacturers have struck an appealing balance between flotation and low-profile designs that don't obstruct movement by keeping the bulkiest part of the PFD low on the torso, away from the shoulders and upper chest. Specialized rescue vests offer a releasable harness system and various other safety features that are recommended for more advanced river running (see the "Rescue" segment of this book). Talk to someone at the store who has been trained in Coast Guard approval ratings, and read the labels inside the PFDs so you are informed about what you are buying. Paddling "vests" are not rated as "life preservers"—this is to say that they are not designed to float your head above the surface when you're unconscious. They do offer various amounts of flotation; at least fifteen pounds of buoyancy is a common recommendation for the average person. Cost: US $75–$250.

Spray Skirt

The spray skirt is responsible for sealing off the cockpit of your kayak and keeping water out of your boat as you paddle. This is a pretty important job, so when shopping for a spray skirt, you should be looking for one that is comfortable, effectively keeps water out, stays on but comes off when you need it to, and will last. Most companies now offer them with a reinforced layer around the outside of the skirt, where the cockpit rim puts the greatest stress on the material. These reinforced skirts are a bit more expensive, but you'll find that they last much longer.

The first thing to know when choosing a skirt is that cockpits of kayaks are not all uniform in size, so you'll need to be sure to get a skirt that fits your particular boat. There are skirts with adjustable shock cords that can be used on any kayak. Although these adjustable skirts might seem like a good, economical option in the beginning when having a good seal isn't overly important, it won't be long before you need to upgrade to a skirt that is specifically sized to your boat. These skirts have a stiff rubber rand or perimeter-sewn bungee that may be a little harder to get on, but will keep you much drier. Skirts of this kind generally have two sizes associated with them—the tube (waist) size, and the cockpit size, which refers to the kayak that it is designed to fit. Most manufacturers have a fit list that specifies what skirt/ cockpit size is best for each kayak model. Make sure you pick a size that is not only snug around your boat, but snug around your waist because it will stretch! Cost: US $75–$200.

Dressing for Warm Conditions

For those of you lucky enough to be dressing for warm conditions, your biggest challenge will be to keep the water out of the boat while staying cool and protected from the sun. The best solution is to have some form of light short-sleeved under layer and either a "shorty" splash top or dry top outer layer. Shorts of any kind are fine for the lower body.

There is a variety of specialized materials designed for paddling now. Lightweight polypropylene (available in many brand names and styles) is the classic under layer, but rash guards have become more and more popular and are often worn without a layer over top. Rash guards won't stop water from getting in your boat, but they provide a great means of staying cool and protected from the sun. Although a splash top can work quite well, short-sleeved dry tops do the best job of keeping water out and letting you play uninterrupted for longer. Their only downside is that they can be quite warm on a hot summer day.

Cost: Rash guards, US $40–$85; shorty splash tops, US $50–$200; shorty dry tops, US $200–$300.

Dressing for Cold Conditions

"A good dry top is worth its weight in gold if you are in a cooler environment. Staying warm is just as important as a PFD or a helmet." (James Mole)

Under Layers

As with under layers for any outdoor sport, it's preferable to have a material that wicks moisture away from the skin, as opposed to absorbing it and holding it against you. As mentioned above, various blends of lightweight polypropylene, polyester, spandex and neoprene are available in both short-sleeved and long-sleeved tops and bottoms (as it gets colder, you'll want to start covering your legs). For an even warmer layer, micro fleece tops are available in all sorts of thicknesses. Layering is always the best option as it allows you to fine-tune your temperature throughout the day. In other words, as a general rule, wear more than is necessary as you are much better off being too warm than too cold. Being cold on the river will zap your energy, your enthusiasm, and your ability to enjoy your paddle. Cost: US $40–$120.

The first layer against your skin should be a wicking layer, which pulls moisture away from the skin.

Outer Layers

Long-sleeved splash tops and pants or dry tops and pants are most effective in cold conditions. They are constructed using different thicknesses of rip-stop nylon with various types of breathable or non-breathable water-resistant treatments. Dry tops and dry pants have tight latex or neoprene gaskets at the wrists, ankles, and neck to prevent water entry.

Because latex wears quickly in the sun, the gaskets should be protected by other material. The seams of dry tops and pants should be taped for the best seal. For the absolute driest and warmest day on the river, consider a dry suit. Dry suits don't come cheap, but they provide an unrivalled level of comfort on even the coldest and wettest days.

Cost: Splash tops, US $65–$250; dry tops, US $200–$350; pants, US $65–$250; dry suit, US $600–$1200.

LATEX GASKETS

The latex gaskets on dry tops, pants, or suits are designed so that you can customize their fit by cutting rings off along pre-marked lines. When doing so, use a sharp knife or pair of scissors and make clean cuts, because as nicks in the latex will allow the gasket to rip when stretched. When deciding how much to cut off, don't go too big too fast! Keep in mind that the material will stretch a little over time and you can always make another cut later, but you can't add material. If for some reason a gasket does tear on you, it can be replaced by cutting away the damaged one and gluing a new one on. You can find replacement gaskets in some retail stores or order them directly from the manufacturer.

ACCESSORIES

Nose plugs

Nose plugs are great little pieces of gear that can make life a lot more pleasant for some paddlers. By preventing water from shooting unmercifully through the sinuses, you'll not only save yourself a running nose for the following few days, but you'll probably find yourself much more relaxed when underwater, which can make a big difference when going for a roll! Be sure to get specialized kayaking plugs that won't come off. Cost: US $5–$10.

Earplugs

Earplugs are always a great idea, as they will help prevent ear infections and the longer-term issue of exotosis, which is the closing of the eardrum in

response to repetitive cold water shock. There are now earplugs on the market with small holes or valves that allow you to hear quite clearly while keeping all water out. Cost: US $6–$50.

River shoes or booties

It's always important to wear a good pair of water shoes that provide traction on wet rocks. Not only do they keep your feet warm and serve as protection to you both in and out of your kayak, they will allow you to move around quickly on shore to help others if the need ever arises. Cost: US $50–$100.

Most river shoes are quite thin and flexible so that your feet fit comfortably into your kayak.

Sunglasses

If you plan on spending a significant amount of time on the water, then you may want to invest in a good pair of sunglasses. The reflection of the sun off the water is intensified and can be very damaging to the eyes. Make sure that your glasses are attached to you so they won't fall off. Some companies now make sunglasses specially designed for sports like kayaking. Cost: US $20–$200.

Pogies, mitts or gloves

Pogies, mitts or gloves are the best way to keep your hands warm while paddling. Pogies cover the hands and attach by Velcro onto the paddle shaft. The nice thing about pogies is that they allow your hands to be in direct contact with the paddle. Gloves and mitts on the other hand are considerably warmer. Cost: US $15–$50.

Skull cap

A skull cap is a thin, insulating layer that fits under your helmet. This simple piece of gear can have a huge impact on your comfort level on the river, and is never a bad idea to bring along in cooler conditions. Cost: US $20–$35.

SAFETY GEAR

Throw rope/bag

A throw rope/bag is a bag to which one end of a rope is attached and then coiled inside, making carrying the rope more convenient and the throwing of a rope more accurate. It is one of the most versatile pieces of safety gear you can carry, and so it's worth having a good one. The bag should be made from a durable material and have a wide opening for easy repacking, which can be closed easily and securely. The rope that gets coiled inside should be a tightly woven polypropylene or spectra cord, fifty-five to seventy-five feet in length. The exposed end should be "clean," i.e. have no handle or pre-tied knots or loops—which have a habit of getting snagged on things. Also, to prolong the life of your throw rope, take the time to hang your rope up to dry in the shade whenever you can.

First aid kit

A first aid kit is always a great thing to carry in your boat; it will need to be held in a waterproof bag or container of some sort. But just having it isn't enough; you need to be trained in the use of the tools. If you haven't taken a first aid course, sign up for one now.

The type of paddling you do will dictate the safety equipment you use. For example, on steep creeks a helmet that provides full face protection is prudent to use.

Tow line

A tow line provides the greatest means of towing a boat around and is especially valuable on big-volume rivers. It's attached to your body by a quick release belt that wraps around either your waist or life jacket and has a relatively short piece of webbing with a carabiner on the end that can be clipped onto one of the grab loops of another boat very easily.

Breakdown paddle

Breakdown paddles come in two, three and four pieces. A four-piece breakdown paddle will always fit best in the smaller boats that now dominate the river. These paddles can easily ride along in the back of your boat and can come in very handy should someone in your group break his or her paddle. The number of breakdowns you should have within a group is determined by the remoteness of your river trip. Is walking out an option? If not, then you should probably have a couple of breakdowns in your group, just in case.

Whistle

You need a loud enough whistle to hear over the noise of the river—not one that relies on those little balls, or that is made of anything that might rust.

Duct tape

Not an entire roll. You can wrap some around your water bottle, paddle shaft, or just around itself. This wonderful stuff will come in handy more often than you would ever think.

Pin kit

A pin kit comprises all the tools that you'll need to set up a simple Z-drag with your throw rope. Of course, a pin kit is next to useless if you don't know how to use it, so take a swiftwater rescue course and prepare yourself for all the situations that can arise on the river. A basic pin kit should include the following tools, which should be carried in a small, waterproof bag.

Carabiners: At least two "beeners," made of either stainless steel or aluminium so they won't rust. These come in handy for many rescues as well as towing, and hanging and clipping things into your boat.

Tubular webbing: At least three metres (ten feet); long enough to wrap around a tree. The ends can be pre-sewn together to form a loop or "sling," which makes for a quicker anchor set-up.

Prussic: At least one; can be a low-diameter rope (at least one metre or three-and-a-half feet long) or a newer self-jamming pulley (quicker and easier to use). A prussic is a device that will either slide along a rope or grip onto it securely, depending on the force applied to it.

Pulley: At least one; make sure it's one that you can put on the middle of a rope and not one that you have to feed the end of the rope into. Pulleys allow for the frictionless redirection of a rope in a rescue operation.

Knife: Whether you carry this in a secure holder attached to your PFD or in your rescue kit, you'll want to have something sharp to cut through rope or other material if necessary. Good scissors can also do the trick.

BEFORE HITTING THE WATER

SITTING IN A KAYAK

As a general rule, your boat should fit like a good pair of shoes: snug yet comfortable.

When you are sitting in your kayak, your legs should be in front of you, splayed out so that your knees are flexed and under the thigh hooks. Your feet should be resting comfortably and securely against their supports, and the back band should be supporting your lower back, encouraging an upright sitting position, but not preventing you from leaning back.

When sitting upright like this on the water, your kayak should be "trimmed out," which means that the bow and stern should be equally out of the water. If you find your stern is lower in the water, you'll need to move yourself forward in your kayak by sliding the seat forward and/or tightening the back band slightly. If you find your bow is lower in the water, or that you are short on foot room, you will need to move the seat backwards slightly or loosen the back band.

CUSTOMIZING YOUR KAYAK

The outfitting of your kayak will have a large impact on both your control and your comfort in your boat. You need to consider the support that is provided to your feet, legs, butt, hips, and lower back.

When outfitted correctly, your kayak should feel like an extension of your body.

Foot Support

Depending on the model of your kayak, it will have foot pegs, a secured bulkhead, or an unsecured bulkhead system.

Foot pegs are small plates that slide forward and backward along a track to accommodate different leg lengths. These are the most easily adjusted form of foot support, although sand has a tendency to get caught in the track, making their adjustment more difficult over time. The downside of foot pegs is that they provide a smaller platform to push on and with any serious head-on impact this can easily result in broken toes or

even ankles. They also offer more potential for your feet to get temporarily stuck while trying to exit.

A secured bulkhead is a wall of plastic that slides forward and backward and then gets locked into place. Secured bulkheads are generally the safest and most reliable form of foot support, but they don't tend to work well in playboats where the goal is to minimize the volume in the ends of the kayak.

Unsecured bulkheads come in the form of foam, air bags, or bean bags that are stuffed into the bow of the kayak, creating a wall of support for your feet. These bulkheads can be quite comfortable and are usually the best option in playboats, as the tapered ends of the kayak often force your feet into a position that won't accommodate foot pegs or secured bulkheads.

Leg Support

Your legs should fit comfortably under the thigh hooks with even pressure across your thigh. Most thigh hooks can now be adjusted to fit a wide range of leg girth and length, but older outfitting will require some customized padding. Though it is most important that your thigh hooks provide your legs with a surface to squeeze in against for support and to pull up against for edging, it is also very important that your legs are supported from the outside and from underneath. This additional support provides more control and helps reduce hip discomfort.

Butt Support

There's no doubt that your butt is one of the most padded parts of your body, but this doesn't mean that it won't appreciate a little tender loving care. Many seats now come equipped with seat padding, but if yours does not, then placing a quarter inch of mini-cell foam on your seat will make for a much more comfortable day on the water. Some paddlers who are short in the torso will glue considerably more foam

Lift the kayak onto your thighs.

Grab the far cockpit rim with one hand.

to their seat to raise their centre of gravity and give themselves more control over their edging. This can be very helpful for some, but beware that you don't raise yourself too high, as this will make you very tippy.

Back Support

Back support is absolutely critical for both comfort and performance. Back bands are by and large the most functional and effective systems and should be used in any kayak. The back band should fit above your hips and be tightened enough to prevent you from sliding backwards without impeding your ability to lean right back. The best back bands are those held in place with heavy-duty webbing and with rounded hardware that won't create weak points or potentially cut any of the straps.

Hip Support

Much of the control you have over your kayak stems from the hips, so it is vital that they are well supported. It's also very important that your hips aren't being squeezed too tightly, as this can cause your legs to fall asleep or just be downright painful. Your hip padding should be snug enough to prevent your butt from sliding from side to side, but no tighter.

It's also very helpful if your hip pads cup over your hips and upper thighs, providing some support from above. This provides additional edge control over your kayak and helps keep your butt from falling out of the seat when you are upside-down. Of course, you need to be sure that your hip support still allows an easy escape from the kayak if needed. Generally, if you can get into your kayak without too much effort, then you can be almost sure that you'll be able to get out more easily when the need arises and the adrenaline is flowing.

Kick the boat up and onto your shoulder.

Rest the cockpit rim on the PFD's padded shoulder strap.

Some other things that you might want to make a permanent feature in your boat are a sponge to remove any water from your kayak, and a screwdriver that will allow you to tighten the screws on your kayak or make any small adjustment to your outfitting.

CARRYING YOUR BOAT

Carrying your boat is a bit of an art form! One way to carry the boat is by resting the inside of the cockpit rim on your shoulder and holding onto it with the same hand for control. The best way to get your kayak on your shoulder is to approach it from the side, grab the close side of the cockpit coaming, and then lift the boat onto your thighs so that the cockpit is facing outwards. You'll then grab the far edge of the coaming, kick the boat up with your knee and roll

the boat up and onto your shoulder. To put the kayak back down, simply reverse these steps. It's a good idea to wear your PFD while carrying your boat on your shoulder, as it will provide a little extra padding.

Other cultures have taught us to carry boats on our heads as well. This is achieved by turning the boat backwards and adjusting its angle so that the back band rests comfortably on your forehead. Again, one hand can be used to balance the boat while the other carries gear.

You can also throw some teamwork into the mix. Having one person at either end holding onto the grab-loops, with the gear thrown into the cockpits, makes for quite a civilized carry.

Finally, if you have to carry your boat for any major distance, you may want to try a specialized carrier that lets you throw your kayak on your back like a pack.

WARMING UP AND STRETCHING

As with any physical activity, your body is your most important tool. The healthier, stronger and more flexible you are, the more you'll be able to accomplish. This doesn't mean that you need to be Arnold Schwarzenegger or that whitewater kayaking is necessarily a high-impact sport. In fact, it's amazing how far good technique will get you. In the same breath, power and flexibility will pave the way to getting the most out of your kayak. It should go without saying that warming up and stretching are invaluable ways of keeping the body healthy. Unfortunately, many paddlers completely ignore their lower bodies. The lower body is actually just as

important as the upper body to warm up for a day on the water. In particular, tight hips will impede your boat tilts, and tight hamstrings can dramatically affect your ability to lean forward. Keeping your body strong and limber will definitely help improve your paddling, but it will also make sitting in a kayak a lot more comfortable.

GETTING IN AND OUT

Even though whitewater kayaks have large cockpits, getting in and out of them can be tricky because of the outfitting. The trick to getting in is to keep your legs straight for as long as possible as you are sliding

kayaks offer less aggressive thigh hooks, which might solve the problem. Otherwise, you'll want to find a different boat to paddle.

The river environment will frequently throw a twist into things; realistically it won't be often that you are getting in and out on a nice sandy beach! You'll learn a few of your own tricks as you gain experience, but here are some general tips that may help you.

When getting in or out while the boat is in the water, don't sit too far back on the boat—it will inevitably sink the stern and flood your boat. In some situations, you can use the paddle as a brace by placing it perpendicular to the boat with one blade on shore and the shaft resting behind the cockpit. This works well when the water is not fluctuating much, but can be frustrating if it is! A common choice on the river is to find a friendly looking rock as close as possible to the water to launch from, or to pull up on or brace against in order to get out.

On a steep rocky shoreline, use your paddle as a brace on shore to get in or out of your kayak.

in and then twisting your whole lower body to get a leg at a time under its respective thigh hook. If you are still having trouble, try loosening the back band. You can retighten it once you're in. Getting out is actually much easier. With your hands on the sides of the cockpit at about your hips, push down and back. Keeping your legs straight, you should be able to slide them right out of the boat. Of course, if you can't get out of your boat relatively easily on dry land, it's probably not the best boat for you. Some

PUTTING ON YOUR SKIRT

When putting on any skirt, it is critical that you leave the rip cord out so that you can easily grab it at any time. Simply getting to this stage can be tricky though, as today's skirts, particularly those with a Kevlar-reinforced trim and a stiff rubber rand, can be hard to put on. One trick that tends to help is wetting the skirt before getting in. This seems to soften up the neoprene, making it a bit more flexible.

Seal Entry

The seal entry involves sliding off the shoreline and dropping into the river. The seal entry is a fun way to start your day and, on rivers with steep banks, it can be the only way of getting on the water. If done right, you can seal launch from fairly high up, but the higher you go, the smaller the room for error and the bigger the potential consequences. A botched seal launch from any significant height is a great way to hurt your back or damage your boat.

Seal launching is a skill like any other, and just as you wouldn't start by running a twenty-foot waterfall, you shouldn't start with a ten-foot seal launch. The first order of business is establishing whether or not the potential seal launch spot has a deep landing zone. You then need to pick your line, which means choosing where you want to slide off the rock. This will of course dictate where you get into your kayak. Ideally, a buddy can hold your boat and paddle while you get in; otherwise you'll have to find a flat spot or something to brace against. When it comes time to launch, there's a good chance this same buddy will be eager to give you a push off the rock. This can sometimes be helpful, but unless he or she has some experience in launching paddlers, it's probably better to do it yourself. At least this way you will only have yourself to blame!

When launching, hold your paddle with your control hand and use your other hand to push yourself off. This push-off will play a huge role in the success of your seal launch. The speed and trajectory with which you launch will be different for every situation, but the desired result of your seal launch will be the same. Ideally, you'll enter the water straight, with your kayak on a seventy- to eighty-degree angle so that you pencil into the river. This slightly off-vertical angle will let the rocker and the buoyancy of your kayak bring your bow to the surface in a smooth arc. If you launch with too little speed, your kayak is likely to stand up too vertically, or even rotate past vertical, which is referred to as "going over the handlebars." If you launch with too much speed, there's a good chance that you'll land flat and hard on the water, which is particularly dangerous for the back.

The last thing to consider is where to hold your paddle as you hit the water. The goal is that when you make contact with the water, your paddle doesn't come up and whack you in the face or strain your shoulders. With this in mind, you can hold it slightly over your head or along one side of your kayak so that it pierces the water like your kayak does. Holding your paddle just above your head can be appropriate for small drops, but avoid holding it too high. Never hold your paddle right in front of your face, either—you won't be the first paddler to finish a seal launch with a bloody nose!

THE MENTAL GAME

We were taught early on that good paddling technique is as important as having strong paddling muscles. What we weren't taught right away is that kayaking is as much a mental game as it is a physical one and that in order to improve you need to develop both of these elements. Since you're reading this, you have already shown the mental capacity to be a great paddler, because at some point you made the decision to explore a sport that is falsely considered by many to be reckless and dangerous. Whether you're already paddling or just getting into the sport, you've probably already learned that whitewater kayaking is like any other outdoor adventure sport in that it can be as dangerous and exciting, or as relaxed and enjoyable, as you choose it to be.

The mental game is a dynamic and unique attribute of this sport. Early on, you need to teach yourself to do many things that are counter-instinctual, such as keeping your head down while rolling, getting more aggressive as the current gets stronger, and using rocks as your friends. As your mental game improves, your confidence could progress more quickly than your actual physical skills. This of course can result in poor decisions that create dangerous situations. On the other hand, you may end up with skill sets that surpass your mental game. It's a lot easier to gauge where your physical skills are, but it's very important that you take the time to consider how your mental game is doing. Remember that the goal is to have fun with one of Mother Nature's most incredible natural playgrounds. How you do that is a very personal thing and should not be dictated by how others feel.

USING YOUR PADDLE

As we mentioned earlier, the paddle evolves into an extension of your arms and is probably the piece of gear you will become most intimate with. You're

Whitewater kayaking is as much a mental game as it is a physical one.

more likely to go through a few boats than you are to change paddles, especially once you've found your match. We've already discussed how to choose a paddle, so now let's look at how to use it.

A kayak paddle should be held with your hands an equal distance from the blades and slightly more than shoulder width apart. Having your hands too far out makes for very awkward strokes, while having your hands too far in toward the centre will cost you substantially in the amount of force you can apply at the blades. A great way to establish the correct hand placement is to position the centre of the paddle on top of your head and then grip the paddle so that your elbows are bent at approximately ninety degrees.

Your "control" hand keeps a firm grip while the "grease" hand is loose enough to allow the shaft to rotate within it.

As the "control" hand lifts, the "grease" hand allows the shaft to rotate.

Knowing roughly where your hands should be, the next thing to look at is whether or not your paddle has any feather to contend with. Feathered paddles have blades offset at different angles. As one blade pulls through the water, the angle of the other blade allows it to slice through any wind. Feathered paddles are traditional and can make a small difference if you're paddling in an area with high winds, but they are less intuitive to use and by no means essential. We're now going to look at how to use a heavily feathered paddle since the same concept gets applied when using a non-feathered paddle, but to a lesser extent.

First of all, being left- or right-handed has an important impact on your paddling, as it dictates which is your control hand. Quite simply, for a right-handed paddler, the control hand is the right; for a left-handed paddler, the control hand is the left. Having said this, it's becoming increasingly common for all paddlers to learn with right-handed control paddles. The reason for this is simple: left-handed control paddles are very uncommon, so finding a replacement is highly unlikely in the event that you break, forget, or lose your paddle. Your "control" hand is the hand that grips the shaft firmly at all times, which is why we also call it the "glue" hand. The opposite hand, in contrast, is often referred to as the "grease" hand. The control hand's grip should never change whether you're forward paddling, bracing, rolling, playboating or running waterfalls. It's your reference point for how the paddle will react and you need to be able to rely on it automatically. The big knuckles of your control hand should be aligned with the top edge of your paddle blade. After taking a stroke with your control hand side, you'll loosen your grip with your grease hand so that you can rotate the shaft within it. This rotation is necessary to accommodate the feather of your paddle, and lets you place the next blade in the water squarely. This loosening of the grease hand and the rotation of the shaft within it takes place between each stroke.

If you're using a paddle with no feather you can get away with not rotating the paddle between each stroke. However it is ideal to use this same technique in a scaled-back way because there is naturally a small amount of rotation associated with paddling. If you don't let the paddle shaft rotate a little in your grease hand, you'll find that wrist doing small curls while you paddle, which can gradually result in an injury or strain.

On a final note, it's important that you keep your control hand grip on the paddle secure, but as light as possible. A light grip will let you paddle more comfortably for longer and is instrumental in avoiding overuse injuries such as tendonitis in the wrist and elbow.

INDEX YOUR PADDLE

Most paddles will have some degree of an oval shape to the shaft at the control hand to help "index" your grip. This lets you grip your paddle correctly without having to look down at your hand. You can add to the index by taping some additional material in a position underneath the knuckles of your control hand. The oval shape of the shaft also helps to prevent the shaft from turning in your control hand. You can supplement your control hand's grip with grip tape or paddle wax.

THE ESSENTIALS 3

THE WET EXIT

A wet exit refers to the act of getting out of your kayak when it's upside-down, and it's one of the first skills that any paddler should learn.

To smoothly exit an overturned kayak, the first thing you'll do is lean forward and find your skirt's rip cord with one hand, while the other hand firmly hangs on to your paddle. Now yank the ripcord forward and up to pop your skirt. Next, slide your hands back to your hips (still holding the paddle), and while staying leaning forward, push yourself out. You'll end up doing a bit of a forward somersault out of the boat.

The trickiest part of this manoeuvre is fighting the instinct to lean back as you slide out of your kayak. The problem with leaning back is that it raises your butt off the seat and presses your thighs against the thigh hooks, which will actually make it harder to slide out, and slow down your wet exit.

The entire process of wet exiting will only take a few seconds, and the more relaxed you are, the more smoothly it'll all go. The first few times it may feel as if you'll soon be short of air, but in reality you have lots of time, so relax and practise sitting there for a few moments before popping out of the boat.

Propping one end of your kayak on shore is usually the easiest way to empty out your kayak.

EMPTYING THE BOAT

When emptying a boat full of water a little technique can make a big difference, but any way you slice it, emptying the boat is one of the most tiring parts of learning to paddle. First of all, getting the boat to shore can be challenging, especially when you are in moving water and/or far away. In this case, you'll likely need some help. If you're close to the bank, leave the boat upside down (where it's full of air and thus lighter) and push it to shore. Now try to get one end up out of the water. Just by raising one end, water will have drained from at least half of the boat. Take care in getting the end up on shore, especially if the boat is full, as it can be very heavy. If you have friends nearby, this may be a good time to call on them for help. Now lift the lower end to dump the bulk of the water out through the cockpit. To drain the rest of the water, you can prop the centre of the boat up on your knee and rock it back and forth.

Most kayaks now have a drain plug in the stern that you can unscrew and drain the water out from by gradually lifting the bow higher and higher. A sponge

The trick to a smooth wet exit is tucking forward and pushing yourself out of the kayak with your hands at your hips.

will also come in handy for getting the final drops out and, more importantly, it will let you pop your skirt while you're sitting in your kayak and remove any water that entered your boat while you were paddling.

BOAT-OVER-BOAT

The boat-over-boat technique is a method of emptying a boatful of water from a kayak. It's a useful skill to have when a capsized boat is far from shore and the water isn't too rough. It involves dragging the upside-down kayak over your own cockpit and rocking the boat back and forth to dump the majority of the water out. If the kayak has float bags in the stern, then it is easiest to do this by pulling the bow over your kayak first. Either way, it will certainly be useful to have the swimmer help push the boat across your kayak. Once the boat is empty, you can flip it upright and off your kayak. At this point you can tow the boat to shore or provide the swimmer with an aided re-entry, which we discuss in more detail in the rescue chapter.

Something to keep in mind when doing a boat-over-boat rescue is that the upside-down kayak can do damage to the rescuer's skirt when it's pulled across their boat. This is where a Kevlar reinforced skirt makes a big difference.

THE THREE GOLDEN RULES

The Three Golden Rules will apply to your paddling from here on. Whether you're running your first river or surfing a huge wave, you need to separate your body movements, use the power of your torso, and maintain control of your kayak with an active blade. These three rules will serve as a checklist for you to refer back to as long as you paddle. You will notice them being applied to virtually every technique we discuss in this book. Let's have a closer look . . .

1. Separate Your Body Movements

The best kayakers have mastered the art of letting their upper and lower bodies work independently, yet cooperatively with each other. This means there needs to be a distinct separation of movements at the hips. Early on you will become comfortable with this separation as it applies to leaning forward and backward. As you progress, it will become a key ingredient of balancing your boat on edge and staying ahead of your boat as it spins.

By letting his upper and lower bodies work independently but cooperatively with each other, Ken tilts his boat aggressively during an eddy turn.

To cut back while surfing a hole, Nicole rotates her upper body in the direction she wants to go and plants her paddle securely in the water. Her stomach muscles can now help turn the boat.

2. Use the Power of your Torso

To make the most of each stroke, you'll need to use much more than just your arm and shoulder muscles. Whether you're propelling the boat or turning it, your goal is to harness the power available from your entire upper body. We refer to this as torso rotation. It is the way you get your front and side (oblique) stomach muscles involved with your strokes. Using these larger muscle groups will maximize the strength of each stroke, and will improve your stamina as your efforts are spread over more muscles.

There are three components to torso rotation: the winding up of the body, the planting of a pivot blade, and the unwinding of the body. To wind up, turn your upper body at the hips in the direction you want to go. At this point, your stomach and chest should no longer face the direction that your kayak does. Once your body is wound up, plant your paddle blade completely in the water as a pivot. As you push or pull on this pivot blade, draw on your stomach muscles to force the body back to its (unwound) position of rest.

This act of using the stomach muscles to return your body to its position of rest is what we refer to as

unwinding the body. One applicable analogy is that of an elastic band. The further you stretch it, the more it will sting when it makes contact! Similarly, the more you wind up, the more power you will have available to you. It would be excessive to fully wind up your body for every single stroke, but your stomach muscles should always be involved.

Torso rotation is also an important way of protecting your shoulders from injury. As a rule of thumb, you want to keep your hands in front of your upper body. By turning your whole torso, you can reach as far back as you want with a blade and still be in a safe position, while at the same time harnessing more power for your strokes.

3. Maintain Control with an Active Blade

Today's whitewater kayaks are incredibly responsive. As such, they are very easy to manoeuvre, but are more susceptible to being pushed around by even the smallest river features. Whereas longer boats can cruise through waves or different currents with less

An active blade allows steady control while paddling through a large and breaking wave train.

effort, smaller boats don't track or maintain their speed as well. The only way to truly control them is to have an active blade in the water. This means it's important to get your next stroke in the water as soon as the one you are taking is finished. Having a blade in the water allows you to take an active role in deciding what your boat will do, rather than reacting to the things that happen to it. Keeping this rule in mind will help you paddle in a straight line, carve smooth eddy turns, punch through crashing waves, and perform increasingly advanced moves.

PADDLING POSTURE

Paddling posture refers to the different ways your body positioning can help with the control and balance of your kayak. As with most dynamic sports, posture plays an important role in paddling performance. For example, if you are familiar with skiing you know what it feels like to stray from the proper body position. When you get caught leaning back, your weight is on the tails of the skis and you lose control. When you fall over to one side, you go into survival mode trying to recover. When your weight is too far forward, odds are your tips dig in, or you go for a nasty yet acrobatic tumble. Similarly in kayaking, the goal is to maintain control of your centre of gravity to prevent crashing and burning. There are two aspects to paddling posture: lateral balance (edge to edge) and body position. Both rely on the first Golden Rule of upper-lower body separation.

Lateral Balance

Lateral balance involves keeping your weight over the centre of the boat and not off to one side. In flat water this is fairly straightforward, but in whitewater it requires that you be loose at the hips and allow the boat to tilt on edge without your upper body doing the same. A classic analogy of this technique is the belly dancer, who can wildly fling the hips while remaining

Photo by Trevor Lisoi

A moderately aggressive position provides the most flexibility, balance, and control.

An aggressive body position keeps Ken upright while breaking through a large wave.

perfectly still in the upper body. Whitewater can act in many ways to rock your boat from edge to edge, but if your hips are loose and your body stays over the boat, you will be fine. It's when you stiffen up or let your weight fall to one side that you're likely to take the plunge!

Body Position

Body position refers to your lean along the length of the boat, again assuming separation at the hips. In this context, an aggressive position is a strong forward lean; a neutral position is sitting straight up; and a defensive position is leaning back. Acknowledging that you will inevitably spend some time recovering, the goal is to paddle as often as possible in the position that best prepares you to deal with dynamic situations. You want to sit in a position that allows you the most flexibility, balance, and control to minimize the amount of time your spend recovering. This default body position in kayaking is sitting with a moderately aggressive lean. To achieve this, sit up straight with your butt against the back band and then bend slightly forward at the hips. Pretend a rope secured to the bow of your boat was attached to your belly button and someone pulled the slack right out of it. It is not a slouch—your stomach muscles need to be turned on and ready.

The most common problem paddlers have is "getting in the back seat." When this happens, your weight shifts onto the stern edges, which causes you to sink slightly and exposes you to all the weird and wonderful effects of river currents. The back seat position also compromises your control, making it difficult to take efficient strokes or balance the boat on edge.

SHOULDER SAFETY

The shoulder dislocation is to kayaking what a blown knee is to skiing. Why is this injury so dreaded? The pain factor doesn't seem to drive the fear into paddlers' hearts; it's more the thought of having to go through surgery, of sitting idle through months of therapy, of the shoulder never again being as strong as it was. Unfortunately these are substantiated concerns, as a shoulder dislocation is often accompanied by damage to the joint that requires real care, and sometimes surgery, to heal. These are all good reasons for us to take a good look at how to keep our shoulders safe.

It goes without saying that having well-conditioned muscles around the shoulder will go a long way towards keeping the joint in place. It should be noted that paddlers often have much stronger back shoulder muscles than front, as these are the muscles used primarily for forward paddling. Seeing as the majority of shoulders dislocate forwards, your goal should be to make the front muscles equally as strong as the back. This is where back paddling practice comes in. But even with Superman's shoulders, a dislocation can easily happen, though there are two simple rules that, when followed, will go a long way towards keeping your arms intact. The first: don't overextend your arms. The second: maintain a "power position" with your arms. Let's look at both of these in more detail.

1. The idea of not overextending your arms is a simple concept to appreciate, but it isn't always so simple to apply. When you're getting tossed around in whitewater, the desire to keep your head above the water can easily override any safe paddling practices. Try to stay as relaxed as possible and fight the urge to use massive "Geronimo" braces.

2. So what is the "power position"? When looking at your body from above, let's imagine an invisible line that passes through both shoulders. The power position simply involves keeping your hands in front of this line. In so doing, you'll maintain a rectangle (often called "the box") with your arms, paddle, and chest. With this rectangle formed, you get the most power from your paddle and your shoulders stay in the safest position.

When a hand falls behind you, the arm is in a very vulnerable position. Does this mean that you can't

A stroke is planted at the back of the boat without any torso rotation.

The same stroke is planted at the back of the boat while maintaining the power position.

Staying loose at the hips is the key to edging. This lets you keep your head and weight over the kayak, even when your kayak is being aggressively edged.

safely reach to the back of your kayak? Not at all! It means that in order to reach to the back of your kayak you'll need to rotate your whole torso so that your arms stay in the power position. This act of rotating your whole torso is fittingly named torso rotation. Torso rotation is not only responsible for keeping your shoulders safe, but it is one of the Three Golden Rules of whitewater paddling (see "Three Golden Rules" section).

EDGING

Much of your time kayaking will be spent on one edge or the other, depending on what you're doing. Peeling out into the whitewater, ferrying across the current, side-surfing in a hole, or paddling through a wave train all require you to keep balanced while the boat is tilted on edge. To tilt a boat on edge, shift your weight slightly over to one butt cheek and lift the opposite knee. Moving your weight over to one side and staying balanced will involve keeping your torso vertical while shifting your whole rib cage over to one side. You'll find that your stomach and side muscles have to work to hold this position, while your leg muscles hold the boat in its tilted position.

As you progress, it becomes more and more important to be able to tilt and hold the boat on edge quickly, and then transfer from one edge to another. You can practise this on the water by paddling in a straight line with your boat held on a steady edge. After five to ten strokes, switch to your other edge without losing your paddling rhythm. This is a great drill for improving your balance and edge control while strengthening your stomach muscles.

AN INTRODUCTION TO SPIN MOMENTUM

A couple of the most prominent features of modern whitewater kayak designs are their shorter lengths and their flatter hulls. While these combine to make the boats more manoeuvrable (and fun!), these two features can also leave you spinning in circles without the right technique. A boat with forward speed left to coast on its own will skid out to one side and quickly lose its forward momentum because it does not have a centre line or keel in the water to keep it on track. It follows that whenever you give a boat forward or backward speed, you are also giving it potential "spin momentum." This is true of any boat left to coast, but the difference with modern whitewater kayaks is that their spin momentum will take over immediately because that is what they are designed to do! Of course, turning or spinning your boat also establishes momentum in one direction. Once established, spin momentum will continue turning the boat until there is no energy left or until something is actively done to change it. Learning to control and use this spin momentum to your advantage is one of the most important whitewater kayaking skills to learn.

The only way to prevent your kayak's spin momentum from taking over is to have an active blade in the water.

When your kayak is on edge, it will carve a turn.

SKIDDING VS. CARVING

Now that you understand the concept of spin momentum, it's important that we look at the different ways it will turn your kayak. Modern whitewater kayaks are designed to turn very effectively in two different ways. Their wide, flat hulls allow them to skid, while the sharp edges allow them to carve. Both of these features come in really handy in different situations. Just as with downhill skiing or snowboarding, the key to carving is getting on edge and preventing your tail end from sliding out. Most paddlers have a tougher time carving than spinning out because it requires balancing on edge.

When your kayak is kept flat, it skids to a stop.

STROKES

4

PROPULSION STROKES

Forward Stroke

Whitewater kayaks are designed to turn efficiently, so mastering a stroke that is supposed to make them go straight isn't going to be easy. When you're learning, there's a good chance that you'll find paddling in a straight line next to impossible, and so you'll probably be happy to hear that you're not the only one. In fact, no one can paddle a whitewater kayak in a straight line. Even the best whitewater paddlers are turning back and forth slightly with each stroke. What happens is that as you get better, you start anticipating any corrections rather than reacting to the actions of your kayak.

Although any stroke that gets your kayak moving forward is fine, by learning correct technique you'll be able to get where you want to go more efficiently and with the least amount of wasted effort. Having said this, we're going to be looking at what could be considered the ideal forward stroke. The reality is that each of your forward strokes will need to be modified slightly to accommodate any correction that is needed.

The forward stroke can be broken down into three parts: catch, rotation, and recovery.

The Catch

The catch refers to the start of the stroke, when you place a paddle blade in the water. Sitting up straight, with a relaxed grip on your paddle, reach to your toes and plant your blade fully in the water. This reaching action involves both your arms and your shoulders. Do not lean forward at the waist to reach to your toes, but rather twist from the waist. If you're reaching for a stroke with your right blade, you'll push your right shoulder forward while reaching with your right arm. This shoulder-reach causes you to rotate your upper torso or "wind-up" your body. As we already know, this torso rotation lets you harness the power of your front and side stomach muscles for strokes, rather than just using your arms. With your body wound up, you'll plant the full blade in the water, pull on your paddle and unwind your upper body to drive your boat forward.

One of the most common mistakes is pulling on the forward stroke before the blade is fully planted in the water. If you're doing this, you'll notice your strokes creating a lot of splash, which means that you're actually wasting energy pulling water past your kayak, rather than pulling your kayak forward through the water. To understand this better, imagine that you're planting your paddle in cement when you take a stroke. The paddle shouldn't really move anywhere once it's planted. Instead, you're pulling yourself past that paddle blade. The only way this will work is if you have fully and securely planted your whole blade in the water.

Rotation

Your body is like an elastic band in that once it's wound up, you'll have a lot of potential energy at your command. Rotation refers to the way you'll use this energy to power your forward stroke.

As described above, when taking a forward stroke, your body gets wound up and your paddle is planted at your toes. You'll now pull on your paddle and drive your kayak forward using as much of your large torso muscles as possible, rather than relying on your comparatively weak arms to do the work. In fact, a good way to think about this is that your arms are just a supplement to the power of your torso. True power comes from your stomach, side, and back muscles. To get a feel for this, try paddling forward with your arms locked completely straight at the elbows. Although it won't be comfortable to paddle like this, you can really get your boat moving using only the rotation of your torso to power your kayak forward.

Now that you're engaging the most powerful muscles, let's take a quick look at what the rest of your body will be doing. With elbows bent and staying low, pull on the paddle with your arms as you

Rotate your whole upper body to plant your blade at your toes.

Plant your blade deeply in the water to get the most power.

The top arm stays bent with the hand around eye level as you unwind your torso and pull the blade through the water.

The more vertical your paddle stays during the stroke, the more power it will offer.

When the blade reaches a point beside your hip, slice it out of the water out to the side.

Wind up for the next stroke by reaching with your other arm and shoulder.

take each stroke. The range of motion for your arms will be quite small since your torso will be doing the bulk of the work. As a general rule, the more vertical the paddle shaft is while taking a forward stroke, the more forward power you're getting from it. To get the paddle more vertical, bring your top hand higher and further across your boat. In contrast, the less vertical your paddle shaft is the more directional control you are exercising, which means that the stroke will be more effective for course correction at the sacrifice of forward propulsion. Since, as we already discussed, whitewater kayaks are constantly turning and therefore in need of correction, the verticality of your strokes will be in constant flux

Recovery

The recovery is the point at which your forward stroke ends and the blade is removed from the water. This happens at your hip, which is earlier than most paddlers think. When your stroke reaches your hip, slice your paddle out of the water and get ready for the next stroke. At this point, your body should have unwound past its position of rest, and be wound up, ready to catch your other blade on the opposite side.

Now that you understand the upper body motions involved with the forward stroke, it's important to look at the actions of your kayak because it is an important factor in the effectiveness of your forward stroke, particularly when paddling in current and/or when using a short kayak with low-volume ends. In both cases, by paddling forward with a moderately aggressive forward position (the default body position), there is a significant chance that your bow will dive underwater. To avoid this, there are two things that you can do. First off, you can tilt your boat a little and very briefly into each stroke that you take. Doing this will pull your stern slightly underwater and lift your bow upwards. This forward paddling technique will come in really handy when ferrying, or when paddling through wave trains, but keep in mind that your forward strokes are most effective with a level boat—so minimize the amount of tilt you use. Although this is an incredibly effective means of keeping your bow on top of the water sometimes it just won't be enough and you'll have no choice but to lean back as well. For instance, you may need to lean back when crossing eddy lines, or when paddling against the current as you do when ferrying. It's important to understand that there's no problem with leaning back, as long as you return to your neutral or moderately aggressive position as soon as it is possible.

Although you might have figured that the forward stroke would be the easiest stroke to master, there are a remarkable number of things that you need to think about. In fact, entire books have been written just on the forward stroke! Try focusing on each component individually and don't get frustrated when your boat doesn't respond the way you want it to. Remember that whitewater kayaks were not designed to go straight.

Back Stroke

Most paddlers will develop a forward stroke that is powerful enough to get them where they need to go, but very few paddlers ever reach that same level of comfort with their back stroke!

Taking the time to practise your back paddling will go a long way toward improving your overall skills. Not only will the practice make your stroke more effective, you'll have an increased awareness when you find yourself backward on the river. Working on the back stroke is also a great way to help prevent shoulder injuries. For anatomical reasons, shoulder dislocations are anterior (forward) over 90% of the time. The back stroke strengthens important front shoulder muscles that the forward stroke misses. This may not stop a dislocation from happening, but it can certainly help prevent it. So let's take a look at a few things to keep in mind when practising backward paddling.

Your back stroke will begin just behind your hip and end at your toes. At first you'll probably find that your top hand is quite low during your strokes because

Keep your weight forward as you rotate your upper body and plant your back stroke just behind your hip.

Tilt your kayak slightly into your back stroke to lift the stern out of the water.

The back stroke ends when your blade reaches your toes, at which time your boat should be level.

Stay forward, wind up for your next stroke and tilt your boat slightly in the opposite direction.

of all the corrections you're making to keep yourself moving in the right direction. Although there's nothing wrong with this, it needs to be understood that the ideal back stroke has your top hand between shoulder and eye level, where you'll get the most push from your stroke.

It should come as no surprise now that the power for your back stroke doesn't come from your arms alone, but from torso rotation. This means you need to wind up your upper body to plant every back stroke. You do so by turning your chest to face the knee on the stroking side of the kayak. Now with your paddle blade planted fully in the water, push on your back stroke and unwind your torso by driving your back shoulder forward.

Now that we've looked at the stroke dynamics, let's look at some of the practical issues that you'll need to deal with.

Staying on course tends to be one of the first problems encountered. The key to doing so is to alternate looking ahead and then behind you. To see behind you, choose one shoulder to look over, and do so every few strokes. You'll find it's easiest to look over that shoulder as you reach to take a stroke on that same side, since your body will be turned in that direction during the wind-up phase of your stroke. When not looking behind, you can keep a steady course by using landmarks in front of you. For example, you could choose a tree in the distance and be fairly certain that if you keep that tree in the same position relative to the direction in which your bow is pointing, then you should be on track.

Another common problem encountered with the back stroke is having the stern dive underwater or the stern edges catching—an issue that is amplified in playboats with aggressive edges and low-volume ends. For this reason, maintaining a moderately aggressive forward position while back paddling is imperative as it helps keep your stern edges up and out of the water. Even still, you need to become proficient with the same boat tilt method that we discussed for the forward stroke.

By tilting your boat a little and very briefly into each of your back strokes, you can pull your bow slightly downward, which lifts your stern upward. The amount you'll actually tilt your boat and pull your bow underwater will depend on the situation, but keep in mind that your back stroke will be most efficient when your boat is kept flat to the water, so don't overuse this boat tilt technique.

Power Stroke

Now that you understand the concepts of spin momentum, it's time to start talking about how to control it and make it work for you. The first thing we can do is use edging to help our kayak stay on line. As compared to a flat hull, which planes across the surface, an edge literally digs into the water. The channel that it carves out acts as a track for the boat to stay on. The effect this has on controlling spin momentum is best illustrated in the power stroke exercise.

The power stroke is a vertical forward stroke designed to help your kayak accelerate while carving a steady path. The stroke has some very important practical uses, which you'll see later in this book, but furthermore, the practice drill for the power stroke is fantastic for developing balance and edge control—two of the most important paddling skills.

The goal of the power stroke exercise is to paddle in a circle using only power strokes on the inside of the turn. Start by getting some forward speed and then initiate spin momentum in one direction with a light sweep. Now, instead of letting the boat stay flat and skid to a halt, lift the outside knee to drop the edge on the inside of the turn. From this point on, you'll use only vertical forward strokes (power strokes) on the inside of your turn to keep your boat carving in a circle. Your success will depend on your ability to balance your kayak steadily on edge and your ability to take forward strokes with a vertical paddle shaft. These vertical forward strokes focus your power on propelling your kayak forward. Anything less than vertical will act to turn the boat in the other direction. The key to making your forward strokes vertical is reaching across your kayak with your top hand, while keeping your bottom hand in close to

Power strokes are vertical forward strokes that are used to propel
you forward without altering your kayak's spin momentum.

the kayak. This is a very committing position to put yourself in, as your paddle won't offer much in the way of bracing support, so you'll need to keep your centre of gravity over the boat.

Committing to this exercise will likely result in a few flips! It may be frustrating at first, but keep practising on both sides until you get it. Once you do, try adding as much power as you can to each stroke and tilting the boat more aggressively on edge. There are a couple of ways you can add power to your power stroke. Most obviously, you can pull harder on your

paddle although it's important that you keep your strokes short—between toe and hip. To get the most power from your power stroke, you'll need to get your whole body into the act. Try thrusting your hips past the paddle and pushing forward with your toes. You'll finish the stroke leaning back slightly, which isn't a problem as long as you recognize that this isn't where you want to stay. You need to get back upright right away and reach forward for the next stroke. This hip thrust technique will come in incredibly handy down the road when you start considering river running skills such as eddy turns, or even for more advanced skills such as running waterfalls.

LATERAL STROKES

Draw Strokes

Although there are a variety of draw strokes that we'll be looking at in this chapter, this segment focuses on the draws that move your kayak sideways. These most basic forms of the draw stroke are useful for pulling up beside someone or something or lining up your kayak in river situations.

Basic Draw Stroke

The basic draw involves rotating your torso to face the direction in which you want to draw yourself. You'll then reach out to the side of your hip and plant your paddle about two feet away with the power face towards you and the paddle held as vertically as possible. The more you can twist at the hips, the easier this will be to achieve. The boat should remain flat to avoid catching an edge. When your blade is completely in the water, pull your lower hand in towards your hip. Your top hand will stay very stationary, acting as the pivot point for the stroke. Before your paddle hits your boat, you'll need to finish the stroke by slicing the blade out of the water towards the stern. Be careful that you do not bring your paddle too close to the side

To add power to your power stroke, thrust your hips forward as you pull on the paddle.

DRAWING CIRCLES

One of the most common problems people have with the draw stroke is that they find that it turns their kayak rather than moving it only sideways. If you experience this problem, it generally means that you're pulling your draw too far forward or too far back. If you're pulling your draw too far forward (towards your knee instead of your hip) you'll pull your bow towards your paddle. If your draw is too far back, you'll pull your stern towards your paddle. Drawing your paddle towards your hip is a good guideline, but every kayak reacts differently and you can expect to need to make some fine adjustments to keep your boat moving perfectly sideways.

of your kayak before finishing the stroke, as it can get pinned and throw you off balance. The paddle should exit about three to six inches away from the side of your kayak.

T-Stroke

Once you're comfortable with the basic draw, you're ready for the T-stroke. The only difference between the two is that instead of slicing the blade out of the water towards the stern, you'll keep it in the water, curl your wrists forward ninety degrees and slice the

1. Plant your draw stroke directly out to the side of your kayak, with your head and body rotated to face the shaft, and your paddle held as vertical as possible.
2. While your top hand stays very still, your bottom hand pulls in towards your body until your blade is 6" away from your boat.
3. The T-stroke involves curling your wrists forward and slicing the blade back out to where it started.
4. Notice how aggressively the upper body stays turned towards the draw stroke.

blade back out to its starting position. This in-water recovery will help develop valuable paddle dexterity, but more importantly, it allows you to follow the third Golden Rule—keeping an active blade in the water. By doing so, you are maintaining steady control of your kayak—effectively keeping your hands on the steering wheel.

Sculling Draw

The most advanced and powerful technique for drawing your kayak sideways is called the sculling draw.

The sculling draw is set up in the same way as the T-stroke—with your upper body rotated towards it, your paddle shaft positioned as vertically as possible, and your blade fully planted in the water at ninety degrees from your hip. The difference between the two strokes lies in how you'll pull on your paddle. Instead of pulling your blade directly into your hip, you'll use something called a sculling motion. This sculling motion lets you pull steadily on your paddle, and bypasses the recovery phase that the T-stroke requires.

The key to sculling is keeping your paddle blade moving along a short path forward and backward about a foot or two out to the side of your kayak, with a blade angle that opens your power face to the oncoming water and pulls your paddle away from your kayak. This unique blade angle is commonly referred to as a "climbing angle." Climbing angle means that the leading edge of your paddle blade is higher than the trailing edge. It's the same as spreading jam on toast: picture the knife's angle as it glides over the bread's surface, leading edge higher than the trailing edge. To maintain a climbing angle on your blade while performing the sculling draw you'll cock your wrists slightly back as you slice your blade forward. You'll then make a quick transition and curl your wrists slightly forward as you slice your blade backward. Keep in mind that the change in blade angle is subtle. If you open your power face too much, you'll be pushing your kayak forward and backward rather than drawing it sideways.

Using this sculling technique, you can apply steady drawing pressure with your paddle blade and move your boat laterally at a surprising speed. Don't

Sculling involves maintaining a climbing angle on your blade, which you do by cocking your wrists back as you push your blade to the bow and curling your wrists forward as you pull the blade towards the stern.

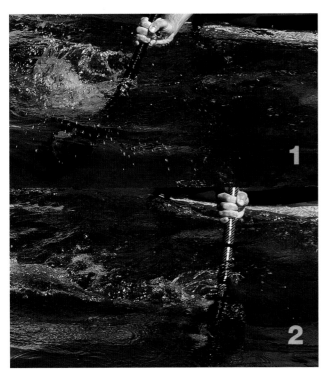

Notice the climbing angle is quite subtle as the blade is sliced towards the bow with the wrist cocked back.

forget that just like any other stroke, the power for your sculling draw comes from your torso rotation. This is why it's so important that you turn your body aggressively into the stroke. The forward and backward movement of your paddle can then be driven by your torso rotation, while your arms will stay in a relatively fixed position.

TURNING STROKES

Sweep Strokes

Sweep strokes are the most basic and common strokes used to turn your boat. Whereas propelling strokes follow a path very close to the boat with a close to vertical paddle, sweep strokes require you to move the blade out and away from the boat with a relatively horizontal paddle. As you reach further out to the

TORSO ROTATION

Before getting into the techniques of turning, it's important to emphasize one key element of all turns (and you've heard it before!): torso rotation. Of course, torso rotation requires the separation of upper and lower body, so we'll proceed with the assumption that this is understood. One way to think of your upper body is as a steering wheel–you turn it to make the boat go in that direction.

Without rotating your torso, you forego all of the power available from it–like trying to fling a rubber band without stretching it first. You also inevitably let the boat turn ahead of you, which leaves you recovering after the turn instead of ready for whatever is next. Finally, not using torso rotation could put your shoulder at risk. When your hands are in front of your shoulders, you are generally in a safe position. Rotating your whole upper body allows you to maintain the "box," or "power position" throughout a turn. However, extending your arm without rotating the torso can put it outside of the box and very vulnerable to injury.

The sweep begins at the toes, with the body wound up and facing in the direction you'd like to turn.

Sweep as wide an arc as possible to get the most turning power.

Pull your arm in towards your body as your sweep nears its end.

Remove the paddle from the water before the blade gets pinned against the stern of your kayak.

side, you gain more leverage for your turn. Sweeps can be forward (using the power face) or reverse (using the non-power face); we will have a look at them independently.

Forward Sweep

The forward sweep stroke can be used while stationary, or while moving. The nice thing about using it while moving is that it lets you turn your boat effectively while keeping your forward speed going.

Start the sweep by rotating your torso and head in the direction you want to turn. Now, on the side opposite to that which you are facing, place the blade completely in the water at the front of the boat, as if you were taking a forward stroke. The difference is that you will keep the top hand nice and low with the elbow bent. This hand should remain between chest and chin height to orient the paddle more horizontally than vertically.

For a complete forward sweep, your blade will follow a wide arc that starts at the bow, extends out to the side, and pulls in at your stern. Throughout the stroke (or at least until near its end), your top arm is low and bent, while your bottom arm is straight. To maximize power, when you pull on the blade, try to pull your legs around with your stomach muscles at the same time. This will become more and more important as you progress into advanced techniques.

Once your sweep stroke has reached the three-quarters of the way mark, your tactics will change for what we call the recovery phase. Your goal is to avoid having your paddle get pinned against your kayak, or putting your shoulder in a position of risk. To do these things, you'll pull your back arm in towards your body at the end of the stroke and remove your paddle from the water.

To just change or correct the direction of the boat slightly instead of doing a complete turn, you can use a partial sweep. Do this by starting with your blade anywhere along the arc and finishing at the stern, but still rotate! (See "Stern Draw" for more information on correcting direction.)

Reverse Sweep

The reverse sweep is very similar to the forward sweep, except that it uses the back side of the blade and follows the opposite path—starting at the stern and ending at the bow. Also like the forward sweep, the reverse sweep can be used while stationary or when moving, although it will effectively kill any forward speed, which makes it the ideal braking stroke.

To set up for the reverse sweep, rotate your torso aggressively and look where you want to go. The top arm will be bent and low with the hand held in front of your belly button. The other arm will reach and place the blade completely in the water back at the stern. If you're set up correctly, your paddle shaft should be almost parallel to your boat, with your body wound up enough so that you're maintaining your power position (see "Shoulder Safety"). The blade will follow a wide arc: starting at the stern, pushing out to the side and finishing at the bow. The lower arm is extended and the top arm remains bent throughout the turn. As you push on the blade, focus

A SWEEPING TALE

Whitewater kayaking sweep stroke technique has evolved over the past decade thanks to advancements in boat design that have been based on the acceptance that it is more important for a kayak to turn than it is for a kayak to go in a straight line. Consequently, modern whitewater kayaks are much more manoeuvrable than those of the past. The challenge used to be getting the kayak to turn, and so a sweep stroke technique was taught that encouraged the maximum use of torso rotation. This involved watching the active sweeping paddle blade make its arcing path through the water—and is still a great technique for turning less manoeuvrable kayaks, such as sea and touring kayaks. But, modern whitewater kayaks turn very easily and the bigger challenge lies in controlling the turn and finishing a turn immediately ready for the next stroke. Furthermore, it is of obvious benefit when paddling in whitewater to keep one's eyes on where one is going. This is why the end of the sweep stroke is sacrificed and it is preferable that the paddler keep looking in the direction of their turn rather than watching the active sweeping blade.

on using those stomach muscles to help pull the boat around. To do so, it can help to lean back somewhat during the wind-up phase and then pull your body forward during the sweeping phase.

In many cases, you may not need to use a full reverse sweep to accomplish your goal, and so a partial back sweep can be accomplished by rotating and placing the blade anywhere along the arc.

Initiate the reverse sweep with your blade completely in the water at the stern of your kayak, and with your body aggressively leading the way.

Sweep as wide an arc as possible out to the side.

Continue leading the way with your head as you sweep to your toes.

Take your paddle out of the water before it hits the bow of your kayak.

Following a power stroke, the gliding draw gets planted just behind the hip and about two feet out to the side of the kayak with your upper body rotated to face it. This stationary stroke allows your kayak to carve a smooth turn.

Gliding Draw

Now that we've looked at the techniques for drawing your kayak laterally, we're going to take a look at a slight variation of the draw stroke that will let you carve turns when you've got forward momentum. The gliding draw does this by acting like the skeg on a sailboat. It lets your kayak carve a smooth turn without spinning out and losing valuable forward momentum. Just as with downhill skiing or snowboarding, the key to carving a kayak is getting your boat on edge, and preventing your back end from sliding out.

Practise the gliding draw and carving on flatwater first by building up some forward speed then establishing spin momentum with a small sweep. Before your kayak has a chance to spin out, tilt it on edge and take a power stroke to give yourself a final

boost and to keep your kayak carving. Using the same paddle blade, you'll then reach and plant a draw out to the side of your kayak, on the inside of your turn. Since the goal is to keep all your forward momentum, it should make sense that this gliding draw stroke gets planted with the blade parallel to the direction of your kayak, so as to cause minimal resistance. To get the most power out of your draw, your paddle shaft should be held as vertically as possible and your chest should be rotated to face it. In order to keep a smoothly carving turn, plant your draw somewhere just behind your hip, but expect to need small adjustments. If your stern slides out, then your draw is too far forward. If your kayak starts turning in the opposite direction, then your draw is too far back.

When practising the gliding draw, remember that the role of the draw is not to turn your kayak but to maintain the carving turn you've established

An open-faced bow draw.

A closed-faced bow draw.

by preventing the stern of your kayak from sliding out. This means that relatively little pressure will be applied against the water with your gliding draw.

Bow Draw

As you're discovering, a draw stroke is useful for more than simply moving your kayak sideways from a stationary position. A draw can be placed anywhere along the length of your boat—either statically, by keeping it in one place, or dynamically, by sliding it forward or backward. At each position alongside the boat, the draw stroke will have a different effect. One of the most efficient ways to change the direction of your boat is to move your draw forward where it will act to pull the bow around. Not surprisingly, this is called a bow draw.

Start practising the bow draw in your stationary position first by using the T-stroke draw technique, but instead of pulling the draw to your hip, open the power face of your paddle a bit more and pull the blade towards your toes. You should be able to spin the boat in controlled circles with repeated T-stroke bow draws.

The next step is to get comfortable with the bow draw while your boat is moving forward. Start with a little forward speed in a straight line and then plant a stationary bow draw about a foot or two out to the side of your knee and cock your wrists slightly outwards to open the face of the paddle. You'll find that the boat turns towards your paddle without your having to pull it in. Because of your forward speed, placing an open-faced bow draw catches "incoming" water and harnesses its power to act on the boat. The forces at play here are very much the same as those you will encounter in moving water. This leads us into taking a closer look at two distinct forms of bow draws that you'll use on the river: the open-faced bow draw and the closed-faced bow draw. It is important to note at this time that bow draws are usually accompanied by a front or back sweep that initiates your spin momentum.

Open-Faced Bow Draw

The open-faced bow draw is also commonly referred to as the "Duffek" stroke (named after a Czechoslovakian slalom paddler), and is the most

powerful means of turning your kayak when you have forward speed. Since whitewater kayaks are designed to turn very efficiently to begin with, you'll only need to use this stroke in the most aggressive turning situations and when maintaining forward speed is not a real concern, since the stroke acts as a brake. You can plant this bow draw anywhere along the length of your kayak from the very front to directly out to the side of your body. The further out to your side that you plant the stroke, and the more you open the power face, the more powerful your draw will be. By reaching directly out to your side and opening your power face right up, you can catch an incredible amount of water and spin your kayak around very effectively. To harness all this power and keep your shoulders safe at the same time, you'll need to rotate your head and upper body to face your draw. This effectively winds up your body, keeping your hands in front of you in the power position that we spoke about in the "Shoulder Safety" segment.

Although this technique alone will turn your boat very effectively, there is another technique that you can incorporate to make your turns much quicker still! It involves sinking your stern underwater and using something called "buoyancy energy" to pivot the boat. Not surprisingly, it's referred to as a pivot turn, and is something that we'll be looking at later in this chapter.

Closed-Faced Bow Draw

If you don't need to make an ultra-aggressive turn and would like to conserve some of your forward momentum, then the closed-faced bow draw is your best choice. The closed-faced bow draw involves using a draw that doesn't catch water. Instead of being opened to your bow, the power face of your paddle will actually face your body throughout the stroke. Let's look at this stroke starting with a gliding draw—a very common transition. While performing a

The open-faced bow draw, or Duffek, is the most powerful means of turning your kayak when you have forward speed. Notice how aggressively the head and body lead the way. This lets you draw on the power of torso rotation, while keeping your hands in front of your body, and therefore your shoulders safe.

gliding draw, your paddle will be planted just behind your hip and a foot or two out to the side with the blade parallel to the length of your kayak so that it will slice effortlessly through the water. Your head and upper body should of course be turned to face your paddle, which keeps your shoulders safe. Now slice your draw forward by unwinding your upper body, and as the blade passes your hip begin pulling in on your draw. As you do so, your boat will begin to turn towards your paddle. Assuming that the angle of your paddle blade remains constant, then as your boat turns into it, your paddle blade will actually become "closed" relative to the incoming current and the direction of your boat. Another way to think about this is that the power face will continuously face your body as you slice the blade forward and pull it inward. This closed-faced draw doesn't act as a brake because it doesn't "catch" incoming water. In fact, it can actually provide your boat with a small amount of added forward momentum.

C-Stroke

The C-stroke is different than the other strokes we've looked at as it represents a series of strokes that when combined, allow you to propel your kayak and carve a steady turn without removing your paddle from the water. The "C" of the C-stroke could stand for a variety of things. It could mean; constant, combination, carving, or circular. It could refer to the shape the paddle blade draws in the water. Regardless, it is an important skill to develop as you will use it frequently in whitewater situations.

The best way to practise the C-stroke starts with the power stroke drill we looked at in the "Propulsion

1. The closed-faced bow draw starts from a gliding draw, which slices forward and pulls towards the body.
2. Make sure that the power face continues to face your body as you slide the draw forward so that it doesn't catch water and slow you down.
3. The further forward you slice the closed-face bow draw, the more aggressively it will turn your kayak.
4. Finish the stroke by pulling it in towards your toes, in position for a power stroke.

Strokes" segment of this chapter. Establish some forward speed, initiate spin momentum with a small sweep stroke, tilt your boat on its carving edge and take a power stroke. This time, though, instead of reaching for a second power stroke, when the stroke reaches its end (at your hip), curl your wrists forward and slice your paddle blade out to the side and into a gliding draw behind your hip. After gliding for a moment, continue with the closed-faced bow draw technique we just looked at. This involves slicing your draw forward and pulling it to your toes while keeping the power face facing your upper body so as not to catch incoming water. Once your draw reaches your toes, you're back at step one and ready for another "power" forward stroke. In so doing, the circle has been completed with your paddle remaining active in the water at all times.

The C-stroke will be explored further and put into more practical use in the "River Running" chapter. Before long, I'm sure the C-stroke will be one of your most valued river running techniques.

Stern Rudders

Stern rudders are one of the most effective ways to make small adjustments to your direction of travel, because it turns the boat without taking away your forward momentum. They're also the best way to control your kayak when surfing a wave. There are two forms of the stern rudder: the stern pry, and the stern draw. Both strokes start from a similar position—with your body wound up and your paddle planted somewhere behind your hip.

Stern Draw

You're now becoming an expert on draws, and have likely already figured out that the stern draw is performed at the stern and acts to pull it around. In effect, this is the same as the last portion of a forward sweep.

The stern draw is initiated with your paddle blade planted somewhere between your stern and directly out to the side of your hip. Of course, the further from the stern you start, the longer and more powerful your stroke will be. As you sweep/draw the stroke to your stern, you'll punch across the kayak with your front arm with your hand at eye level to maximize the power of the draw. As your stern draw reaches its end, remember to remove your paddle from the water before it hits your stern to avoid having it get pinned against your boat. You'll do so by pulling your back arm in towards your body with your elbow bent. Throughout these motions it's important that you keep your eyes on where you're going instead of watching your active blade. This will feel a little awkward because your upper body will be aggressively rotated towards your paddle while you take this stroke.

The stern draw involves pulling the stern towards your paddle and requires that you reach right across your boat with the front arm.

The stern pry is initiated with the body wound up and uses the back side of the paddle to push the stern away.

Stern Pry

The stern pry is much more powerful than the stern draw and so you'll tend to use it more often, to make small course corrections while running a rapid or to control your kayak when surfing a wave. The stern pry is essentially the first part of a back sweep and so it starts at the stern of your kayak with your body wound up and your paddle held parallel to your boat. To turn your boat, you'll simply push away from the stern, applying force on the water with the back side of the blade. Something to note is that the further out to the side you push your stern pry, the more water you'll be catching with your blade. This means you'll turn more quickly, but your stroke will also be acting as a brake.

Pivot Turns

One of the most important features of whitewater kayaks is that they have less volume at their ends than at their centre, and pivot turns are the fundamental reason for this. Pivot turns are the most powerful and effective means of turning the kayak in nearly all situations, whether river running or playboating. They also form a crucial element of the foundation you'll need to keep progressing. A pivot turn is basically an ultra-effective sweep stroke during which one end of your kayak is pulled underwater, bringing the other end into the air. This facilitates the turn by reducing the amount of resistance or "drag" on one end, and taking advantage of buoyancy energy that is created by submerging the other end (which we will discuss below). This can be accomplished by either submerging the bow end (bow pivot turn), or the stern end (stern pivot turn).

The pivot turn technique combines four skills we have discussed so far: balance, edging, recruiting power from the torso, and a choice of turning strokes (sweeps or draws). Before proceeding, make sure you understand them thoroughly. There's a lot happening at once during a pivot turn and there are many ways to break it down, but we will try to keep it simple throughout by just separating the initiation of the turn from its completion.

Buoyancy Energy

Buoyancy energy refers to your kayak's desire to be on the surface of the water due to all the air that is trapped inside. When one end of your kayak is underwater, it will have a lot of buoyancy energy and will want to take the quickest path back to the surface. Using your edges, you can dictate in which direction

Learning to use buoyancy energy to your advantage is a key element of any playboating move that involves sinking an end of your kayak.

this end will return to the surface. This energy can be a very powerful tool, but if misdirected it can also work against you. You'll need to learn to harness the power of buoyancy energy for any playboating move that requires having an end of your kayak underwater (which is most of them!). It will also come in handy in a variety of ways while river running. We're going to start by looking at how buoyancy energy can be used to optimize one of the fundamental paddling strokes, the sweep stroke. A sweep stroke that takes advantage of buoyancy energy is referred to as a "pivot turn."

Stern Pivot Turn

We'll start with the stern pivot turn because it's easier than a bow pivot turn. The stern pivot involves slicing the stern underwater to elevate, "release" or "free" the bow, and in doing so, you should be able to turn a full 360 degrees or more with just your single initiating stroke. Although there are small variations of the stern pivot turn, we're going to look at the most basic and common technique which uses the forward sweep as the initiating stroke with your kayak starting in a stationary position.

Initiating your stern pivot turn involves starting with your regular forward sweep technique—remembering, before you start the sweep stroke, to edge the boat by lifting the knee on the side opposite to that which your stroke is on. With this tilt, the stern is set to slice underneath the water when your sweep begins. Now, just as you start pulling on the blade, you'll want to thrust your weight backward to help sink the stern. This happens right at the beginning; and then you should literally bounce back into the forward position. Something else to consider when initiating the stern pivot is that although it does not change in relation to the boat, because your kayak is on edge, your sweep stroke will be pulling downward on the water as it sweeps its arcing path. This is important, because it helps lift your bow into the air.

Now that you've pulled the stern underwater and started your boat turning, your ability to deal with buoyancy energy will either kill your pivot turn, or give your turn an incredible boost. To deal with buoyancy energy, you need to make a quick adjustment of the edge to sustain the momentum of your spin because if you were to keep the initial tilt on the boat after you reached the end of your sweep stroke—when there is no longer any force pulling the stern downward—it would immediately begin to resurface in the direction it came from. We refer to this (a lot!) as "hitting the wall." It happens because you've created a significant amount of "buoyancy energy" by submerging plastic and air. This energy wants to force the stern back up to the surface following the easiest available path. With your boat on its current tilt, that path is straight back up in the direction that it came. The way to prevent hitting the wall is by levelling the boat out just before you reach the end of your initiating stroke (the sweep in this case). To do this, think about lifting the knee that is on the same side as your sweep stroke until the boat is flat again. If you do this quickly and correctly, your spin momentum will not have been interfered with and the stern will gradually corkscrew back up to the surface in the direction of your turn. You will have taken advantage of the buoyancy energy you created to help you complete the spin! Be careful not to overdo the edge transition by tilting the boat completely on the opposite edge. This will send the stern straight up to the surface and kill the spin as well.

A final tip that will help you succeed at this exercise and will be crucial in whitewater is to "rewind" your torso once the initiating sweep stroke is complete, and to always look ahead to where you are going. By the time the blade comes out of the water at the end of your stroke, the boat will be spinning ahead of you. Quickly rotate your body so it's leading the boat again. This will help pull the boat through the rest of its turn and prepare you for whatever comes next. Practise this drill in flatwater on both sides with the goal of spinning a full 360 degrees using only one stroke. As you improve, see how vertical you can get the boat while staying balanced and in control.

Variations of the Stern Pivot

The stern pivot doesn't only work with a forward sweep as the initiating stroke. This technique can be practised and used with the reverse sweep and bow draw as well.

When using the reverse sweep, there are a few important differences to recognize. First of all, instead of lifting the knee opposite your stroking side, you'll lift the knee on your stroking side to tilt your kayak on edge. Your back sweep can then push your stern underwater. Furthermore, your reverse sweep must be started with the blade deep in the water so you can push up and out on it throughout the stroke, instead of down and out as you did with the forward sweep. Otherwise, the technique is much the same; you'll have to wind up your upper body very aggressively and thrust your weight back when you initiate the sweep to help sink the stern. Similarly, you'll need return your body to the forward position and level the boat off before the stroke is finished to avoid hitting the wall. Finally, rewind your body once the blade leaves the water to help pull the boat around and to prepare yourself for whatever is next.

An open-faced bow draw can also be used to initiate a stern pivot turn. In fact, this is how you'll make the

Wind up for the stern pivot turn by rotating your upper body and looking in the direction you're going to turn.

With your boat tilted towards your stroke, sweep hard downward and outward and throw your weight to the back edge to sink it.

Level the boat before your sweep stroke finishes.

With your boat level, your kayak will continue to turn as your stern works its way towards the surface.

Rewind your upper body to lead the turn once again.

The single sweep stroke should spin your boat a complete 360 degrees.

A stern pivot turn initiated with a back sweep—otherwise referred to as a stern squirt.

open-faced bow draw stroke that we looked at earlier in this chapter the most effective turning stroke. Like the reverse sweep technique, you'll need to lift the knee on your stroking side to tilt your kayak on edge and throw your weight back momentarily as you take the stroke to help sink the stern. The further out to your side that you plant the draw, and the more you open the power face, the more powerful your stroke will be and therefore the more aggressively you'll be able to slice your stern underwater. Of course, remember to keep your shoulders safe by rotating your head and upper body to keep your hands in front of you—in the power position.

Keeping Your Stern Pivot Turn Going

The bow draw is not only used to initiate a pivot turn, but it is the best way to keep a pivot turn going. Immediately following the initiation stroke, you'll plant the bow draw on the inside of your spin and pull aggressively to your knees. Remember that the more vertical your paddle shaft is, the more powerful the draw stroke will be. It also helps to open your power face to catch more water. Before your bow draw hits your kayak, release the water by cocking your wrists inward, and then feathering the blade back out to the side of your kayak where you can open your draw, catch water, and repeat the process. Be sure to keep your body wound up throughout the turn, which

Although it follows the same rules, the bow pivot turn is more difficult than the stern pivot turn because a kayak's bow has more volume than the stern and the move gets initiated with the less powerful reverse sweep stroke.

helps you use the power of torso rotation and maintain a safe shoulder position. Furthermore, the rules for dealing with the buoyancy energy of your kayak remain the same. This means that as you're actively pulling on your bow draw, you can edge your kayak slightly and work the stern more deeply underwater. Before your draw stroke has reached its end, you had better level off your kayak or else the stern will shoot back to the surface.

Bow Pivot

A bow pivot turn follows the same routine as the stern pivot turn, only this time you'll pull your bow underwater. This is a trickier skill to master, because a kayak's bow is always larger in volume than the stern, which means you'll have more buoyancy to submerge, and more energy to control, as soon as it's underwater. You'll also need to use a back sweep to initiate the turn, which is less powerful than the forward sweep that primarily gets used for the stern pivot turn. To compensate for these obstacles, you'll need to be less aggressive with your edging and will need to level off your kayak earlier to avoid hitting the wall.

Now let's look at the bow pivot turn in more detail. To submerge your bow, you'll need to do a couple of things as you take your back sweep. You need to tilt your kayak into the stroke and throw your weight aggressively forward. As soon as your bow enters the water you need to begin levelling off your boat tilt in order to avoid hitting the wall. When practising the bow pivot turn, it's difficult to keep your head and body wound up because they naturally unwind as you push on your back sweep. There's no problem with this as long as you "rewind" your torso once the initiating sweep stroke is complete. This will help pull the boat through the rest of its turn and prepare you for whatever comes next. Like the stern pivot turn, practise this drill in flatwater on both sides with the goal of spinning a full 360 degrees using only one stroke. As your technique improves, apply more power and see how vertical you can get your boat while spinning your boat the full 360 degrees.

STABILITY STROKES

Braces

No matter how good your balance is, sometimes you will lose it. A brace is a stroke used to recover when you've been thrown off balance. There are two basic forms of braces: the "high" and "low" brace. Both involve reaching out to the side of your kayak with your paddle and slapping the water with one blade, which provides the support needed for your body to right the boat. The only major difference between the two is the position of your paddle. It's critical to understand that the slap of the paddle just provides momentary support. It's your body that's responsible

Low bracing while side surfing.

for the rest. Let's take a quick look at how it does this.

As you flip, the only way to right the kayak is by pulling up with the knee that is going underwater. The only way to pull up with this bottom knee is to drop your head towards the water in the direction that you're flipping. Doing this is extremely counter-intuitive, but it's absolutely essential. Your head should be the last thing to come back up on a well-executed brace. If, instead, you lift your head up, you'll inadvertently pull on your top knee, which simply flips you even more quickly. To make sure that your head drops towards the water, try watching your slapping blade as you brace. It's hard to lift your head if you're looking down.

Low Brace

The low brace is so named because the paddle is kept very low. To set your paddle up for a low brace, sit upright and roll the paddle under your elbows so that your forearms are virtually vertical. Think of a push-up position. From here, you'll reach out to ninety degrees so that one hand is at your belly button and the other is out over the water. You'll then smack the water with the non-power face or backside of your paddle blade. Practise slapping the water on alternating sides, making sure that your paddle hits the water flat. If your paddle has any type of feather, you'll need to rotate the paddle in your grease hand in order to slap the water with a flat backside of your blade. After slapping the water, slide your paddle forward and inward, and roll your knuckles upward to clear the blade from the water.

When you get comfortable with these motions, start edging the boat slightly in the direction that you brace. As you slap the water, drop your head in that direction and pull up with your lower knee to level off the kayak. Keep practising these motions until they become natural, and then start pushing your boat tilts further and further.

The low brace is a great reactionary brace that can be thrown in at less than a second's notice. Once you're comfortable with it, the low brace will become your best recovery technique, and it also keeps your shoulders really well protected from injury.

High Brace

The high brace is definitely the most powerful of the recovery techniques. A good paddler can even use the high brace to recover when their boat is almost completely upside-down! The problem with the high brace is that it's easy to rely on it too much, which can put your shoulders at risk. So the first thing to keep in

The low brace uses the back side of your paddle against the water, which means rolling your paddle and hands into a push-up position.

Dropping your head toward the fall lets you completely right your kayak with your lower body.

Clear the blade from the water by slicing your paddle forward and upward.

The high brace uses the power face of your paddle against the water, which means rolling your paddle into a pull-up position.

Drop your head towards the water so that you can hip-snap the boat upright.

The high brace can be very powerful, but remember to keep your hands low and your shoulders safe.

mind is that despite its name, you need to keep your paddle and your hands low and in front of your body. Otherwise, the high brace follows the same rules as the low brace; only for the high brace you'll use your paddle in a "chin-up" position, instead of the "push-up" position. This means you'll be using the power face instead of the backside of your blades to contact the water.

Starting with a flat boat, keep your elbows low and roll your paddle up until your forearms are almost vertical. You'll now reach out over the water at ninety degrees, with your inside arm low, in what is sometimes called the "nose pick'" position. It's important that this hand stay low so that your paddle blade is as flat to the water surface as possible when it makes contact, offering you the most support. After slapping the water, pull your paddle blade inward and out of the water.

Once you're comfortable high bracing on both sides, start tilting your boat slightly, and combine the head drop and knee pull-up with your motions. This means that as you slap the water, you'll drop your head towards the water and pull up with your lower knee to right the kayak. Remember that looking at your active blade is a good habit to get into as it helps keep your head down.

As you perfect the high brace, you'll be amazed at how powerful it can be. Just remember that for even the biggest high braces, you've got to keep your hands low to keep your shoulders safe from injury.

ROLLING A KAYAK

5

Rolling is one of the most important skills for any whitewater kayaker to master. Once you can reliably roll in whitewater, your confidence will soar, and your paddling will dramatically improve. This doesn't mean that you shouldn't expect to swim every once in a while. Sometimes you won't have a choice, but swimming should be one of your last resorts. Aside from being tiring, frightening, and humbling, swimming makes you much more vulnerable to hazards. So, next time you miss a roll, set up and try it again. When the time does come to swim, make sure you haven't waited until you're completely out of air and exhausted. You're still going to need enough energy to get to shore.

We're going to look at three forms of the kayak roll. There's the standard C-to-C and sweep rolls, the back deck roll, and the hand roll. We're going to take a look at each of these techniques independently, starting with the standard roll. We'll then look at

how to roll in whitewater situations. But first, we're going to look at a common element that provides the foundation for all types of rolls—the hip snap.

THE HIP SNAP

The hip snap (or hip flick) refers to the action of rotating your hips to right your kayak. The hip snap is without a doubt the single most important technique to master in order to have success with your braces and your roll.

The idea behind the hip snap is simple. By staying loose at your waist (applying the first Golden Rule by separating your upper and lower body movements), you can use your knee to roll your hips and your kayak upright while your body remains in the water. In order to do this effectively, you'll need some form of support for your upper body. For most rolls, your

HIP SNAP PRACTICE

This drill involves practising the hip snap technique while holding onto something for support. It can be done alone or with the help of a friend. Alone, you can use the side of a pool or dock. With a friend, you can use an end of his or her kayak. The idea is to hold on to whatever aid you have available, and then to lean right over on your side and lay your cheek on your hands. Relax your hips as much as possible and pull your top knee over so that the kayak collapses on top of you. You'll know that your hips are loose enough and that your kayak has flipped over all the way when you feel its cockpit rim come into contact with your side.

Lay your head on the bow of a friend's kayak and use your knees to pull the kayak completely upside-down. Keeping your head down, roll your boat upright using the lower knee while pushing as little as possible on your friend's kayak.

paddle provides this support. For a hand roll, your hands provide the support. The fact that your hands can provide enough support against the water to roll your kayak is a testament to how important the hip snap is for the roll.

THE ROLL – AN OVERVIEW

The idea behind any roll is quite simple. To roll a kayak upright from the upside-down position, you're going to extend your body out to the side and get yourself as close to the surface of the water as possible. From this position, your paddle (or your hands in the case of the hand roll) will act like a brace and provide the support needed to hip snap your kayak upright. When practising your hip- snap (which we just looked at), the support needed to do it came from a friend's kayak, or from the side of a pool or dock. In

the description of the hip snap drills, we stressed the need to maximize the hip movement while exerting the least amount of pressure on your hands. This is all the more important when attempting an unassisted roll—you'll get far less purchase from your paddle than you did from the kayak or the pool side.

As your hips roll your kayak upright and under your body, your head, upper body, and lower body work together to finish the roll. This is where the bracing technique we looked at earlier comes in, and where I'll again emphasize the importance of dropping your head towards the water. By dropping your head to the water, you allow your bottom knee to continue to pull your kayak upright. At the same time, dropping your head keeps your centre of gravity low while your body moves over your kayak. If you lift your head instead, you'll pull on your top knee, which will effectively pull your kayak back upside-down.

Now it's time to right the boat again. Keeping your cheek on your hands, pull the trailing knee (the one that's underwater) up toward your body and roll your hips and kayak to an almost upright position while minimizing the amount you push with your hands. For this drill, you're going to maintain your grip and repeat these steps, so once you feel the lower cockpit rim come into contact with your side, that's as far as you're going to right the boat, and it's time to start over. Ideally this drill is done off the bow of a friend's kayak, as the bow will sink if you push off too heavily with your arms. You should be able to do this drill while keeping the deck of your friend's kayak dry.

When you get comfortable with your hip snap on one side, practise it on the other. Having an effective hip snap on both sides will come in handy for kayak rescues, and it will provide you with an even better understanding of the technique.

Raising your head will cause you to push down on the bow of your friend's kayak and makes rolling the kayak upright much more difficult. You should be able to keep their bow dry.

Again we'll acknowledge that dropping the head towards the water is extremely counter-intuitive—but we'll also restate that it's absolutely essential! Your head should be the last part of your body to come back up.

THE STANDARD C-TO-C AND SWEEP ROLLS

The C-to-C and sweep rolls are the two most popular rolls for new paddlers to learn and the most common rolls that you'll see being used in real life. What makes them so popular is the fact that they break the roll into a series of three defined, easy-to-understand steps. There is an ongoing debate about which roll is best to learn first (and which we're not really going to get into). What we will tell you is that we consider the sweep roll to be the more effective of the two because it requires less set-up, the paddle doesn't usually end up as deep in the water, and the paddle gives you a longer-lasting support. With that said, the sweep roll can be slightly more difficult to learn, because two steps from the C-to-C roll are combined into a single motion, which opens up a bit more room for error.

Whatever you learn, your "natural roll" will just be the one you feel most comfortable with and typically use the most often. It is normal for your "natural roll" to be redefined over time as you develop other skills and preferences. This means that although you may prefer to learn the C-to-C roll first, over time your roll may evolve into a sweeping style.

We're now going to break down the C-to-C and sweep rolls into three distinct steps, while at the same time looking at the differences between the two rolls. The three distinct steps are the set-up, the catch, and the recovery.

The Set-Up

The C-to-C and sweeping rolls both start from the same set-up position. Regardless of how you flip over, your first order of business is to get into this

The ideal set-up position involves placing your paddle alongside the kayak with the forward blade flat to the water's surface and your head and body turned towards your paddle.

position. It's best to start on flat water, getting into the set-up position before flipping over. The set-up position has your paddle placed alongside your kayak with the forward blade flat to the water's surface and power face up. Which side of the kayak you set up on is generally determined by which is your control hand (the control hand being that which stays glued to your paddle). Most people prefer to set the paddle up with their control hand closest to the bow. As most paddlers use right-hand control paddles, the paddle is most often placed on the left side of the kayak with the right hand closest to the bow.

Tuck your head and body forward and try to push the paddle right into the water (still flat and parallel to the boat). There are a couple of good reasons for starting with this set-up position. For one, tucking forward provides you with the most protection while underwater, as your helmet and life jacket are between you and any looming rocks. Secondly, being upside-down can be very disorienting, so the set-up position is a consistent starting point from which you can always get your bearings.

There are a couple of cues to be aware of when setting up underwater. Your forearms should press against the side of your kayak and your hands should be in the air. You should also be extending your body out to the side so that your head is as close to the surface as possible. The further out to the side you can get your body, the more easily your hip snap will be able to right your kayak.

ROLLING TIPS AND TRICKS

Use nose plugs! There are few things as unpleasant and panic-inducing as the rush of river or pool water up the nose. Aside from being distracting, you'll also blow air from your nose in an attempt to stop the flow of water, which ultimately leaves you out of breath and will cause you to rush your roll.

Try a diving mask or goggles! Although I personally don't open my eyes underwater, it can be very helpful for some people to see what they're doing down there. With goggles, you can clearly see if your paddle is near the surface or if it is diving and can make the required corrections.

The Catch

The catch refers to the part of the roll where you grab water with your blade to support your upper body while you hip snap your kayak upright. The catch is also where the sweep and C-to-C rolls start to differ.

We must emphasize that the catch is not about grabbing water to pull yourself upright. Your paddle just won't supply enough support to do this, and trying to do so will put an undue amount of stress on your body. Remember how, when practising the hip snap, you had to minimize the use of your arms. If you were successful in doing this, then you have felt

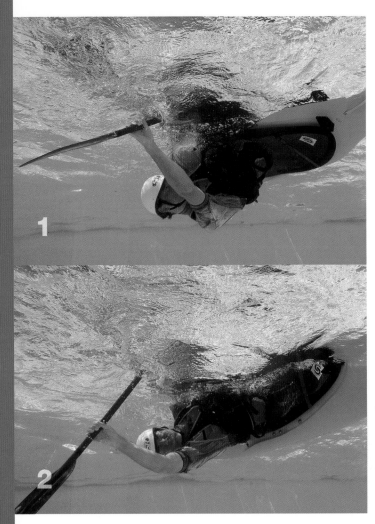

With your paddle blade out at ninety degrees and as close to the surface of the water as possible, you can pull downwards on your paddle and "catch" water in a position that provides you with the most leverage.

Your paddle actually goes through very similar motions for the sweeping roll. The difference is that you start applying downward pressure on the blade sooner, and so have a longer period of leverage from your blade. You'll also swing the paddle blade out to ninety degrees in a wider arc to maximize leverage on your blade. This means that the forearm will not remain against your kayak as a pivot. Instead, keep that arm bent, close to your body, and relatively passive as it sweeps out from your kayak.

The catch phase during a C-to-C roll.

how little pressure is needed from your paddle to roll the boat upright with your trailing knee (the knee that will be last out of the water when you roll upright).

You will get the most support or leverage from your blade when it's out at ninety degrees (perpendicular) to your kayak.

The C-to-C roll starts by swinging your control hand out to ninety degrees while your other forearm acts as a pivot against the kayak that keeps the other blade over the bottom of your upturned kayak. Make sure you maintain your power position at all times while doing this. This means that as you swing your control arm paddle blade out to ninety degrees, twist your upper body to keep your hands in front of your body.

The catch phase during a sweep roll.

As with the C-to-C roll, you absolutely must maintain your power position at all times. Your arms should actually stay in a relatively fixed position while your torso rotation drives the sweeping motion of your paddle.

Keep your blade near the surface of the water while you sweep and pull downwards on it. This will be one of your biggest challenges and the only way to do it effectively is to maintain a slight climbing angle on the paddle blade. This means keeping the leading edge of the blade slightly higher so that it wants to "climb" to the surface. You don't need very much climbing angle on your paddle, because you won't be applying too much downward pressure on it, right? It's also important to understand that your paddle won't provide as much support at the beginning of its travels (just as a brace planted at the bow of your kayak wouldn't give you much bracing power), so don't try to snap your hips too aggressively too early.

Without having started the hip snap yet, you'll find that even the initial pressure you apply on your paddle will draw your head and body slightly closer to the surface, and start your kayak's rolling motion. This action alone can roll your kayak a good twenty degrees up before you even start your hip snap. As your paddle sweeps further out, you'll gain more and more leverage, and you can begin snapping your hips to right the boat. Because this sweep gives you an extended period of time with support, you can snap your hips in a smoother, slightly less "jerky" motion than is required for the C-to-C roll.

A last issue to consider during the catch phase of the roll is how the body is involved. As you should already know from the first golden rule, all kayaking skills require the use of your arms and upper body separate from, but in conjunction with, your lower body. By relying on your arms alone, you lose an incredible amount of power and can potentially put your shoulders at risk. In the "Shoulder Safety" segment, we learned that keeping your hands in front of your body is instrumental in protecting your shoulders. You need to apply this rule to your roll.

One of the best ways to keep your hands in front of your body is to watch your active blade through its C-to-C or sweeping motions. If you don't like to open your eyes underwater, then just imagine that you're watching the blade! Turning your head in time with your active blade will naturally turn your upper body at the same rate. This gets the power of torso rotation involved with your movements and keeps your shoulders safe.

GET A GRIP!

At times, your paddle might get knocked around in your hand, or you may just lose grip with one hand. This turn of events can be disastrous for your roll, as your hand position is what dictates your blade angle. Poor hand positioning on the paddle often results in knifing, which means the blade is angled so that it slices through the water when it's pulled upon. If you feel no support or resistance when you pull on your paddle, you need to double-check your blade angle. The best way to do this is to slide your control hand over to the blade and feel for its position relative to the surface of the water. Remember it should be flat to the water's surface.

You might also want to place an index on the control handgrip of your paddle. This index can be a small strip of foam or wood that is taped to your paddle shaft so that it fits under the fingers of your control hand. Over time, you'll be able to recognize when your hand positioning is off just by the feel of the index. Many paddles now have built-in indexes or oval shafts, which serve the same purpose.

The Recovery

The recovery is the final stage of your roll. If you have set up properly and initiated the roll well with a powerful hip snap, then it's a relatively straightforward step. Having said that, a poor recovery is also one of the biggest reasons for a failed roll, and it all has to do with teaching yourself not to prematurely raise your head out of the water. As you've already seen in both the hip snap and bracing segments, lifting your head causes you to pull on your top knee, which effectively cranks your kayak back upside down. By dropping your head to the water, you allow your bottom knee to continue to pull your kayak upright while at the same time keeping your centre of gravity as low as possible.

Watching the active blade throughout the roll ensures that your head is the last part of your body to return to its position over your kayak.

There is some debate about the recovery path your body should take after the catch and the hip snap. Most people find that it helps to lean slightly backward during the final stages of the roll because it lowers one's centre of gravity. Others believe that the roll should be finished with your body swinging forward over the bow of your kayak to help protect your face from rocks. We are strongly against swinging the body forward because it raises your centre of gravity and hinders your hip snap, making the roll more difficult and less reliable. This means there's a better chance of blowing your roll and going back underwater. Furthermore, it's questionable that swinging your body forward provides additional protection to your face, because when the roll is executed properly, your head should stay close to the surface and well-hidden behind your arms and paddle throughout the roll. It is the awkward transition into the set-up position immediately after flipping upside-down that puts your face in the most vulnerable position—and that neither of these rolls can avoid. (In this regard, the back deck roll has a distinct advantage, and is why we use it most of the time...but that's another story.)

If all has gone well, then you should recover from your roll with your head turned to face your active paddle blade (which keeps your shoulders safe and promotes torso rotation), and with your head also being the last part of your body to return to its position over the kayak. The boat comes up, and then the body, and finally the head. You're now in a stable position and ready to go.

THE HAND ROLL

The hand roll is a roll done without the help of a paddle, requiring a highly effective hip snap and careful timing. The hand roll is a great move to master for a number of reasons. Most importantly, it's a confidence booster, and (if you haven't figured it out by now), whitewater kayaking is as much about confidence as it is about skill.

We're going to go over the hand roll with the assumption that you already have a reliable roll. As we did with the C-to-C and sweep rolls, we will break down the hand roll down into three unique parts: the set-up, the catch, and the recovery.

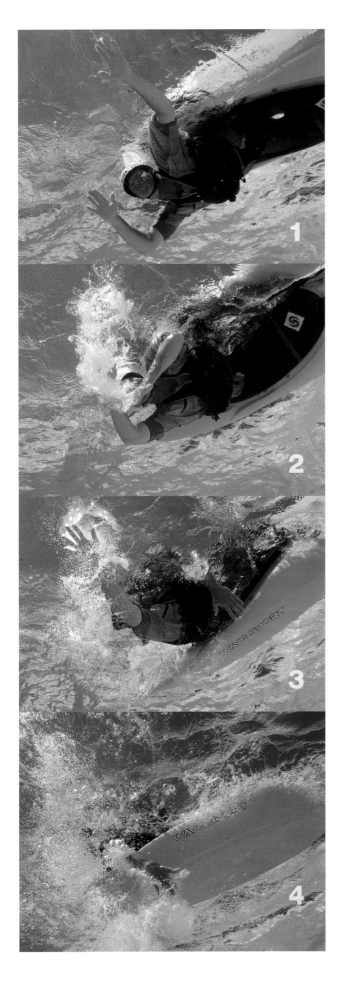

The idea behind the set-up for the hand roll is the same as that for your basic C-to-C and sweep rolls. You need to get your body out as far to the side of the kayak and as close to the surface as possible to maximize the potential of your hip snap. Though the concept is the same, the position of your body is quite different. This position has you leaning out to the side with your head and chest facing downward instead of up towards the sky. Your arms should be up and in front of your face. Most paddlers are stronger rolling up on their right side, which means leaning out to the left with the left arm closest to the bow of the boat.

Now that you're set up, the hand roll can be initiated in one of two ways: by using a two-handed or double-pump technique. These two techniques differ in the same way that the C-to-C and sweep rolls do. The two-handed roll is like the C-to-C roll in that you'll set up to use a single quick and powerful brace from which your hip snap can right the kayak. The double-pump technique uses one arm at a time in a two-step motion that resembles the climbing of a ladder, and which provides longer bracing support just like the sweep roll does. As you may have guessed, you'll probably find the easier of the two techniques to be that which corresponds with the standard style of roll that you prefer. For example, if you're used to getting longer-lasting support from a sweep roll, you'll probably prefer the double-pump hand roll. We're going to look at both of these rolls together, because the differences between the two forms are very straightforward.

The key to the catch phase of either roll is to extend out from your set-up position with your hands, arms and body as far out to ninety degrees from your kayak as possible. For the two-handed roll, push downward aggressively with both your hands and

1. Set up with your chest facing downward with the body as close to the surface as possible.
2. The double-pump technique involves pushing down on the water with one arm after the other.
3. As the second arm pushes downward, swing your head and body over the top of the kayak.
4. Keep your body as low as possible as you bring it back over your kayak.

arms, and you'll drop your head as you hip-snap the boat upright by pulling upward on the trailing knee (the right knee for those rolling up on their right side).

The catch phase for the double-pump technique is slightly different, and in our opinion it is the most effective and reliable hand rolling technique because it gives your hips more time to roll the boat underneath your body, and it forces you to keep your head down throughout the roll. Assuming you're rolling up on your right side, the first step involves pushing down aggressively on the water with your left hand. This first push draws your body further out to the side and to the surface of the water, while at the same time providing the purchase necessary for your hips to start snapping the boat upright. As soon as this hand begins losing its effectiveness, you'll reach out and push downward with your right hand and continue to rotate the boat upright with your hips. Remember to keep your head down throughout this process. As you begin sweeping downward with your second hand, you've reached the recovery phase of the roll and it's time to swing your body back over top of the kayak.

HAND ROLL HANG-UP

Through my first few years of paddling I would sometimes deliberately let go of my paddle underwater and hand roll myself up. I did this is because it was quicker to set up without the paddle and I knew it was just as reliable. Of course this left me without a paddle in the middle of a rapid, but at the time that was a secondary concern. I got by like this in Class 2 and 3 whitewater, but I knew this approach wasn't going to work as the whitewater got more adventurous and more continuous. Without knowing it at the time, doing this led me to develop my back deck roll technique, but I'll discuss that later on. (Ken Whiting)

As with the C-to-C and sweep rolls, there is some debate about whether the ideal recovery position is in leaning forward or backward over your kayak. Again, our preference is to recover over the back deck, for the same reasons: by leaning backward you lower your centre of gravity and can roll your hips more easily than you can if you lean forward. Whichever technique you choose, make sure that you keep your body as close to the boat as possible, and leave the head for last!

THE BACK DECK ROLL

The back deck roll evolved from the need to roll as quickly as possible, which it does by skipping the set-up step that other rolls require. It's not uncommon to hear people comment that though it's a quick roll, it's a dangerous one that leaves a paddler's face exposed, and puts the shoulder at risk. It's true that your face isn't quite as well protected, but you spend a LOT less time underwater, and your head stays much closer to the surface throughout the roll. Also, for much of the time you are underwater, your arms are actually in a very protective position in front of your face. With regard to shoulder safety, there is the potential for the shoulder to be put in an awkward position, but if you keep your hands in front of your body and don't overextend your arms, this roll won't pose any more risk to your shoulder than the standard C-to-C or sweep rolls. So when should you use the back deck roll? I use it almost all the time, and once you master it, it just might become your standard roll as well.

Before I get into describing the roll, it is important to note that the back deck roll is easiest in whitewater kayaks with low-volume (non-bulbous) ends. This feature allows the kayak to rotate around your body as much as your body rotates around the kayak. For example, you will find that your stern will be forced underwater during the recovery phase of the roll, which lets you keep your centre of gravity lower and leaves more room for error.

Because of the right-handed offset on most kayak paddles, it's easiest to perform the back deck roll

The back deck roll in action.

The only way to get comfortable rolling in current is to practise.

flipping to the left, with your right blade doing the work. Start with your paddle held low in front of you, with elbows hanging down, forearms held horizontally, and wrists cocked back quite aggressively so that the right paddle blade is facing directly down. You've now formed a rectangle with your arms, paddle and chest. This rectangle should stay relatively intact throughout the roll. Now lean back and aggressively turn your head and upper body to the left. As weird as this sounds (or maybe not for some), think about trying to kiss the stern of your kayak! This keeps your head turned and your neck cocked back. With your head and body aggressively leading the way and your kayak committed to flipping, plant the power face of your right paddle blade in the water as early as possible. Once planted, you'll push your right blade out in a wide arc over your head, and then out to the side and all the way to your toes. If your wrists

remain cocked back as they should be, then your right blade will be on a climbing angle that keeps it near the surface and provides the brace your hips need to roll the kayak upright.

If all has gone well to this point, your hips will have snapped your kayak over your head and your head and body will continue to lead the way as your right blade sweeps out to the side of your kayak. The rectangle between your arms, chest, and paddle should remain intact. For the recovery, swing your body forward as you sweep your right blade in an arc to your toes. When your right blade finally reaches your toes, your boat should be completely upright and your body should be in an aggressive forward position, ready for the next stroke.

When watching the best paddlers use their back deck roll, you'll probably notice that their kayaks seem to flip and roll back up in one fluid motion. The key to an ultra quick back deck roll is committing yourself to flipping once you've passed the point of no return (the point at which no brace will save you efficiently or safely). This commitment involves throwing yourself on the back deck of your kayak and leading the way with your paddle and body. If you can do these two things before you've completely turned upside-down, then you can start the process of rolling yourself upright before your kayak has even finished flipping over!

ROLLING IN MOVING WATER

Rolling in current can be tricky at times. The first thing to know is that the most difficult place to roll a kayak is on an eddy line. Eddy lines have unpredictable currents that can make it difficult to get the paddle into a decent set-up position, or even to get good purchase on the water with your bracing blade. If you find yourself caught upside-down on an eddy line and are having trouble rolling, you're usually best off to relax, be patient, and wait a few seconds. Unless you are caught in a particularly powerful eddy, you'll likely drift downstream. The water will be calmer, the eddy line will get progressively weaker and wider, and rolling will be easier.

Rolling in the main current is generally a lot more straightforward. If you think about it, when you're floating in current, you're moving at the same speed as the water. This means that the water is effectively still, relative to your kayak, and that rolling in current is no different than rolling in flat water. If you're paddling downstream faster than the current, or have just peeled out of an eddy into the current and have not yet reached the same speed as the water, you'll feel the water tugging at your body and paddle when you flip over. This will only last momentarily as you get accelerated or decelerated to the same speed as the current. The best paddlers will actually use these forces to help their roll, but for most paddlers, the best option is to relax and take the time to set up the roll correctly.

If you're having trouble rolling in moving water, then the best thing to do is to practise flipping and rolling in light current and deep water. You can start by flipping in your set-up position, but ultimately you'll want to practise rolling in current without setting up beforehand. Take your time and build your confidence slowly. On the physical side, there are two things that can cause problems with your roll. By trying to roll up on the upstream side, current has the tendency to force your active blade underwater more quickly. This doesn't mean that it's impossible to roll; it just means that you will get relatively less brace from your paddle and will have to have a quick and effective hip snap.

Waves are another potential source of problems for rollers. Large waves, or, in particular, breaking waves, can push the boat around and make it more difficult to get your paddle set up on the surface of the water. To minimize the effects of the current or waves, the ideal scenario is to set up and roll on the downstream side of your kayak. On the downstream side, you are pulling against the current, which can even provide added bracing power (not that you really need it!). As we already mentioned, with good technique you can usually get away with rolling on the upstream side of the kayak, but this is where an offside roll comes in handy.

ROLLING IN A HOLE

Rolling in a hole can be either one of the easiest things to do, or it can be virtually impossible. It all depends on which side of the boat you're trying to roll up on. If you're trying to roll up on the upstream side of the boat, you might as well give up! You're not going to get anywhere. On the other hand, if you are setting up on the downstream side, then there's a good chance you'll be upright before you know it. The reason is that the green water rushing under the foam pile can hit the power face of your paddle and literally push you upright with minimal hip snap involved.

You might even have seen someone unintentionally do a full revolution in a hole (otherwise referred to as "window shading"). This happens when a paddler is

When upside-down in a hole, your only option is to roll on the downstream side. There, the green water will actually give your roll a boost, and you'll likely find yourself upright more quickly than expected.

rolled upright more quickly than was expected, with the help of the hole. In the true window shade, the stunned paddler then catches their upstream edge and gets flipped right back upside-down!

Since it is imperative that you roll up on the downstream side of your kayak, it's not up to you whether you roll up on your natural side, or on your offside. This is why it's a good idea to develop an offside roll before you go playing around in holes.

ADVANCED ROLLING

When you watch good paddlers roll, you might be surprised at how quickly they resurface. It's almost as if they didn't bother setting up. Well that's because they often don't go through the complete set-up routine. As long as you get your paddle in a position to grab water, and get your body in a position that will allow your hips to roll the kayak upright, then you can roll in all sorts of different positions. Only practice will teach you what you can and can't get away with, so get out there and start rolling!

THE ANATOMY OF WHITEWATER

6

One of the most fascinating and challenging aspects of whitewater kayaking is learning about nature's most powerful medium. The river is a complex, dynamic environment with enough energy to offer you a lifetime of enjoyment. The more you understand it, the more equipped you are to work with it and harness its power. Volumes have been written on hydrodynamics, but we'll just focus on the aspects of current and specific river features that affect you as a kayaker.

FLOW

For this rudimentary discussion, flow refers to how the water is moving, particularly at or near the surface, where it affects us. There are three basic types of flow that interest us: laminar, helical and turbulent. It is important to understand at least the fundamentals of each so you know why the water is affecting your boat the way it is. As your paddling evolves, the lens through which you see rivers will be modified to distinguish these flows. This capacity to understand flow will gain importance as you progress, helping you to make key decisions either while descending a river or playing on a feature. Learning about flow is the first step in developing an intuitive capacity for anticipating its effects on your boat.

Laminar flow refers to the streamline motion of water as it moves along a consistent path. This is what we generally know as the "current" of a river. It is caused by the gradient of the riverbed, and is affected by the width, depth, and course of the river. Its most common form is the basic downstream flow that, on its own, has the simple and predictable effect of turning and/or carrying your boat downriver.

Helical flow is the circular, spiralling, or tumbling motion of water that results from one force acting on it in one direction while another force acts on it in an opposing direction. To simplify this concept, imagine the forces being applied by your two hands on someone's arms if you were to spin her around as

if to make her dizzy. As we'll see, this type of flow can affect us in a variety of ways—giving us both grief and serious enjoyment!

Turbulent flow is more irregular and less predictable than laminar or helical flow. Whitewater is pretty turbulent in general, but this term specifically refers to disturbances in the water that usually last for an instant, or not much longer. They might be repetitive, but are slightly different each time they happen. For this reason, their effects on your boat vary.

Volume is expressed in cubic feet per second (cfs), or cubic meters per second (cms), and refers to the amount of water that passes a point over a second in time.

VOLUME

When paddlers speak of different rivers, one of the major descriptions is whether they are high, medium or low volume. They are essentially talking about how much water there is in a river. Volume is measured by how much water passes by a given spot in a given time. Its units are either cubic feet per second (cfs) or cubic meters per second (cms). Volumes range from as low as 100 cfs (a small creek) to over 100,000 cfs (a large river). A high-volume river is typically characterized by faster flows, deeper rapids, and bigger waves. A low-volume river would generally have slower flows, shallower rapids with more obstacles, and smaller waves. The actual volume will give you some indication of a river's character, but it needs to be combined with information about its width and gradient before you know much about it. For example, two rivers may have the same volume, but one could be wide, slow, and shallow with small waves, while the other could be a narrow canyon with fast flows and huge waves. Volume is just one piece of information available about a river's character.

GRADIENT

In simple terms, the gradient is the amount that a river drops vertically over a given distance. It gives the average for a section and is most often measured in feet per mile (ft/ mile). Rivers that are regularly paddled range in gradient from flat to over 600 ft/mile. In general, steeper rivers are more challenging, but gradient is not a sufficient indicator of difficulty on its own. For instance, a section may have a gradient of 100 ft/mile and be either an easy low-volume run or a juicy high-volume challenge. The same gradient may describe a section of river that is relatively flat with a couple big drops. Once you know the volume and gradient of a river, it is time to start collecting more specific information about the rapids.

Horizontal distance =10 feet
Gradient = 10,560 feet per mile

DIRECTIONS

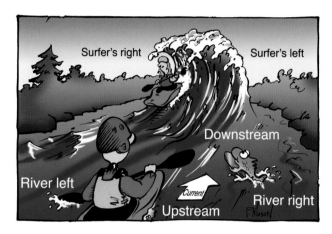

"Surfer's right" and "river right" refer to two very different sides of the river.

Like any sport, kayaking has its own lingo (actually, one that it shares for the most part with all other forms of whitewater recreation). We've already covered some of this lingo in the discussion of river dynamics above. Another essential component of it consists of directional vocabulary used on the river. The following are most commonly used by paddlers to refer to different directions:

Upstream/downstream: Pretty straightforward— upstream is where the flow is coming from and downstream is where it is going. In other words, the net flow of water is from upstream to downstream. This does not change!

River right/left: These directions refer to the corresponding side of the river when looking downstream. They are the most frequently used indicators.

Surfer's right/left: These directions refer to the corresponding side of the river when looking upstream. They are used mainly by playboaters, who spend much of their time oriented upstream while surfing.

A large-volume river can feel like an ocean, while creeks can sometimes feel like natural waterslides.

TYPES OF RIVERS

One of the best things about paddling is the variety of experiences it has to offer. From today's urban river parks to jungle creeks, from enormous cascading waterways to remote granite canyons carved deep into the mountains, there are so many different settings to experience. As we discussed above, there are big-water or high-volume runs right down to low-volume steep creeks. Rivers also vary in their continuity. Some have continuous rapids that are sustained for long distances in tight canyons, while others are "drop and pool," meaning they have distinct rapids separated by calm sections. Some rivers are fed by glacial or snow melt from the mountains and have really cold water even on the warmest summer days. Others are fed by wide expanses of farmland and rolling hills, with water that

12 o'clock: Directions on the clock can be very handy in visualizing different angles you might want to set up with respect to the current. If your bow is pointed at 12 o'clock, it is pointing directly upstream. At 3 o'clock, your bow is pointing to river left (surfer's right) and at 9 o'clock, it's pointing to surfer's left (river right).

has lots of time to warm up each season. Still others are controlled by hydroelectric dams and only flow on certain days of the week with water temperatures that are determined by whether the hydro company releases from the bottom of their reservoir or the surface. You never know where you might end up paddling!

RIVER CLASSIFICATION

Whitewater is rated on a scale of increasing difficulty from Class 1 to Class 6. This classification system provides a useful guide to the technical difficulty of a river, but there are so many other variables that can have a huge impact on the difficulty or danger of a river. Is it continuous in nature or drop and pool? Is the water warm or freezing in temperature? How remote is the run and how far away is help? Can you walk out if need be, or is it in a canyon? Is portaging an option for all rapids, or are you committed to running everything? As you can see, there can be massive differences between two rivers of the same class. For this reason, it's your responsibility to find out more about any river you're considering paddling. For many areas, there are guidebooks with detailed descriptions and images of the rivers, and more of these are available each year. It's always a good idea to pick one of these up. You can also ask questions on on-line chat boards or stop in at the local retailer for information. You can never be too well informed.

The classification system is still very useful for giving a river a general level of difficulty. It must be accepted that this system is in no way an exact science, and that it's open to interpretation. Here are some general guidelines for the whitewater classification system.

Class 1 (Easy): Fast-moving current with small waves and few obstructions that are easily avoided. Low risk. Easy self-rescue.

Class 2 (Novice): Straightforward rapids with wide-open channels that are evident without scouting. Occasional manoeuvring is required. Trained paddlers will easily avoid any rocks or medium-sized waves. Swimmers are seldom injured.

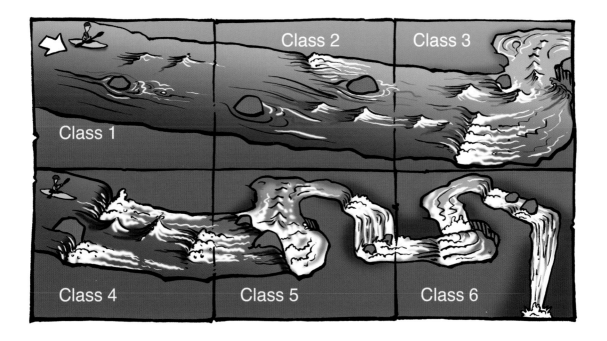

Class 3 (Intermediate): Rapids with moderate, irregular waves, strong eddies and currents. Complex manoeuvres and good boat control are required. Major hazards are easily avoided. Scouting is recommended for inexperienced paddlers. Self-rescue is usually easy and injuries to swimmers are rare.

Class 4 (Advanced): Powerful, turbulent, and predictable rapids with large, unavoidable waves and holes or constricted passages. Fast and reliable eddy turns and precise boat handling are needed to navigate safely through. Scouting is necessary, and rapids may require "must-make" moves above dangerous hazards. Strong Eskimo roll highly recommended, as there is a moderate to high risk of injury to swimmers. Self-rescue is difficult, so skilled group assistance often needed.

Class 5 (Expert): Extremely long, obstructed, or violent rapids with exposure to substantial risk. Expect large, unavoidable waves and holes, or steep, congested chutes. Eddies may be small, turbulent, difficult to reach, or non-existent. Reliable Eskimo roll, proper equipment, extensive experience, high level of fitness and practised rescue skills essential for survival. Scouting highly recommended, but may be difficult. Swims are very dangerous and rescues are difficult.

Class 6 (Extreme): These runs exemplify the boundaries of difficulty, unpredictability and danger, and have almost never been attempted, if ever. The consequences of errors are very severe and rescue may be impossible. Only expert teams with ideal conditions and extensive safety systems should ever consider these rapids.

RIVER FEATURES

As a paddler, you'll inevitably find yourself one day among a group of bystanders pulled over along a scenic road to look down from a bridge at a beautiful river or creek. Just as a mountaineer sees a knife-edge ridgeline, or a windsurfer sees a white-capped lake on a blustery day, you will not be seeing what those around you are seeing. You'll observe a wonderful system of dynamic components, each one acting in its

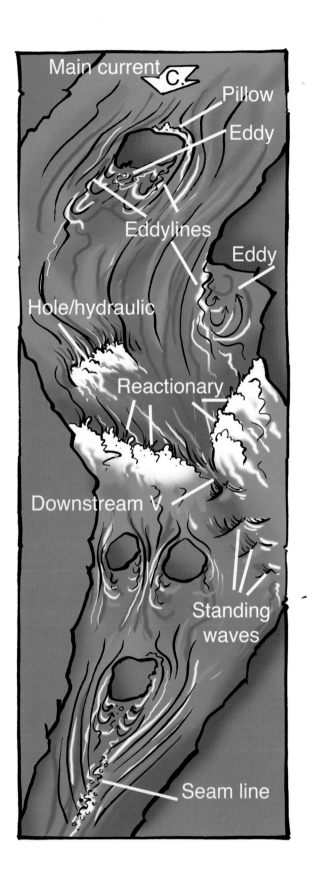

own unique way. As you progress, you'll dissect this scene, analyzing each feature, deciding which ones are worth further contemplation. You'll finish by coming up with a plan of action, whether imaginary (because you are with your grandma on a Sunday afternoon and have no gear) or not. You're going in!

The more you know about river features, the better equipped you are to have fun and be safe on the river. We'll cover some basics here, and they're important to understand, but we're limited to merely expanding your awareness with text. The knowledge becomes truly ingrained only with experience, and then you can use your intuition to anticipate the river's next move.

Eddies

An eddy is a pocket of water directly downstream from some form of obstruction, for example, a rock or a part of the river bank that juts out. The deflection of water by the obstruction creates a relatively calm area below—a paddler's parking spot. The concept is quite simple. When water is deflected, it's pushed away from one area and towards another, creating a differential in the amount of water between the two areas. Because of gravity, the river naturally wants to equalize this differential by flattening itself out. To achieve this, the water circles back into the area that it was originally deflected away from. The result is an eddy on the downstream side of the obstruction. This flow creates an upstream current (from bottom to top) in the eddy that can vary in strength from being almost unnoticeable to very powerful. In big enough eddies on high-volume rivers you can actually have Class 3 whitewater, or an eddy within an eddy! Very small eddies, just big enough to accommodate a kayak, are commonly called "micro-eddies."

Eddies Lines

The eddy line forms where the upstream-flowing water of the eddy (the eddy current) meets the downstream-flowing water of the river (the main current). This meeting of opposing currents creates a helical (whirlpool-like) flow that can be really fun or really bothersome, depending on the situation. The eddy line is narrowest and most crisply defined at the top of the eddy; it dissipates toward the bottom of the eddy. Reading eddy lines is a crucial skill to develop.

Downstream-V

The "downstream-V" is a general term used to describe the path of least resistance through a rapid. This is the point where the water is naturally being directed and therefore deepest; it is most commonly the place that kayakers choose to be. For example, when there are two boulders across from each other, the water is deflected diagonally away from the obstructions, creating this V-shaped path between them.

Reactionaries

As water flows into obstructions, it reacts by deflecting off to one or both sides. This causes a reactionary (or "diagonal," or "lateral") wave that is angled downstream and away from the obstruction. Reactionaries, especially big ones, act to push a kayak in the direction they are reacting. A downstream-V is generally formed by two converging diagonals.

Pillows

On larger boulders, before reacting off to the side, the water can be pushed back upstream. This forms a unique breaking wave or pillow just above the boulder. It is so named because it cushions the blow! This pillow can be a weird and wonderful place to surf or can provide a facilitated detour of the rock. Significant pillows are generally a big-water occurrence.

Seam Lines

At the point where the two channels of a river that has been split come back together, or at the confluence of two rivers, a seam line is formed. Because the currents are not directly opposing, there is less of a helical (whirlpool-like) flow than on an eddy line, but the two are otherwise quite similar. When the currents meet, they collide and move primarily in the only direction they can—downward. This is why it's a common sight to see someone who is swimming in a river get sucked down periodically if they encounter a seam line. It's also why seam lines can be fun play spots. The seam line dissipates slightly downstream of the point of confluence.

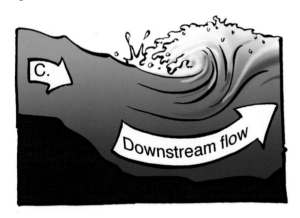

Hydraulics

Also known as "holes," "stoppers," or "reversals," hydraulics are formed when the water flows over an obstacle at a steep enough gradient to cause a recirculating flow downstream. As the water drops over the ledge or rock, it creates a depression or "trough." Because of the river's natural tendency to flatten out, water flows back upstream to fill up the trough. Tumbling over the drop and then recirculating causes the water to become aerated, so hydraulics are always white and bubbly. Where this aerated recycling water meets the incoming dark or "hard" water is called the "seam" of the hole. Holes come in a huge variety of shapes and sizes, depending on the gradient of the drop, the volume and depth of water,

and nearby obstructions. In general, holes formed by steeper drops have a longer recirculating component ("recirc" or "backwash") and a stronger capacity to hold a kayak (see "Pourover" segment).

A hydraulic is one of the most intimidating yet important river features to get comfortable with. You spend much of your time on the river avoiding them, punching through them, or playing in them. The better you know the anatomy of a hole, the more equipped you'll be to do all of these. One important concept is that the hole is a surface feature, which means that the water below it is still flowing downstream (except for some vertical drops that reach the bottom before recirculating—you generally stay away from these!). So if you were to reach underneath the aerated backwash, you would feel the current pushing downstream. Try throwing a piece of wood into a hole. It will usually bounce around for a minute, and then get one bounce that sinks it enough to catch this current below. A second later it will emerge downstream. This is also one way for a person to get out of a sticky spot (see the "Safety and Rescue" segment).

Most natural holes will have weak spots on the sides and/or in the middle, depending on their shape, location and the proximity of obstructions that might affect the flow. We refer to the sides of holes as

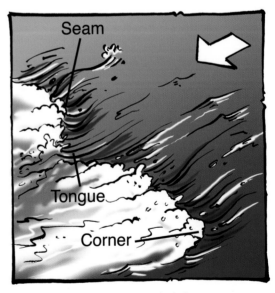

The anatomy of a hole.

"corners" and to a weak spot in the middle (where the recirculating flow is broken) as a "tongue." These both present potential exit points when you want to get out of a hole; and are also very useful for playboating. The lack of natural weak spots is one of the things that make man-made hydraulics like dams and weirs so dangerous.

Pourovers

Watch out for these! Pourovers are formed when water flows over a vertical, or nearly vertical, drop. The water pours over the ledge and straight down, making a deep depression in the river. This causes more water to recirculate from farther down. Pourovers often do not have tongues, so on top of being strong recirculators, they are usually pretty hard to get out of. Some pourovers are fun to play in, but more often than not, we like to avoid them or "boof" over them (see the "Boofing" segment).

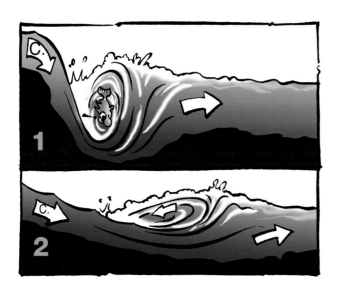

1. Pourovers are formed when water flows over vertical, or nearly vertical drops. Pourovers usually represent the nastiest form of holes for kayakers.
2. Long, shallow, sloping holes are more easily navigated and can be swum through more easily, as most of the water is flowing under the hole.

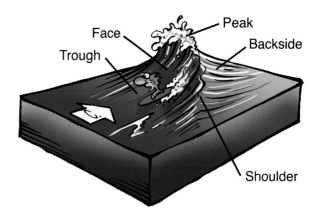

The anatomy of a wave.

Waves

In general, waves are swells that result from a combination of increased flow and some physical feature of the riverbed. Waves are even more varied in their forms than hydraulics, and their causes tend to be a bit more mysterious (at least to paddlers!). They can be flat or steep, smooth or breaking, stationary or dynamic, predictable or explosive.

Regardless of their type, waves all have some common features. The "face" of the wave is the upstream side of the swell. The depression at the bottom of the face is the "trough." The very top of the face is the "peak" or "crest," which then drops off to the "backside." Mountaineers have peaks and valleys; paddlers have crests and troughs!

For now, we'll look at a few of the most common types of waves.

Rolling Waves

When water speeds up, it acquires energy, and a bumpy riverbed or narrowing of the channel can cause it to rise and fall slightly, like rolling hills. These rolling waves are not steep enough to have whitecaps (or to "break"), but they provide a gentle up-and-down ride that is great for starters. These are often found at the top or bottom of rapids, where the gradient is not very steep.

Standing Waves

When fast water is slowed down somehow (e.g., by a pool below a rapid, by submerged boulders, or by a narrowing of the channel), it gets pushed upward to form a stationary standing wave. These waves are in sets of at least three and are more like defined faces and peaks than rolling waves. Depending on the volume of the river, these waves can be small or gigantic. One great thing about them is that no matter how big they get, standing waves are pure fun and present no hazard on their own.

Breaking Waves

When a wave is steep enough, water will begin to tumble down its face from the crest toward the trough and become aerated. On some waves, the break is very slight and remains up near the crest, while on others the break is all the way down to the trough. This creates a feature similar to a hydraulic, because the water is tumbling upstream, often with enough force to stop and hold on to a kayak. The difference is that the breaking wave is not recirculating from downstream of its face, whereas hydraulics are recirculating from

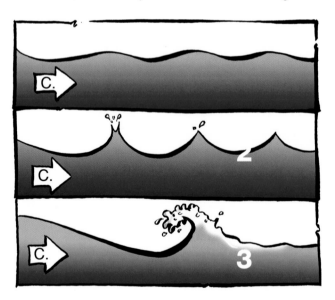

1. Rolling waves 2. Standing waves 3. Breaking wave

downstream. The effect is that breaking waves are usually not as sticky as a hole, though they can still give you a big, bouncy ride! Some large, unique waves form a curling or "tubing" break that is more reminiscent of some ocean waves. These can provide an awesome surf—or an equally awesome thrashing!

Surfing a big breaking wave.

Exploding Waves

Exploding waves are formed when, in addition to the normal causes, fluctuating or unstable factors, such as surging side currents, make them continuously yet unpredictably build and crash. An exploding wave will start out as a smaller wave, and then swell until it finally becomes unstable and crashes (the explosion). It repeats this cycle over and over, but with only an ounce of predictability. Quite often, you'll watch one for a while, and just when you think you've got it figured out, its pattern totally changes! This is generally a big-volume phenomenon and can be one of the most exciting features on the river because it keeps you guessing.

For personal reasons, we can't broach this topic without briefly mentioning "Mundaca." Mundaca is a fantastic exploding wave on the mighty Futaleufu River in Patagonia, Chile, our home away from home. We have witnessed this wave render hundreds of paddlers euphoric, in awe of the feature itself, and in awe of themselves for paddling right into it! This is the power of an exploding wave.

Boils

Sometimes the effects of the riverbed are a little more mysterious and cause random, funny things to happen. The most recognizable is a boil, which gets its name from the bubbles in a pot of boiling water. A boil occurs when the current is forced directly upwards to the surface, often in unpredictable surges. One specific type of boil is found below a waterfall, where aerated water is finding its way back up to the surface after having plummeted toward the bottom. Boils are also found in constricted rapids or canyons, and randomly on large rivers. They usually last for only as long as it takes them to settle out. The best way to get through them is discussed in the "Big Water" segment.

Mariann Saether prepares to land in the big boils at the bottom of this waterfall.

Playing around in a whirlpool.

WHIRL POOLS

The term whirlpool describes the action of water flowing in a downward spiral. It's caused by the collision of opposing flows, as with an eddy line. While small, the whirlpool is at most an unstable place for a paddler, but when the currents involved are powerful enough, the whirlpool can become a very entertaining or intimidating phenomenon. Big whirlpools can suck a person and even a kayak underwater, which can be fun if done intentionally, but not so fun if it's a surprise!

HAZARDS

The bottom line is that although there are real objective hazards inherent in the whitewater environment, kayaking is as safe or as dangerous as you make it. It's important to learn from professionals, to be informed and aware of your surroundings, to make sensible decisions based on your skills and training, to communicate with those around you, to carry the right equipment for the situation, and to promote safety on the river. Knowing what features present hazards and how to identify them in rapids is an integral skill for staying safe. This knowledge is something you both learn and gain from experience. Never rush into situations you're unsure of. If you're careful and sensible, you can stay safe your entire life on the river.

Shallow water is a basic hazard, but it's one of the most common causes of injury and broken equipment among paddlers. You can tell water is shallow either by being able to see the bottom, or by the little rippled waves that are caused when rocks are close to the surface. If you're unsure, try to get a better look or figure out a way to test the depth. If the water is shallow, take extra care not to flip or plant your blade deeply. Be especially careful if you notice that the rock on the banks looks sharp, as this is usually an indication of sharp rock in the river as well.

Flipping in shallow water exposes your entire upper body to trauma. To minimize the potential for damage when upside-down, keep your body as shallow as possible by tucking it up to the boat, and roll as quickly as you can.

If you're swimming in shallow water, always resist the urge to stand up. A "foot entrapment" is when your foot becomes lodged in between rocks or anything else on the riverbed. Because the current will not cease, this can very quickly present a life-threatening situation, as you're being forced down by the current and getting increasingly tired. It's easily preventable by staying in the "bodysurfing position" in shallow water. In this position, you're flat on your back with your feet downstream, keeping your bum up, and using your arms to steer if necessary. This keeps you as shallow as possible, and lets you push off any obstructions with your feet. It's the recommended position for defensive swimming.

As you're running a rapid, especially a steep rapid, it's possible that your kayak may become pinned on a submerged or exposed rock. In the case of a steep drop, the boat may become vertically pinned if the bow or stern gets lodged in the rock. This most often happens as a result of the shape of the rock, a crack in the rock, or a gap between two rocks. Regardless of which, there is just enough room for the end of the boat to become stuck. Otherwise, your boat may be broached sideways against an obstruction. In both cases, the rock was in the path that you chose to run (or ended up running, if it was not intentional). Because of the force with which the river pushes against your

boat, pins can be very dangerous situations. The main risks are that your boat may give way and bend, or that you cannot be rescued quickly enough.

Vertical pins are one of the biggest dangers on steep, shallow creeks.

Scouting a rapid from shore will always give you the best view of potentially hazardous spots. When you scout a rapid or waterfall, always look for signs of rocks just below or above the surface that may interfere with your run. When they're exposed, they are easier to detect, but when they're submerged, you have to resort to your ability to identify the signs. In general, the water will look "funny"; like it's not doing what it's supposed to. There may be strange ripples, or, halfway down a rapid, there may be a big "rooster tail" spraying water up into the air, or a strange, rigid bump in the water. Below a waterfall, the water will usually plunge downward and then boil back up just downstream. If there's a rock at the bottom, there will be less or no boil activity and some splatting or spraying of the water. These and other abnormalities are indications that you should beware of potential pinning rocks.

Undercut Rocks

Undercuts are rocks that have been eroded by the flow of water over time. They are most dangerous when the river level is such that the erosion is right underneath the surface, forming somewhat of an underwater cave that is very hard to detect until it's too late.

The degree of hazard presented by undercuts depends on several things. If the rock is facing directly upstream, it's likely to be more dangerous than if it were angled downstream, because water is forcing you straight into it. This makes it more difficult to get out or to be rescued; and also it is more likely that logs and other items will be stuck in there that might complicate your situation. Larger rocks, a stronger current, and prevalence of wood in the river are other factors that increase the hazard posed by an undercut.

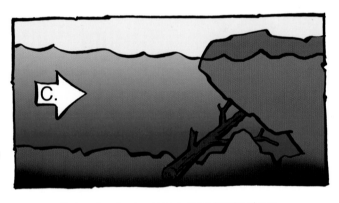

Undercut rocks should be avoided like the plague.

Detecting and avoiding undercuts are challenging things to do. The first choice is to get local information about any major hazards. You also need to be aware of the characteristics of the river. Are the rocks eroded along the banks? Are they sharp shelves of sedimentary rock, or old, rounded granite walls? Are they smooth or jagged? Are there potholes or other peculiar features? Have you noticed wood jammed up against rocks or floating in eddies? These are all valuable pieces of information.

If you are unsure about a particular rock, compare what the water is doing when it flows into it with a rock you know is not undercut. In bigger water particularly, water flowing into a boulder will often create at least a moderate pillow or surge up against the rock. An undercut will often lack this pillow as water is allowed to continue flowing underneath it. You can check for boils or other signs of water emerging from the downstream side of the boulder, another sign of an undercut. Avoid any suspicious boulders or walls.

Sieves/Strainers

Named after the device we use to keep pasta in and let water out, these nasty river features also let big things in (like kayaks or people), but let only water out. Sieves pose a significant hazard to paddlers and can be very difficult to detect.

Again, the first thing to do is ask locals if they know of any major hazards. Otherwise, be aware of the type of rock around you and any oddities. Are there a lot of cracks? These are the main causes of rock sieves, as water is allowed to flow through them, but anything bigger can get stuck. Ominous cracks in rocks, small channels between boulders, abnormalities in the flow above slabs of rock, and evidence of water emerging downstream of boulders are all potential signs of rock strainers. Needless to say, it's best to steer clear of these features.

Log-Jams

Where one log gets broached, subsequent logs flowing down the river can result in a pileup of wood that creates a specific kind of strainer. Water will flow through this log-jam, but anything bigger will get caught up in it. If you see a pile of logs, stay away!

A strainer lets water through, but stops bigger objects... like you!

Bad Holes

Bad holes are holes that won't let go of your kayak easily. The worst holes will hold you even when you're swimming. As we discussed in the section on hydraulics, those with steep entries (like pourovers and waterfalls) typically have the strongest backwashes. Because the water is dropping so steeply into the trough, there is not much downstream momentum—even in the current below the backwash. Usually, if push comes to shove, swimming down into the current below the backwash is a way to escape. When

this current is not able to provide much help, the hole is considered more dangerous.

One of the scariest things about really steep holes is that they are almost impossible to see as you approach them—at most there may be a little hump or roller just above them formed by the ledge or boulder. These holes are one of the reasons why scouting any unknown water is important. Other bad holes are big, powerful ones that may not be as sticky, but have enough force to injure you, or are so violent that breathing can become an issue.

Although the steepness of the green water pouring into a hole plays the largest role in determining its severity, the "smiling" factor of a hole will also provide some insight. The "smiling hole rule" is simple. If when looking downstream at a hole it is shaped as a smile, with the sides of the hole being further downstream than the centre, then the hole will be safer than its ugly counterpart. The "frowning" hole has corners that are further upstream than its centre, forming a frown when looking at it from upstream. A hole will always want to feed paddlers to the furthest point downstream. Therefore, in a smiling hole a kayaker will be fed to the corners where they can escape, whereas in a frowning hole paddlers will be fed into the centre of the hole where things can be a little bleaker.

Waterfalls can present their own unique hazards. The water flowing over the waterfall (the "curtain") can create a "double hole" (recirculating both ways) if it's landing away from the wall behind it, which has often been eroded away to form somewhat of a cave. It's possible in this case that a paddler may end up, either in or out of the boat, behind the curtain and in a very difficult rescue situation. You can usually tell if there's a cave behind the curtain when scouting.

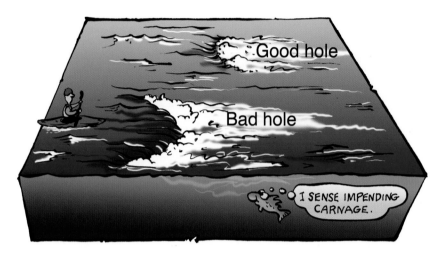

The "smiling hole rule" says that if when looking downstream at a hole, it's shaped as a smile, with the corners of the hole being further downstream than the centre, then the hole will be safer than where the hole is in the shape of a frown, with the corners of the hole being more upstream than its centre.

Man-made Weirs/Dams

Aside from the fact that there may be all sorts of dangerous hidden materials and that you often are at the mercy of those controlling the water flow, man-made weirs and dams are inherently dangerous. Because the flow is generally carefully controlled and contained by barriers on both sides, the hydraulic formed ends up being free of any natural weak spots. The water entering the drop is smooth, the angle is usually steep and creates a dangerous backwash, and there are no natural corner or tongue formations. The majority of deaths on rivers are caused by people flirting with man-made dams and weirs, and then by untrained people trying to rescue them. If you choose to play here, no longer are you dealing with the laws of nature—so beware.

Some waterfalls have been eroded on the backside, which is clearly not a good place to find yourself.

RIVER RUNNING

7

For this "River Running" segment we're going to start by looking at eddy turns and ferries in their most basic and ideal forms. We're then going to look at other skills and techniques that will come in handy, including the scouting of a rapid and the picking of a line.

EDDY TURNS

Eddy turn refers to the action of moving from the main current into an eddy, or vice-versa. This is also commonly referred to as "peeling" in and out, or "eddying" in and out. Whether you're eddying in, or peeling out of an eddy, your goal is to break completely through the eddy line and to carve a smooth, arcing turn in which your kayak maintains its forward momentum.

To this point, we've looked at the individual components that are required to make a smooth eddy turn. It's now simply a matter of piecing these skills together with the right plan of action. This plan of action is determined by your end goal and by the power and variety of the currents that you're dealing with.

As you may have already learned, and as we will discuss further in the "Picking a Line" segment, your success in running rapids relies heavily on your ability to look ahead and take actions that set you up for what is coming next. For simplicity's sake, let's assume that you're pulling out of an eddy and into a mild current without obstacles. Your goal is to carve a smooth turn into the middle of the current and then head downstream. You now need to decide on how much speed, angle, and spin momentum is necessary to achieve this goal. Again, these decisions depend on the strength of current that you're dealing with. As a general rule, you always want to cross eddy lines aggressively. The stronger the current, the more aggressive you'll want to be. This might seem like a simple enough rule, but the reality is that as currents get stronger, paddlers often become more timid. An

aggressive approach is vital, though, as it ensures that you'll break right through the eddy line and into the main current. Breaking through the eddy line, as opposed to getting stuck on it, means avoiding one of the most unstable and unpredictable spots on the river.

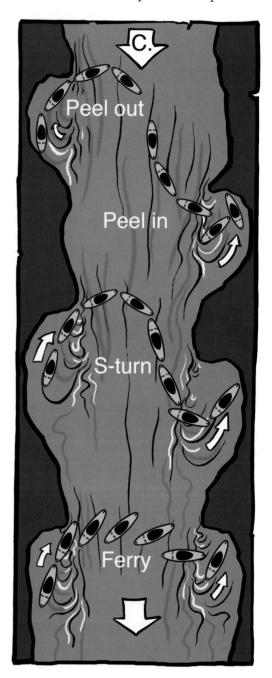

Seeing as we are considering relatively mild current for this example, you will be taking a moderately aggressive approach.

Clearly, every situation will require a slightly different approach, but the basic eddy turn we're going to look at can be slightly modified to work in any circumstance. Your plan of action involves building up enough forward momentum to take you completely across the eddy line at about a forty-five-degree angle. As you break through the eddy line, you want your kayak to carve a smooth arc and end up facing downstream. This basic eddy turn starts with a good set-up position and the right angle, forward strokes to build forward momentum, a stern draw to establish the boat's carving direction (spin momentum), a power stroke to pull the boat completely across the eddy line, and a gliding draw to carve a smooth turn downstream. Let's look more closely at each of these steps.

A good set-up position gives you time to build adequate forward momentum that will take you across the eddy line at around a forty-five-degree angle. There are a couple of things to consider when deciding on your set-up position.

Firstly, it needs to be recognized that the inside of an eddy provides the calmest water and will result in the least amount of "drift" on your approach. Drift is the movement of your kayak by the current in a direction other than the one in which you wish to go. The outside of an eddy has the quickest current and will thus result in the most drift. Learning paddlers have a tendency to hang out on the outside of eddies, where they are closest to shore. This actually complicates their set-up as they will drift more on their approach.

A second issue to consider is that eddy lines are most defined and narrowest at their source (the top). This makes it the preferred area to cross, because there is less "funny water" and the water is more predictable there.

Having established a good set-up position and built up some forward speed, you then need to give your kayak a slight amount of turning momentum before

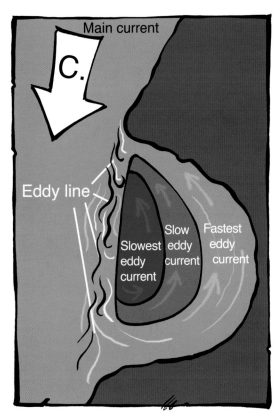

When setting up your eddy turn, keep in mind that the inside of the eddy is the calmest, and the best place to begin your approach.

you completely cross the eddy line. This turning momentum ensures that your kayak will carve in the right direction. Because whitewater kayaks turn so easily, and since the main current will be helping to turn your boat downstream, you won't need to use a full sweep stroke to accomplish this. A light stern draw on the upstream side should be enough to do the trick. With turning momentum established, your focus is now on pulling yourself completely across the eddy line and into the main current, which is where the "power stroke" that we practised in Chapter 4 is so effective.

Recall that the power stroke is a vertical forward stroke designed to provide maximum forward propulsion with minimal impact on the kayak's turning momentum. The only difference when using

1

2

A small stern draw establishes turning momentum into the current.

Reach across the eddy line to plant your power stroke.

3

4

The power stroke pulls you across the eddy line.

Feather the power stroke into a gliding draw.

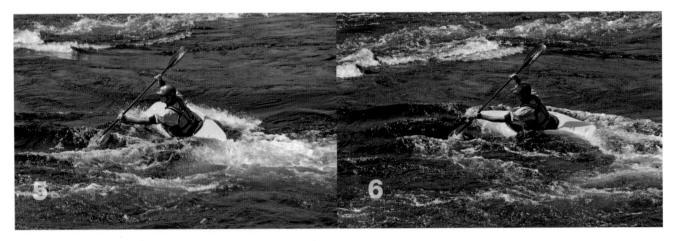

5

6

Slice the gliding draw forward to turn the kayak more aggressively.

Use a closed-faced draw to finish the turn.

The "Duffek" lets you grab a substantial amount of water, and pivot around very quickly.

it to cross an eddy line is that the timing of the stroke is important. You need to plant the power stroke across the eddy line in the main current. You can then pull yourself completely across the eddy line. As you do this, you must be sure to have your boat tilted downstream. Holding a steady downstream tilt not only lets your kayak carve, but it prevents the main current from catching your upstream edge. The amount you tilt your kayak and the muscle you apply to your power stroke will depend on the speed of the water that you are entering. The faster the main current, the more aggressive your boat's tilt and the more powerful your stroke will need to be.

So you've now thrust yourself across the eddy line with your boat carving a smooth turn downstream. The final challenge is getting your kayak to continue carving this turn until you are facing directly downstream. You could continue to take power strokes while holding a steady tilt on your boat. This would allow you to continue carving your turn while maintaining your forward momentum, but it is not the most efficient and not always necessary.

To peel into an eddy, you'll use the same technique that we discussed for peeling out of an eddy. The only difference is that you'll have more "drift" to take into account.

THE LEARNING CURVE

One of my biggest revelations about whitewater paddling came very early on. It was during my first season of kayaking, while scouting McKoy's rapid on the Ottawa River. McKoy's was, and will always be, one of the most menacing and mentally challenging rapids for paddlers visiting the Ottawa River. As I looked at the rapid before me, I saw more than just a frightening mess of turbulent water. I saw distinct river features. At the same time I realized that running through McKoy's simply involved performing a fairly straightforward combination of eddy turns and ferries. Was that it? Could running whitewater really be that simple? Having practised my eddy turns and ferries tirelessly, I decided to give it a shot and I slid into my kayak with new found confidence. Unfortunately I didn't really understand how fast the water was actually moving... and the waves were a lot bigger than I expected... In the end, I got thumped in the mighty Phil's Hole and rolled up wide eyed and red faced. When I reached the calm water below I had another major revelation... yes, a rapid could be broken down into some fairly basic eddy turns and ferry manoeuvres, but there were a whole bunch of other techniques that I needed to learn that would come in handy. One of the most important being the ability to pick a good line through a rapid! (Ken Whiting)

Another option is to use the gliding draw that we covered in the "Strokes" chapter of this book. The gliding draw is a fairly static draw stroke that gets planted firmly in the water to help your boat carve more effectively and maintain speed. The gliding draw gets planted about a foot behind your hip and between one and two feet out to the side of your boat with the blade parallel to the kayak, and with your body turned to face the paddle. This is a very committing stroke in its purest form, so you may want to start more conservatively by keeping your top hand over your kayak. As your balance improves and your confidence grows, you can push your top hand across the kayak to get your draw more vertical.

There you have the standard eddy turn technique. As we mentioned before, this technique can be adapted to fit almost any situation. One of the most significant modifications that you can make involves turning your gliding draw into an active bow draw. Using the C-stroke technique we covered in the "Strokes" section, you can turn your boat downstream more quickly while maintaining constant control with an active blade in the water. You can also use an open-faced bow draw after breaking across the eddy line to turn your boat even more aggressively. This open-faced bow draw is commonly referred to as the "Duffek" stroke. It allows you to grab a substantial amount of water to aggressively pull your bow around. By sinking your upstream stern edge slightly, you can also use your Duffek stroke to perform a stern pivot turn. When would you use this stroke? A Duffek gets used when we need to move from an eddy into the main current and face downstream as quickly as possible.

We will now take a quick look at pulling out of the main current into an eddy, otherwise known as "eddying out." You'll use the same technique that you used for peeling out of an eddy, although your set-up is trickier because you have a large amount of "drift" to take into account. Your goal is to break through the eddy line as close to its source as possible, with your forward momentum breaking you through it on a forty-five-degree downstream angle. To reach this goal, you need to account for the speed of the current that's taking you downstream. It is a simple notion that if you point your kayak directly at your destination, then the downstream drift will take you past your target. For this reason, you need to aim

With your angle set, build up some forward speed and use a power stroke to pull yourself through the eddy line.

Keep your boat on edge and keep paddling as you cross the main current.

upstream of your target enough so that the drift and your forward momentum lead you directly to your target on the eddy line. An important tip is to keep your eyes on where you're going when catching an eddy. Don't get caught staring at the hood ornament of your kayak!

Of course practice is the only way to become truly proficient at reading whitewater and plotting a course to the next eddy, but there are a few key things you can keep in mind. It's essential to establish lateral momentum (momentum across the river) when catching an eddy, so that you can break right through the eddy line. This means that if you're planning to catch an eddy on the river right, you'll want to start away from that right-hand shore to give yourself a chance to build lateral momentum toward the eddy.

FERRIES

Ferrying is the act of moving from one side of the river to the other with minimal downstream drift. This is accomplished by paddling your kayak on an angle somewhere between directly upstream and perpendicular to the main current in the direction that you want to move. Although every situation will require a slightly different approach, we're going to look at a ferrying technique that can be adapted to fit any situation.

The idea behind the ferry is quite simple. To move across current you can't simply point your kayak to your end destination and paddle as if you were in flatwater, because the main current will pull you

Keep your eyes on where you're going and you can make adjustments to your ferry angle along the way.

downstream. You need to angle your kayak upstream enough so that your strokes work to counterbalance this downstream pull. With experience, you'll learn what boat angle is most effective for the various situations that you come across. As a general rule, the more upstream angle you have (the closer you are to pointing directly upstream), the slower you'll move laterally and the more your paddle strokes will be working to keep you from drifting downstream. On the other hand, the less upstream angle that you have (the closer you are to pointing directly across the main current), the more quickly you'll move across the river and the less your strokes will be working to keep you from drifting downstream. To start, you need to come up with an action plan, which is determined by your end goal and by the

power and character of the currents you're dealing with. To keep things simple, we'll consider ferrying from one eddy to another across fairly mild and wide current that has no significant obstacles to contend with. Your goal is to reach the eddy on the other side of the river. The success of your ferry will rely heavily on your set-up position and angle. You'll also need to break through the eddy line in control, maintain an effective ferry angle, hold a steady downstream tilt on your boat as you ferry and successfully break through the eddy line into your destination eddy. We'll now look a bit more closely at how you'll accomplish these things.

The most important part of your ferry is your entry into the main current. The key to ferrying is converting the upstream momentum you establish on your approach into lateral momentum as you cross the eddy line. This means that the less upstream angle you can get away with using, the better off your ferry will be. If you have too much upstream angle, you'll fight the main current more than is necessary. For the scenario we're considering, your set-up and approach will be very similar to an eddy turn, although you might decide to approach with a little more upstream angle.

Starting near the middle of the eddy where you'll experience a minimal amount of drift, aim high on the eddy line (near its source) and build up some forward speed. As you cross the eddy line, establish a small amount of turning momentum towards the main current with a small stern draw on the upstream side. This turning momentum helps you break through the eddy line and convert your forward speed into lateral momentum.

Continuing just as you would with a peel-out, tilt your kayak on its downstream edge, and use a power stroke to pull yourself completely across the eddy line. This power stroke will also be responsible for establishing your ferry angle by preventing the main current from turning your boat downstream. This means that the power stroke you use for the ferry may not be quite as vertical as the power stroke you used for the eddy turn, because in the ferry you need this stroke to provide some turning power. Be careful that your power stroke doesn't provide too much turning power, as this would angle your kayak too far upstream or even back toward the eddy.

Now that you're in the main current with a good angle on your kayak, you're well on your way. At this point, your job is to maintain your ferry angle and your forward speed while holding a steady downstream tilt on your kayak that prevents your upstream edge from catching. The scenario we are considering involves a wide section of river, so you need to keep paddling your way across the current while balancing your boat on edge. As you do this, keep glancing at your target. Keeping track of your destination will let you know of any adjustments you need to make to your ferry angle along the way. If you find yourself moving

upstream of the destination eddy, this means you have too much upstream angle and you must ease it off a little. If you're drifting downstream of the eddy, this means you need to use a more aggressive upstream angle that fights the current more (turn the kayak more upstream).

As you get closer to your destination eddy, you have to make plans for punching through the eddy line and deep into the eddy. Do this using a version of the eddy turn technique that we covered earlier. To minimize your drift downstream, you'll ferry until you get fairly close to the eddy line. You'll then sweep your bow downstream and punch through the eddy line and into the eddy, pulling yourself completely across with a power stroke.

Recall that you want to break through the eddy line on a forty-five-degree downstream angle with forward speed. You also have to remember to switch your boat tilt as you cross the eddy line to carve into the eddy and prevent your outside edge from catching. The temptation is there to just ferry right into the eddy, which may work in some situations, but in others you may not have enough lateral momentum to break completely through the eddy line. You'll then get stuck on the swirliest, most unstable water on the river, which becomes less and less of a good thing as the whitewater you paddle gets harder.

S-TURNS

An S-Turn is a ferrying technique used for crossing narrow current. This can be tricky, because you need to peel out of an eddy in a way that sets you up quickly for breaking into the eddy on the other side. Remember that for punching into the second eddy, you want to hit the eddy line with a forty-five-degree downstream angle.

This S-Turn is basically two linked eddy turns. Because your timing needs to be quite precise for the S-turn, keep a close eye on your destination eddy so that you can make any small corrections to your boat angle along the way. The gliding draw that you used

An S-turn across a narrow stretch of current.

for your basic eddy turn technique comes in very handy for the S-Turn, as it lets you keep constant control over your boat's path and allows you to make small corrections. If you need to turn more quickly to establish the downstream angle needed to punch the destination eddy line, then you can slide your blade forward and use it as a bow draw temporarily. When you reach the destination eddy line, pull yourself completely through with a power stroke as you tilt your kayak onto its other edge and carve your way into the eddy.

TURNING MIDSTREAM

We've looked at how to carve in and out of eddies and how to ferry across the river; now it's time to consider how to make directional changes while in the main current.

There are two types of turns that you're likely to have to make: casual turns and aggressive turns. There really aren't many rules to consider for casual turns. Your basic sweep strokes will turn your boat quite effectively, especially if you combine a little edging with your sweeps to pivot the boat around. The ideal spot to turn is usually near the peak of a wave, but it's certainly not your only option. The advantage of turning at the peak of the wave is that you have the best view of the rapid ahead, which obviously lets you make the most informed decision on how much to turn your kayak. Furthermore, a large part of your boat will be out of the water at the peak of the wave, making your boat easier to turn. The reality is that any recent whitewater boat is designed to turn very well, so you don't need to restrict yourself to turning at the peak of a wave. If you need to turn, you should be able to turn your boat very effectively at any point.

When you want to turn your boat more aggressively, your best option is the pivot turn. This is a skill that we've already looked at in depth and that you really need to master. Let's consider a situation where you are floating sideways pointing to river right, when

An upstream pivot turn is usually the quickest way to pull your kayak onto the needed ferry angle. This is the same pivot turn that you learned to do on flatwater.

you notice a massive hole in front of you that needs to be missed to the river left. You could just back ferry away from the hole, but let's say you saw it last minute and are too close to avoid it with a back ferry. Instead, you can use a stern pivot turn to pull your boat aggressively upstream and onto a ferry angle to the river left. The pivot turn that you'll use in this "combat" situation is no different than that which you use on flatwater. This means you'll aggressively lead with your head and body and pull the stern of your kayak underwater so that the bow can swing around effortlessly. To sink the stern, you need to tilt your kayak into your forward sweep stroke and throw your weight back slightly. The tricky part of this turn is making the right changes to your boat tilts. You need to maintain a downstream tilt on your kayak throughout the turn, or you'll catch your upstream edge. This means that once your sweep has pulled your bow past 12 o'clock, you need to have changed the tilt on your kayak.

You could also initiate your pivot turn with a back sweep, an open-faced bow draw, or a combination thereof. For a review of the pivot turn, see the segment on this skill in Chapter 4. The key is developing your confidence and your edge control to a point where you can use a pivot turn to make quick changes of direction in even the most chaotic whitewater.

BACKWARD AWARENESS

One of the best ways to improve your paddling overall is to develop your comfort level being backwards on a river. When river running, you'll be able to confidently back ferry away from obstacles and will remain in control when spun backwards mid-rapid. Without having developed this backward awareness, you would probably find yourself panicking and struggling to regain control in these same situations. For the playboater, backward awareness is absolutely critical, since most moves involve spinning around—which means facing backward up to 50% of the time. If you are only controlled and comfortable when surfing facing upstream, then you will be at the mercy of the river the rest of the time.

The best way to develop your backward awareness is to practise eddy turns, ferries, and S-turns in reverse.

There's only one way to develop your backward awareness: be backwards! Begin with practising your back paddling and your back sweeps. You can then move on to simple backward eddy turns and ferries. It will feel odd in the beginning and you're almost guaranteed to flip a few times, but keep practising until you're comfortable crossing powerful eddy lines without having to think about which way to tilt your kayak and on which side to take your next stroke. The next step is to practise back surfing. Back surfing is an incredibly powerful skill for the river runner as well as the playboater. Back surfing will let the river runner use waves to help their back ferries and even provides the opportunity to effectively boat scout while surfing. In a more general sense, the fine edge control that you'll learn from back surfing will help take your overall paddling to a whole new level.

SCOUTING

If the fun-to-pain ratio isn't looking good, then why would you run it? (Ken Whiting)

Scouting is the action of looking ahead at a rapid to identify any hazards and to decide on a route. We can scout either from our kayak ("boat scouting") or the riverbank. Of course, scouting from shore is generally the best means, as we can get a variety of different perspectives and a clearer view of the rapid as a whole. On the other hand, boat scouting is much quicker and warmer in some instances. Both of these forms of scouting are skills like any other, and take practice to develop. This practice does involve putting our ideas to the test, and invariably it will mean learning from both good and bad decisions.

When scouting there are four main things to consider: the approach, the rapid itself, the recovery area, and specific safety concerns. We'll start by looking at the rapid itself, as it will have a strong bearing on how you look at the approach and the recovery area. When looking at the rapid, seek out any possible hazards or places to avoid, and identify all the different lines that have potential. Given the required moves, the group you are with and your personal skill level, you should then be able to pick a line that you're comfortable with. Of course if you aren't comfortable with any lines at this point, then it's time to start portaging—no matter what anyone says or how easy anyone makes it look!

With a line picked, turn your eyes upstream and have a look at the approach to the rapid, as it plays a pivotal role in the success of your run. Check the speed and direction of the current flowing into the rapid and where you'll be launching from. How will each of these affect the line that you have chosen? The next thing to look at is the recovery area. What's going on downstream of the rapid? Do you need to be anywhere in particular at the bottom, or is there a large recovery zone? What are the consequences of swimming? These are of course very important things to consider and should have a real impact on your decisions.

The final thing to look at, but certainly not your least important consideration, is how you can run a rapid the most safely. You should be looking at the hazards and considering the worst-case scenarios. Where can you set up effective safety? For a more detailed discussion of safety and rescue considerations, see the "Safety and Rescue" section of this book.

When scouting from shore, try to gain as many unique perspectives of a rapid as possible. It's amazing how varied things can look from a slightly different location. For instance, by scouting from above and looking down upon a rapid, you'll get a great overview, but it is very difficult from this position to gauge the size of river features and the actual gradient of the river. Whenever possible, scout from water level as well as from above.

It's also important to choose useful landmarks that will be recognizable from your kayak. Landmarks are features that you can choose from shore to use as guides as you approach and descend a rapid. A

landmark might be a particular wave, a rock, or even something unique on shore like a protruding branch. After choosing your landmarks, make note of how they look from the different scouting perspectives. When we walk back to our boats to run a rapid that we've just scouted, we'll stop frequently to relocate landmarks, and we'll crouch down to water level so that we know what to expect of the view from our boats.

Boat Scouting

Boat scouting is best done from a calm eddy above a rapid that provides you with the option of getting out and portaging. Trust us when we say that there's nothing more terrifying and dangerous than finding yourself in an eddy that has you committed to running a rapid, yet not being able to see what lies ahead! The biggest problem with boat scouting is that your eye level is so low that it provides a very limited—and often obstructed—view of the rapid. Only with lots of experience can you effectively predict what lies ahead, and even then you'll be guessing and are bound to be mistaken at times.

When boat scouting, you must consider the same issues that you would when scouting from shore. You'll look at the rapid from as many unique angles as possible, which means scouting from as many different eddies as possible. You may even be able to ferry out to a hole or wave in midstream, from which you can sneak a quick look before returning back to your eddy or heading downstream. Continuous whitewater poses more of a scouting challenge, because you can't see what lies below. You must stay in control at all times and have confidence in all the moves that you make. You can boat scout your way down a continuous rapid by hopping from eddy to eddy and re-evaluating the situation along the way. Just remember that you must always leave yourself an escape route. Remember, if you can't see what's coming up past the next eddy and it doesn't look like you can get out to portage from it, then get out of

Picking a line through a rapid is something that anyone can learn to do. The real challenge is in making good decisions about whether or not you're going to run the rapid.

your boat and scout until you know the coast is clear. It only takes one overconfident eddy hop to make for an extremely long day.

Picking Lines

If you've been paddling for any length of time, then there's a good chance that you'll have spent some time on the side of some road, picking lines through some of the nastiest whitewater imaginable! Even though you have no intention of ever running the rapids, you draw upon your knowledge of how you can use river features to your advantage and pick out the lines you'd take if you were ever foolish enough to try. Or you may have looked at a drop and said to yourself: "There's a good line there, and someday someone will take that line!" We both remember looking at a nearby massive two-stage waterfall on the Coulonge River in Quebec, seeing the potential and thinking it might be runnable, although we weren't going to test the theory. The next summer, BJ Johnson and Willie Kern took the plunge and came out clean and smiling! The reason we bring this up is because the importance of this chapter has as much to do with discovering where our own personal lines are as it does with examining the actual rudiments of picking a line.

When picking a line through a rapid, it's important that you break things down into individual moves, all of which you are confident that you can make. You then need to look at how well these moves fall together as a sequence. It must be understood that your success in running rapids relies greatly on your ability to look ahead and take actions that set you up for the future moves that are required. If you focus solely on getting through one feature at a time without real consideration for the next move, then you'll find yourself running rapids in a defensive, reactionary mode. This is a scary way to run rapids, as you are never really in charge of your situation and things can quickly snowball out of your control, taking you from a reactive/defensive state to a survival mode.

With experience we can all pick lines through rapids, but understanding our own personal lines and limits is an ongoing exercise. You need to consider the reason you're on the water to begin with. You also need to be comfortable with the consequences of your decisions. Are you aware of and accepting the costs associated with missing a move and swimming through a rapid? How will your decisions impact the other paddlers in your group?

The bottom line is that picking a good line is something that you can learn to do very reliably, but making a good decision about whether or not to run a rapid is something entirely different. When picking a line, just remember to pick one that you are comfortable with and not necessarily one that others

think is easiest. We all have our own strengths and weaknesses, and this will affect how you perceive a rapid. Of course, this doesn't mean that advice from more experienced paddlers should be disregarded. A smart person will learn from his or her own mistakes, but the smarter person learns from other people's mistakes too! When deciding whether or not to run a rapid, you need to weigh a number of factors. Experience will help you make the right decisions, but even the most experienced paddlers need to continually ask themselves why they are there in the first place.

HANDLING ROCKS

People are often surprised to learn that rocks aren't always your enemies on the river. Rocks can provide valuable, calm eddies amidst the chaos of a rapid. Rocks also slow down the flow of the main current, create weak spots that allow you to escape from holes,

If you find yourself sideways against a rock, lean into it and keep your boat tilted downstream. You can then push yourself laterally off the rock.

TEST YOURSELF

Using a friendly rapid, try as many different lines as you can come up with to learn what you can and can't get away with. The knowledge you'll gain will be invaluable when you are running more adventuresome rapids that are pushing your limits.

and provide ramps or jumps that you can use to clear nasty pourovers. Of course, rocks can also inflict pain, so you need to be cautious around them

In this segment, we're going to look at some of the basic rules for dealing with rocks. We'll then take a closer look at how to use rocks to your advantage in both the "Creekboating" and "Big Water" segments.

When approaching a rock that you wish to avoid, you have a couple of options. The best options are to pivot turn and ferry, or to back ferry away from it; but if it can't be avoided, you need to take actions that once again fight your natural instincts. The natural response to colliding with a rock is to turn sideways and lean away from it, which puts your kayak between yourself and the rock. Unfortunately, this action will have some very undesirable results, as leaning away from the rock means leaning upstream. As soon as your kayak hits the rock or the pillow of water bouncing off the rock, current will pile up on your upstream edge and flip you mercilessly. You'll now find yourself upside down against a rock, in what

You can drive over most rocks that are just below the surface as long as you hit them straight on.

is a very difficult position to roll. So what should you have done?

When drifting into a rock that can't be avoided, you need to keep your boat tilted downstream to prevent your upstream edge from catching the main current. In lighter current, or when dealing with lower-angle, rounded rocks, this might simply mean holding an edge and bouncing into the rock or its pillow at the ready with a brace. You might even get broached and have to push yourself laterally off the rock with your downstream hand. In faster current, or when the rock is more vertical, you may need to lean your whole body into the rock while holding your boat on edge. You may also need to push yourself laterally off the rock with your downstream hand quite aggressively. Of course every situation is different, but the key is always to keep your upstream edge from catching water. Lean into the rock and give it a big hug!

Rocks that are just below the surface can also wreak havoc on unsuspecting paddlers and are common causes of broken paddles. With experience, there's no reason to get caught by surprise by such a rock, as your river reading skills will allow you to recognize them early on. If your path does take you over a submerged rock then you should try to hit the rock as straight on as possible, with enough speed to drive over top of it. This is a good reason to keep your kayak fairly straight with the current in the early learning stages — before your river reading skills have developed.

The last rocks that we're going to consider are those under the water that can have a real "impact" on an upside-down paddler. Fortunately, these are the most seldom encountered rocks. In fact, many paddlers will never make acquaintances with an underwater rock. In the event that you do meet a rock underwater, there are a few things you need to keep in mind in order to minimize the impact. Of course your first line of defence is to roll up as quickly as possible. The less time you spend underwater, the better.

This is where the back deck roll comes into play, as it provides the quickest and cleanest means of rolling upright. It can even be done without getting your head wet, which clearly has its benefits. Contrary to popular belief, the back deck roll will not expose your head and body any more than other rolls, if it's done correctly. The nice thing about it is that your arms and paddle shaft form somewhat of a cage around your face. Although this cage won't necessarily stop you from hitting a rock with your head, it will take a lot of the initial impact and act as a warning. (For more on the back deck roll, see the "Rolling" segment.)

If the back deck roll isn't an option for a quick recovery, then you need to look at other ways to stay protected. Your most protected position while upside-down is tucked forward against your kayak. Your helmet and life jacket will take the brunt of any impact with rock. This is why you learn to move to this protected position when setting up for rolls, waiting for T-rescues, or wet exiting. Injuries usually result not from hitting rocks in this position, but from moving to this position if you're leaning back when you flip, as it requires sitting right up and then tucking forward, which puts you in a very vulnerable position for a moment. If you're faced with this dilemma, you need to consider using your paddle shaft and your arms as your shield, and sit up with this shield protecting your face and head as much as possible.

RIDING THROUGH WAVE TRAINS

When learning to kayak, you're often taught that if in doubt, keep paddling. The reason is simple. Every paddle stroke that you take effectively acts as a brace. When learning, you don't have enough experience to anticipate how the river will push you around, so you're best off paddling and bracing your way through a rapid. As you gain experience and confidence, you gain the capacity to foresee the effects that waves and currents will have on your boat. As this happens, you will change your approach to running rapids. Continuous paddling will no longer be your "default" action. Your default action will now involve floating downstream sideways with your eyes scanning ahead for obstacles.

There are a number of reasons for this. Firstly, a river's current is usually carrying you downstream at a horse's pace without any forward paddling. Unless you're in a hurry or need to build forward speed to clear an obstacle, then there's no real use in speeding up your descent. Secondly, if you do see an obstacle or a danger ahead, paddling forward is just taking you

Jumping a breaking wave by pulling the bow
on top of the break with a small stern pivot turn.

there more quickly! It also means that you have to turn your kayak almost completely around to establish an effective ferry angle. When floating downstream sideways, just a small sweep stroke will move you onto a powerful ferry angle in either direction. You are also moving the same speed as the main current, which means that it will be much easier to catch a wave to help you ferry out of the way. The key to floating sideways through waves is staying loose at the hips so that your kayak can go with the flow, while at the same time avoiding catching your upstream edge.

If the waves start breaking, you need to get a bit more aggressive to pull yourself through. There are a couple of different ways to deal with breaking waves. You can "jump" the wave, or you can pull yourself through. The method that you choose will depend on your personal preference, as well as on your need to set up for future moves. Jumping a wave involves using a small pivot turn to pull your bow up on top of the break so that you skip over it. It's preferable to have some speed when doing this to prevent your stern from catching and sending you into a vertical

stern squirt. It's also preferable to approach the wave on an angle in such a way that when it's time to pull your bow up, that sweep stroke pulls your kayak to face directly downstream. A potential drawback from using this technique is that you are usually carried very quickly into the following waves, making any subsequent quick moves difficult to make.

Pulling through a wave is a slower, but often more controlled means of getting through a breaking wave. The idea is to float into the wave on an angle, ready with a powerful stroke on the downstream side that will pull you through the break. In this case, you actually use the breaking part of the wave to slow yourself down. You can then come through with more control and will even have more time to prepare for the next move. The best approach when pulling through a wave is to float into the wave with a downstream angle and with your boat tilted downstream. In this way, you prevent water from piling up on your stern and squirting you up when you hit the break. This approach also lets you pre-establish which stroke you'll be using to pull yourself through the wave.

Breaking Wave Turn

As you get more comfortable pulling yourself through breaking waves, you can even use them to turn your kayak in the middle of a rapid. If you position your kayak so that only your stern hits

You can use a breaking wave to turn your kayak.

Boofing a hole requires speed on your approach and a well-timed last stroke that pulls your bow into the air and on top of the foam pile.

the breaking part of the wave, then your bow will continue moving downstream as your stern gets held up by the wave's break. This effectively turns your kayak downstream and into the opposite direction. The key, not surprisingly, is to stay loose and let the boat go with the flow. Being relaxed means spending less time bracing and a lot more time looking ahead and taking effective strokes.

MANAGING HOLES

Holes provide your most formidable challenge when running a rapid. More often than not, the line you pick through a rapid will take you around the holes, but sometimes this just isn't an option.

There are three main techniques for getting past a hole; you can "boof" or jump over a hole, you can punch a hole, or you can surf out of a hole.

Boofing is a term most commonly associated with running waterfalls, but the term can be used more generally, as it really just describes the action of keeping the bow of your kayak on top of the water. Boofing is the cleanest and most controlled way of getting past a hole. Unfortunately, it's not always possible. It becomes particularly tricky for big holes with large, vertical foam piles. The easiest holes to boof are those with flatter foam piles, like pourovers. To boof a hole, start with some speed and then take a powerful sweep stroke to pull your bow into the air and on top of the foam pile. To help lift the bow, edge

your boat into your front sweep as you do for a stern pivot, but remember to level off and get your weight forward quickly. A good boof will usually allow you to skip right over the hole. The most difficult aspects of boofing are the timing and set-up of the boof stroke. You need to approach the hole with a slight angle and time your sweep so that it brings your bow on top of the foam pile to point directly downstream (just like the timing of jumping a breaking wave).

Punching a hole is a technique you can use before you have the boat control for boofing, or when the hole's foam pile is so large and vertical that boofing would just land you flat on your back. To punch a hole you need speed, an aggressive attitude, and a well-placed last stroke. Speed is important because you're going to be hitting a wall of aerated water that will try to stop you dead. An aggressive attitude is important because you need to keep your weight forward when you hit the hole to prevent your stern from catching and rocketing you up into a vertical stern squirt. Your last stroke is what will pull you through the hole and it should be taken just as you hit the wall of water. This stroke will also act as a brace, so it's a good idea to punch a hole with your boat tilted slightly towards your last stroke. This helps avoid a surprise flip to your non-bracing side and it also helps prevent your stern from catching the green water in the trough.

A final way of navigating through holes is to surf the hole and manoeuvre out the side. Although this won't be the best option for all holes, there are times when surfing a hole makes a lot of sense. In particular, it makes sense when you want to decrease your downstream momentum. By surfing a hole, you can move laterally to the main current without losing any ground. We're not going to look at the specific techniques required for side surfing and exiting a hole right now, as this is covered in detail in the "Side Surfing" segment. For now, you should recognize that it's not written in stone that holes are always to be avoided; hole surfing is an important river running technique that should be practised.

Punching a hole requires speed, and a well-placed last stroke that pulls you through the foam pile.

White kayak: doesn't establish lateral momentum and can't break through the eddy line. Black kayak: starts on the opposite side of the river and establishes the lateral momentum necessary to break through to safety.

LATERAL MOMENTUM

For most river running moves, lateral momentum is more important to establish than downstream momentum. For example, consider ferrying across the river, pulling into an eddy, avoiding a hole, or breaking through a big reactionary—they all require some lateral momentum.

Once again, we're looking at a concept that goes against your natural instincts. If you need to break into an eddy or punch through a reactionary on one side of the river, it's only natural to want to start on that side of the river. This can be problematic, since the net effect of waves and holes on the side of a river is to push things out towards the centre. In general, to get to one side of the river, you want to start on the other side or at least far enough out to establish the lateral momentum necessary to get yourself where you're aiming. This might even mean crossing above the very feature that you wish to avoid, which can certainly be intimidating. However, without adequate lateral momentum, you might not make the move you are going for.

USING THE POWER OF THE RIVER

When we were learning, we were taught that kayaking was all about technique and that you didn't need to be powerful to do it well. Though there's a lot of truth to this statement, we can't pass on these words of wisdom without first clarifying something. Though good technique is integral to good paddling, there are times when it simply isn't enough to get you where you need to go. At these times, you may need to combine good technique with power, and this power will come from you and/or from the river. The focus of this segment is on how you can use the power of the river to your advantage.

Kevin uses a reactionary to give his ferry a boost.

There are many ways to take advantage of the river's power, but we're going to focus on a few of the most common. We've already looked at a turning technique that uses the river's power in the "Turning Midstream" segment. In this segment we looked at how you can use the break on a breaking wave or hole to slow down one end of your boat while the other end continues downstream uninterrupted. This effectively spins you at the peak of a wave or side of a hole. Now, we're going to look at how to use waves and holes to help your ferries, and then we'll look at how you can use pillows to your advantage.

Using a pillow to get where you need to go.

Waves and holes are the most common river features, and they can also be the most helpful to kayakers. Waves can give your ferry an added kick, and you a quick break. Consider a situation in which you are ferrying from one eddy to another. If there is a wave abutting the top of the initial eddy, exit so that your bow is in the trough of the wave and try to stay up on the face as you surf the wave across the current for a free ride. Be careful when exiting the eddy. If you pull into the current too far above the wave, you risk blowing through it as you come back downstream. If you enter the current downstream of the wave, you'll be pulling onto its backside and risk missing the wave and/or purling your bow underwater.

The backwash or foam pile of holes or pourovers can also be helpful for ferries. Although the aerated water may be quite turbulent, it can provide a great escape from the fast-moving main current. The trick is to stay on the foam pile without getting sucked right into the hole or falling off its backside, which

WATCH AND LEARN

As we mentioned in the beginning of this segment, there are many different ways of using the river's power to your advantage. A great way to learn how is by watching the best boaters as they make their way down rapids. They make things look easy by using every river feature to their advantage. Watch and see which eddies they catch, where they leave eddies, which waves they use to ferry, and how they get around or through holes. You should also take note of which strokes they use to do these things. We're not necessarily suggesting that you copy the lines of better paddlers, but there's no doubt that you can learn a lot from watching them. As we've already mentioned, smart paddlers learn from their mistakes, but a smarter paddler learns from other people's mistakes.

of course takes practice. Each hole has a different backwash, and the real challenge is learning to read this kind of flow. Once you're comfortable, you can use the foam pile to ferry across the river. You can even use the recirculating water to give your ferry a big boost out the far side of the hole.

Pillows are features that can also come in handy. Remember that a pillow is formed as water piles up on itself after being backed up by a rock. You can use this slack water to slow your own downstream momentum and help make your ferry more effective.

PORTAGING

No matter how skilled a kayaker you become, portaging will always be an important factor in your paddling. Sometimes there's no choice but to walk around a rapid. Other times, you may decide to take the high and dry route because you just don't feel on the ball. Deciding whether or not to portage in different situations can be very challenging. You need to evaluate more than just the feasibility of the rapid. You need to look at how you're feeling that day. Are you tired? Are you a little bit off your game for some reason? There's never any shame in walking around a rapid. Furthermore, it's totally unacceptable to make someone feel bad about portaging. Having said this, there's nothing wrong with a bit of friendly encouragement at the right time. Sometimes we all need a little push from our friends to help us achieve our potential, but a friendly push is very different than pressure. As for general portaging etiquette, it's a good idea to start your portage as soon as you've made the decision not to run the rapid, so that the other paddlers in your group aren't left waiting too long at the bottom.

No matter how good you get, portaging will always be a big part of the sport.

BIG WATER
RIVER RUNNING

8

There's no doubt that big water can be the most intense and committing type of whitewater paddling. When you enter a big water rapid, you have to accept the fact that you may not be in control at all times. You also accept that you might spend a good deal of time underwater and could potentially end up swimming. None of these things is really appealing, but they are risks that you must weigh when deciding whether or not to run a big water rapid. Having conjured up some healthy fear, we can now tell you that big water is absolutely exhilarating to paddle and that there are few activities in this world that compare to it!

We're going to take a look at a few issues that need to be addressed for big water paddling. Of course the fundamental skills and strokes that you use don't change. What does need to change is our approach to the rapids, both mental and physical.

EQUIPMENT

The equipment you use when paddling big water can have a real impact on which rapids you might run and which you might walk. Your boat selection is obviously very important, but there are a couple of other pieces of gear that you should consider as well.

Big Water Boat Selection

The most ideal big water boats are fast, stable, forgiving, and responsive. This translates into a fairly short kayak with more volume than a playboat, yet less than a creekboat, with fairly high edges and a flat hull. The problem with the smallest playboats is that they are designed with very low edges to make it easy to submerge the ends of the boat. When running big water, these low edges make them very unforgiving. On the other hand, a creekboat has high edges and is designed to be very forgiving. It also has lots of volume, which helps the boat resurface very quickly to avoid any rocks below the surface. In big water, however, you're not too concerned about

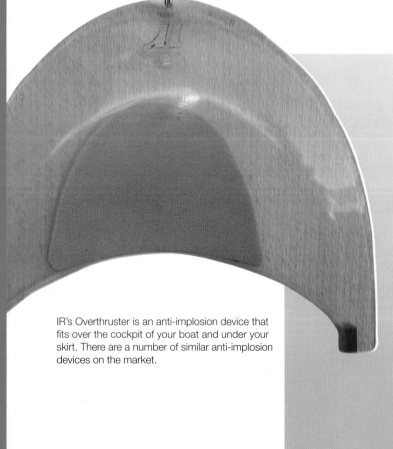

IR's Overthruster is an anti-implosion device that fits over the cockpit of your boat and under your skirt. There are a number of similar anti-implosion devices on the market.

OTHER USEFUL GEAR

There are a number of other pieces of gear that can come in handy for big water paddling. One of the biggest concerns when paddling big water is having your skirt pop. Holes and waves can sometimes break over your kayak and onto your skirts with such incredible force that they blow your skirt right off the cockpit rim. To prevent your skirt from "imploding," it should be supported from underneath. Many skirts now have some form of built-in "implosion bar" that does just this. There are even specific anti-implosion devices available like the Overthruster by Immersion Research and the Bladder by Level Six. The dry top is another good piece of gear for big water as it's inevitable that you'll get very wet. The dry top helps to keep you warm and

Staying loose and relaxed in big water is absolutely essential for staying upright.

energized. It also helps to keep water out of your boat, which is important because having water in your kayak certainly won't make your run through the big stuff any easier!

A final piece of equipment that we highly recommend is air bags, or flotation bags, for your kayak. These can be invaluable pieces of gear if you go for a swim, as getting a boat full of water to shore is nearly impossible. Flotation bags give rescuers a much better chance of getting your equipment to shore before it disappears down the next rapid.

submerged rocks. You'll be much more concerned about getting stuck in a big, trashy hole, which the additional volume won't help you avoid! This is why for big water river running, you should be looking for a boat that is somewhere between a playboat and a creekboat in size and features. We commonly use a bigger playboat than we would normally use for freestyle. The additional size makes it more forgiving, while the aggressive edges keep it responsive and versatile.

GO WITH THE FLOW

The most important rule for paddling in big water is that you need to "go with the flow" more than ever. This means staying loose and relaxed in your kayak and doing your best to anticipate and roll with the punches that the river throws your way. On a similar note, it's very important that you paddle big water with good posture. Leaning back not only puts you in unstable mode, it lowers your stern edges and makes them much more susceptible to catching. This is very important to understand, as the vast majority of flips in big water are caused by the stern edges of the kayak being caught.

KEEP YOUR HANDS ON THE STEERING WHEEL

Paddling through big water can be kind of like being a pinball in a pinball machine. The river is going to knock you around. To stay in control, you need to keep your hands on the steering wheel, which means keeping a blade in the water. When you're actively paddling, this isn't an issue. It's when you're not paddling that it's more important than ever to have an active blade in the water. You generally want this blade on the downstream side of your kayak, ready to brace, sweep, draw, or pull yourself through a breaking wave or hole.

MANAGING BOILS AND WHIRLPOOLS

Boils and whirlpools are right up there with eddy lines among the most unstable spots on the river. In fact, big water eddy lines are often composed of boils and whirlpools, but that's not the only place you'll find them. Whenever water is being constricted or forced to make a quick turn, or when different currents collide, you'll likely find whirlpools and/or boils, along with lots of other nameless, funny water. We're going to take a quick look at how to deal with these features and even how you can use them to your advantage.

The only way to maintain control in big water is to keep your body weight forward and a paddle blade in the water.

Boils

Boils are formed when water is forced up to the surface at speed. It can be water that is pushed up by a submerged obstruction, or turbulent water that has become aerated and is rushing to the surface like boiling water in a pot. Once it hits the surface, this boiling water peaks and then runs off to the side to the lower-lying water around it. Where this shedding water hits the current around the boil, a seam line is created (see the "River Features" segment).

You already know that you don't want to spend time on seam lines or eddy lines, where the water is unstable, so either get yourself clear of the boil or break right across the seam line and on top of the boil. The key to tackling boils is to take them almost straight on (perpendicular to that point on the seam line) with a slight ferry angle in the direction you'd like to go (usually downstream). As you break through the seam line and paddle on top of the boil, it will try its best to push you off to the side. You can use this energy to your advantage by carving a smooth turn on the boil and letting it push you off in the direction that you'd like to go. You'll need to have turned your kayak enough so that you can break through the seam line at a fairly straight angle. When there are multiple boils grouped together, you can even use this boil riding technique to bounce your way downriver, carving off the top of one boil and then the next.

Whirlpools

When running a high-volume river, you'll probably spend a lot more of your time avoiding whirlpools than playing in them, and this isn't always easy to do. In many cases, whirlpools (like boils) can be totally unpredictable and pop up in front of you unexpectedly. Fortunately there is a way to deal with them if you can't miss them.

Boil bouncing is a great way to navigate through boily whitewater. As you drive up on a boil, you'll carve a smooth turn so that as the boil pushes you off itself, you can punch through its seam line and right up the side of the next one.

If you can recognize which way a whirlpool is spinning, you can ride the side of it and use its current to sling shot you right on by. If you fight the whirlpool's current, you'll get sucked into its maw.

You can actually enter the whirlpool and use its energy to your advantage to get through it. The helical flow of a whirlpool offers you a free ride if you make your way into the right part of the swirling water. If you successfully paddle into the part of a whirlpool's swirling current that is moving downstream, then you can slingshot yourself around and out the other side using this current for a nice boost. This slingshot technique uses a similar concept to that which allows satellites to resist the gravitational pull of the earth and maintain orbit. Of course, this means paddling into a side of the whirlpool and not into its centre.

If for some reason you find yourself in the eye of the whirlpool, your momentum will be lost and there's not much you can do but hold on and wait for the opportunity to escape. If the whirlpool is big enough, your boat will sometimes be pulled completely underwater. This can be nerve-racking (or exhilarating), but you can take comfort in the fact that the whirlpool will eventually die out. Sometimes it will take only seconds for a whirlpool to grow and then disappear, while others can last ten seconds or longer.

Invariably, though, the whirlpool will settle out as it moves downstream. This is nice to know when you find yourself upside down in a whirlpool, because it can sometimes be very difficult to roll. If you're having trouble rolling, or even moving your paddle into a set-up position, try to relax and wait for the whirlpool to dissipate. Unfortunately, the only way to really develop your comfort level with whirlpools is to play around in them. So next time you get to that squirrelly spot on your local river, throw on your nose plugs and start messing around.

PUNCHING REACTIONARIES

Reactionaries are diagonal breaking waves or holes, and are a common phenomenon on big water rivers. Reactionaries usually form when water hits shallow sections or obstacles and is redirected towards deeper sections of the river (see the "River Features"

To punch a reactionary you need to establish lateral momentum directed so that you'll break the reactionary at a 90-degree angle.

THE BIG PICTURE

One of the most important and less understood rules for running big water is staying a step ahead of the game. Because the current is so powerful and things happen so quickly, you can end up in a recovery/survival mode in no time at all. To avoid this, you need to always look ahead to your next move, which at the time might seem like quite a distance away, and follow a line that will set you up for that next move. This of course reinforces the importance of scouting and picking a good line from the beginning, particularly in continuous water. By looking ahead and taking the big picture in like this, you'll find yourself fighting the river less and enjoying your trip a whole lot more.

segment). Learning to break through reactionaries is an essential skill that requires an aggressive approach.

Ideally you can break through a reactionary using the "boof" technique that was discussed in the "Managing Holes" segment, which lets you skip right over top of the break. Unfortunately, big water doesn't always let you do this. In fact, as opposed to making it over the reactionary, it's likely that you'll take a big piece of the wave in the chest. If you're not prepared for this hit, the reactionary will stop you dead and take you for a ride at its discretion.

The way to prepare for this hit is by establishing lateral momentum directed so that you'll break the reactionary at a ninety-degree angle. Once you are lined up properly, your biggest concern is having water pile up on your stern, which would quickly send you into a stern squirt. To prevent this, you need to stay in a fairly aggressive position, tilt your kayak downstream slightly, and plant a powerful last

SHORT STORY - A LESSON FROM MOTHER NATURE

by Ken Whiting

Why are many of life's most educational experiences the most traumatic ones? I'm talking about the experiences that turn your stomach to think about, but at the same time had a valuable impact on your life. The thought of what I've gained from such experiences lets me appreciate Conan the Barbarian's philosophy: that which does not kill you will make you stronger. Stronger or not, there are a few experiences I would choose not to relive. One of these experiences took place on the magical Ottawa River on a gorgeous summer day in 1991 . . .

I was sixteen years old, and it was my third year of paddling. My addiction to the sport was quickly turning me into one of the better paddlers on the river, but I severely lacked experience. Sure, I knew the Ottawa River as well as anyone. My buddy Paul and I had done more enders and pirouettes that summer than the river may have ever seen, and we routinely tested the river's tightest lines. After all, it was only the Ottawa River! This was our playground and we

were determined to make the most out of it.

This is how we so easily ignored the warnings of a little voice in our heads (which we later learned to name "Common Sense") and hopped out of our kayaks to swim in the whirlpools at the bottom of "Butcher's Knife." We'd get sucked down, swirled around, then pop back up to the surface like a cork. You can probably guess how these activities became a life-changing experience for me. To put things simply, the river gods spanked me!

After a few enjoyable times getting swirl-o-grammed in the whirlpools, things quickly went sour. Like a lemming making its final leap, I hurled myself into the river and was immediately pulled underwater as a whirlpool formed around me. The awesomely powerful, yet soft, hands of the river tumbled me about. After a short while, the turbulent waters eased their grip on me and I was allowed to make my way back to the surface. But, with the surface only inches away, the river trolls grabbed my ankles

stroke on the downstream side. This stroke will serve as a brace, while at the same time allowing you to pull yourself right through the reactionary.

BIG WATER SAFETY

Big-volume rivers can present the most difficult rescue scenarios because the shore is often quite far away and the current is moving so quickly that you can be washed downstream at frightening speeds. One result is that as the victim you can't always rely on others to help you. To paddle responsibly in big water, you should be proficient with your self-rescue and unmercifully yanked me down into complete blackness. Running out of air, and without any light to guide me to the surface, panic set in swiftly.

I can still remember the events that followed quite vividly, and even after sixteen years, their recollection sends shivers down my spine. I reached a physical stage that I never thought I would reach. I hovered for far too long at a point where I thought I couldn't hold my breath any longer, until finally, I began swallowing water. The darkness that surrounded me was replaced with an even deeper blackness as I passed out.

Moments later, I returned to my senses in a remarkably calm state after such absolute panic. The buoyancy of my lifejacket was pulling me towards the surface, and I watched the first signs of daylight appear as a far-off point. My lungs continued their desperate scream, but I was too confused to focus on that pain. I knew I should be swimming for the surface, but my body was unresponsive. I floated, completely at the mercy of the river gods, and watched in desperation as the light grew brighter. Before I knew what was happening, I broke through the surface and was taking the biggest, most welcomed breath of my life. My buddies were there quickly to tow me ashore, and

I dragged my spent body onto the riverbank.

The events of that day had an immediate and lifelong impact. The nightmares that followed were a nuisance, but most disturbing to me was the effect the experience had on my paddling. I stopped trying new moves and played only in the smallest playspots, as panic would set in as soon as I lost the slightest control. For the first time ever, my confidence was far below my skill level. Fortunately I had a great group of paddling friends that pushed me and helped to rebuild my confidence.

I've often wondered whether this was really a necessary experience. Did surviving an experience like this really make me stronger as Conan believed it would? Well, besides scaring the crap out of me, it did teach me a new respect for Mother Nature. I also learned a lesson that any whitewater paddler should understand. No matter how good you are, and no matter how well you know a river, the river is always in control. All we can do is play as safely and as responsibly as possible with the awesome and humbling power of whitewater.

skills as well as with your rescuing skills. Let's have a look at the most basic self-rescue skill: swimming.

Swimming

If you've ever taken a swim in big water, then you know how frightening it can be. It's very hard to get oriented and you can spend a fair amount of time underwater. You need to prepare yourself for this eventually, and the best way to do so is to go for a swim

The only effective way to get yourself to shore in big water is to swim aggressively.

on your own accord, in a controlled environment. As your paddling advances, this practice becomes even more important as you'll be forced to swim less often, but when it does happen, there's a good chance that you'll be in more serious whitewater that requires you to get out as quickly as possible.

When swimming in big water, getting out of the river is usually your main objective and biggest concern, although every situation is different. The only effective way to get yourself to shore is to swim aggressively. Of course there are times when you'll want to assume the body surfing position to protect yourself from rocks, but you're not going to get any closer to shore like this. It becomes especially important to swim aggressively through eddy lines or seam lines, for the same reason that you paddle aggressively through them.

Big water eddy lines are often accompanied by whirlpools and boils, which can pull you underwater for undesirable periods of time. On that note, you can expect to be pulled underwater when swimming in big water, but you can take some comfort with the knowledge that the features that pull you underwater will usually dissipate quite quickly and allow you to resurface. It's important that you stay as calm as possible when you get pulled underwater. Panic is a downward spiral that not only impairs judgment, but causes your body to use oxygen much less efficiently. Fighting frantically against the downward pull is not usually the best course of action, because the river is just too strong. You need to try your best to relax and wait for that downward pull to ease off, at which time you can swim back to the surface.

Rolling

Your best means of self-rescue is the roll. After reading the swimming section above, hopefully you are even more motivated to master your roll! Not only does a roll prevent a frightening and potentially dangerous swim, but it saves you an incredible amount of physical and emotional energy. I can't stress enough

Your best means of self-rescue is the roll.

how important it is to develop a confident and effective roll before tackling serious big water.

There are a couple of things to consider for rolling in big water. Firstly, big water can make it difficult to set up your roll, as strong currents play games with your paddle. Be patient! If need be, wait a moment for these currents to ease off before attempting your roll. The back deck roll remains the quickest and best way to roll upright, but by no means is it the only one that will work. All other rolling techniques will work fine, although the sweep roll can be slightly more effective than the C-to-C roll, as it is less likely to be foiled by funky currents.

Whatever technique you use to roll, be patient and don't give up if your first one doesn't work. Set up and try again, and if need be try a third or fourth time. If you can, try to get a breath in between rolling attempts. There's no rule for how many times you should try your roll, as every situation is different. But, given the exposure to risk, the time, and both emotional and physical energy you'll save by rolling upright, it's definitely worth trying a few times. At the same time, you don't want to wait until you're exhausted and out of breath before deciding to swim.

Simple words of encouragement can really help calm a swimmer in big water.

Kayak Rescues

When setting up safety for a big water rapid, you need to identify the hazards and set up rescue systems below, because if a situation does arise, the victim will usually be swept downstream very quickly. You need to prepare yourself by establishing an action plan, then putting yourself in the best position to help.

In some situations, a throw line set up on the riverbank can be very helpful, especially when there is pinning potential and the bank is relatively close. But since pins aren't very common in big water, it's usually more important to have paddlers in the water ready to help. You then need to consider your priorities. Of course, the safety of the rescuer is always first, as you are doing nobody a favour if you add yourself as a victim. With the safety of the rescuer secured, the top priority is the swimmer.

Other things need to be considered as well. Are you on a continuous river with limited access? If so, retrieving equipment is quite important, and you'll want to have at least two safety boaters below: one to help the swimmer and the other on gear retrieval. If the river is like the Ottawa River, which is composed of big, drop-and-pool-style rapids, then you won't need to concern yourself as much with the equipment, as it will all end up in the calm pool below where it can be easily collected.

There are a few ways for a rescuer in a kayak to help a swimmer. Simple words of encouragement can be very effective in calming a swimmer. When a swimmer needs more help, he or she can grab onto the grab loop at the back of the kayak and get a tow. If you've ever towed a swimmer, then you know how difficult it can be. If possible, instruct the swimmer to kick and help propel you forward. Be aware that there are situations where having a swimmer holding onto your stern can do more harm than good to both of you. There's no rule for when to tow someone and when not to, but you do need to evaluate each situation as it arises.

Equipment Retrieval

Depending on whether the river is continuous or remote, equipment retrieval will vary greatly in importance. We're going to take a quick look at the best way to retrieve equipment, with the assumptions that the swimmer is safe and the river continuous, so time is of the essence.

Getting a kayak to shore in the middle of a big water rapid can be a discouragingly tricky thing to do. Remember that the kayak will be incredibly heavy when filled with water, so you should consider it a danger in turbulent water. You're best waiting until the river calms down enough that you can safely approach the kayak. For the quickest recovery, you can empty out the boat mid-rapid using the boat-over-boat technique, and then tow it to shore with a tow line.

The boat-over-boat technique involves dragging the upside-down kayak over your own cockpit and rocking the boat back and forth to dump the majority of the water out. After doing so, flip the boat upright and attach your tow line to one of the grab loops. The tow line is a great tool for moving boats around in big water because it allows you to paddle unimpeded. With the quick-release feature, you can separate yourself from the tow line and kayak in a heartbeat if the need arises.

Without a tow line, you'll need to use a bump-and-chase technique for getting the empty boat to shore, which involves repeatedly pushing the empty kayak forward and then paddling after it to until you get to shore. This can work if you're close to shore, but it is not effective over any great distance.

Retrieving paddles is much simpler than boats. You have two good options. The first is to throw the extra paddle into an eddy or onto the riverbank like a javelin. This has the potential of damaging or breaking the paddle, so try to be careful if you can when doing this. The other option is to grasp both paddle shafts in your hand and paddle to shore with the double blades. This can be tricky for smaller paddlers, or when the blades of the two paddles have very different offsets.

CREEKING

9

Creekboating is as much a game of strategy as it is a sport. Half of your time on creeks is spent scouting, and half of the fun comes from picking lines based on how you predict the river will affect your kayak. In this way, creekboating is a lot like a game of chess, and, like chess, there are some important rules that need to be understood. We're going to look at some of these rules, along with a few unique creekboating skills, techniques, and concepts.

On high-volume rivers, rocks can create daunting river features such as big holes, pourovers, and undercuts, all of which you generally try to avoid. On lower-volume creeks, the features that rocks create can often be your best friends, such as micro-eddies that break up a rapid, and ramps for jumping over holes. It's important that you begin looking at rocks as your friends on creeks, not as your enemies. If you're scared of rocks, then you'll end up avoiding them at times when you really should be using them to your advantage. We'll be looking more closely at how you can use rocks to your advantage in the next segment on boofing.

Boofing is the act, or art, of keeping the bow of your kayak from diving underwater, and it is without a doubt the most important skill to learn for paddling creeks. Most notably, you can boof waterfalls and steep drops, but you can also boof holes, pourovers, reactionaries, and even eddy lines.

You should acknowledge from the outset that although boofing is a crucial technique for running drops, it can also be quite dangerous if not done properly. Landing flat from a drop of any significant height is going to shock your spine. This shock has broken the backs of paddlers on surprisingly small drops. Only experience can tell you when or when not to boof a drop.

For now, though, we'll focus on the general boofing technique that will take you cleanly over a small, vertical drop. This technique can be modified slightly to boof over many different features.

The success of your boof relies on two key factors: your set-up, and your boof stroke. As a general rule,

Tyler Curtis uses a rock to help boof over a hole.

you need forward speed directed at the steepest part of the drop, and away from the centre of it. The forward speed helps launch far enough to clear the hole at the bottom of the drop, and aiming for the steepest part makes it easier to achieve this goal. By directing your boof away from the centre of the drop, you are avoiding what is usually the stickiest part of the hole below. In many cases, you can even boof completely out of the main current and into an eddy. This of course requires plenty of lateral momentum on your approach.

This is also a great time to remember that rocks are your friends on creeks. If there is a rock at the lip of the drop, it might prove very useful as a launch ramp. The ideal boof rock is a rock that will give your bow a kick into the air without slowing your forward momentum too much. This means you want to hit the rock with your bow, but not with the rest of your kayak. Do this by establishing lateral momentum on your approach. If you hit the rock with too much force, or approach the rock too directly and catch it with too much of your kayak, then you'll be slowed right down and you'll have difficulty clearing the hole below.

Having successfully set up your boof, let's now take a close look at the boof stroke, which is the last stroke that you take as you drop over the lip. The boof stroke requires a combination of timing and power. The timing of the stroke is fairly straightforward. Plant the stroke just over the lip of the drop, where you can get the most pull away from the falls. On shallow drops, this sometimes means that you actually pull against the face of the falls.

In regard to the actual stroke that you'll use, let's refer back to the "power stroke" that we covered in the "Essentials" segment. The power stroke is a vertical forward stroke that propels your kayak forward without turning it. Since your goal for boofing is to launch yourself over the hole at the bottom of a drop, it should make sense that this "power stroke" will come in very handy. You don't need to worry quite as much about the stroke being perfectly vertical, but make sure it's powerful.

As you approach the lip of the drop, you'll reach

With lateral momentum, you can sometimes boof right into an eddy.

The steepest part of the drop is usually the best spot to boof.

The boof stroke is a power stroke planted over the lip of the drop.

With a vertical paddle, you'll minimize how much your kayak turns while you boof.

As you pull on your stroke, thrust your hips forward to keep your bow up.

Bring your weight forward again for your landing.

Control your boat during the landing with an active blade in the water.

forward and then plant your boof stroke just over the edge. At this same time, the bow of your kayak will begin to drop over the falls. Now is the time to pull aggressively on your boof stroke. As you pull on the stroke, you'll thrust your hips forward and past the paddle blade. The further you pull this stroke, the more lift you'll give your bow. This means that when you want to land the flattest, your power stroke will pull right past your hip and your hips will be thrust hard forward so that you end up in a leaning back position.

Contrary to popular belief, you're not done yet! You now need to prepare for your landing. You always want to land in your default body position, otherwise known as the "moderately aggressive" position. Landing like this helps prevent your boat from being back-endered, it helps you cushion the blow, and it allows you to control your kayak from the moment it touches down. For further control, you should land your boof with a paddle blade in the water at your toes, ready as a brace or to pull you forward and completely away from the hole at the base of the drop.

RUNNING WATERFALLS

Running waterfalls is a unique skill that requires lots of practice and a conservative approach because errors can be very dangerous. Running waterfalls simply isn't for everyone!

If you are interested in running waterfalls we're going to give you some things to think about. Keep in mind though that every situation is different. Even the same waterfall can offer a totally different situation if water levels change or if the path of the water is altered in any way.

BOOFING NON-VERTICAL DROPS

Boofing non-vertical drops is quite difficult. The key is in the timing of your last stroke. Be patient and make sure that your boof stroke pulls your bow up just before you hit the foam pile at the bottom of the drop. The most common error on non-vertical drops is taking your boof stroke too early, which usually means you won't clear the hole at the bottom.

Mariann Saether boofs successfully by waiting until she is half-way down the drop before taking her boof stroke.

There are two basic approaches to running a waterfall: you can boof, or you can pencil into the water more vertically. As a general rule, the higher the waterfall, the more vertically you'll want to enter the water. Since we've just looked at the boofing technique (which doesn't change when running waterfalls), let's start by looking at when boofing is the right approach to take.

Boofing (landing flat) is the only safe approach to take if the landing zone is shallow, but beware, because boofing can put a lot of strain on your back. In fact there are many cases of paddlers breaking their backs by boofing off waterfalls. It is only reasonable to consider boofing from a relatively low waterfall that has plenty of aerated water at the bottom. Aerated water acts like a cushion for you to land on because there is a high level of air mixed in with the water. Every waterfall will have a different amount of aerated water at the bottom, although there's no accurate way to predict how much there will be. Only scouting can provide that answer.

If boofing isn't the right option for running a waterfall, you'll have to pencil into the landing zone. Before going any further on this topic, it's critical that you understand that pencilling into the water at the base of a waterfall is very risky unless you know exactly how deep the landing zone is. A miscalculation on the depth of the water can be a fatal mistake. So, if there's any doubt as to the water depth the only prudent thing to do is to take the high road and portage the drop.

If you decide to run a waterfall that is too high to boof you need to decide on what type of angle you'd like to pencil into the water. As we mentioned at the beginning of this segment, the higher the drop, the more vertically you'll want to enter the water. The aeration of the landing will also dictate your angle of entry into the water. The more aerated the water is, the less vertical you need to be as the landing will be more cushioned.

When boofing a waterfall, it is imperative that there be lots of aerated water at the bottom to cushion your landing.

Regardless of your chosen angle of entry into the landing zone, you should be sitting upright in your kayak so that you can see your landing as you plunge downward. This upright position also lets you make small adjustments while you're airborne. Believe it or not, the best waterfall runners will even take small strokes in the curtain of the falls on the way down to ensure they hit the water at the correct angle.

A last thing to consider is your body position when

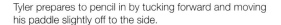
Tyler prepares to pencil in by tucking forward and moving his paddle slightly off to the side.

SCARS AREN'T REALLY COOL

A fairly common injury to waterfall runners is the broken nose. Sometimes it's the paddle that does the damage during the landing, while other times a high impact landing will cause the paddler's nose to connect with the cockpit rim on their front deck. Either way, these are two of the many reasons why avid creekboaters and waterfall runners will wear a helmet with a cage that offers full face protection.

you hit the water. If you're pencilling into the landing zone, you'll need to protect yourself by tucking forward, moving your paddle slightly off to the side (away from in front of your face), and turning your head slightly so that the water doesn't hit you full in the face.

As a final note, please remember that these are just some basic guidelines for running waterfalls. Running waterfalls is a risky endeavour and something that you need to work your way up to. One of the great things about whitewater kayaking is that mistakes usually result in a soaking and a damaged ego, but when running waterfalls, mistakes can have much more serious consequences.

Rockslides come in all shapes, sizes, and levels of difficulty. They are generally best run with creekboats that have plenty of rocker to keep the ends from pinning. It's just too easy for the pointy ends of playboats to catch an unsuspecting rock lip. Running simple rockslides is usually quite straightforward, and your entry into the slide will have the most impact on the success of your run. Once you've entered the slide, it's really hard to make any significant movements because you'll be accelerating very quickly, and the slide is often too shallow for effective strokes. This makes it crucial that you scout the rapid to pick a good approach and line. For longer slides, when there is more room for getting bounced around, it's never a bad idea to probe the run. The best probes are small logs that will float well. You can learn a lot by how a log runs through a rapid, although it can be somewhat depressing when the log has a cleaner line than you!

Once you've picked your line and entered the rapid, your main concern is keeping your kayak straight and upright, two things that do tend to go hand in hand. The best way to stay in control of your boat is to maintain your posture, which gives you the most edge control and allows you to make the quickest corrections. The surest way to flip or get broached on a rockslide is to let yourself get spun sideways or backwards.

Since rockslides are often very shallow, it's not reasonable to think that you can keep your boat straight by having a rudder planted at the back of the boat. Instead, you need to use small "checking" strokes out to the side of your boat. These can be partial sweeps or stern draws. You need to be careful that these strokes stay small and controlled, because cruising down a rockslide is like driving on ice. As soon as you start to spin out, things can quickly get out of control. It's also very easy to overcompensate and send yourself spinning in the opposite direction.

One thing to watch out for on rockslides is a rooster tail or fan, which is a plume of water sent hurling into the air by rock that juts out. These rocks have the potential to pin your kayak—or at least make things very uncomfortable for you. You should also be on the lookout for keeper holes at the bottom of rockslides, which can again be assessed using a test log.

The safety considerations for creekboating are somewhat different from those for big water paddling. Pinning now becomes a main hazard, along with the

do is take a swiftwater rescue course. With that said, here's a short list of some safety gear that can come in really handy.

- throw bag
- breakdown paddle
- pin kit
- first aid kit
- river shoes
- rescue vest
- elbow pads

bodily trauma caused by hitting rocks. One good thing is that most incidents happen within an arm or rope's length from shore, so rescuers can often play a greater role. This is why it's absolutely vital that all creekboaters be trained in swiftwater rescue and first aid. The skills you'll learn could save someone's life someday, including your own!

Equipment

Creekboats are designed to be as safe as possible in steep, shallow whitewater. "Creekboat" is a generic term that refers to any short boat with lots of rocker and lots of volume in its relatively blunt ends—features that cause the boat to resurface very quickly and to bounce off any rocks that it encounters. If you've already spent time on creeks, then there's a good chance you've seen experienced paddlers using playboats on them. It's important to understand that this does not mean that it's a wise thing to do. A playboat simply doesn't give you the same margin for error that a creekboat does.

Unlike big water paddling, creekboating involves a lot of land-based safety. This gives rescuers the opportunity to use a wider range of safety equipment. We'll be looking at different scenarios and how this equipment can be used in the "Rescue" chapter of this book, and it should be re-stated that the best thing to

A throw rope is an essential piece of creekboating safety gear.

Scouting

As we mentioned at the beginning of this chapter, creekboating is similar to chess in that it involves a lot of strategy. You can easily spend more of the day scouting and picking lines than actually paddling. In fact, there are even people who enjoy the scouting and line picking more than the actual paddling! If you've ever done it, then you'll understand why. We wanted to briefly address the subject of scouting, because there are a few valuable lessons we've learned over the years.

As a general rule, you should always scout rapids when you can't see the bottom. It's easy to dismiss this rule when it's a local river that has been run recently, but the fact is that you never know when new wood can appear in a bad place. It's important to understand that the chance of new hazards appearing increases exponentially after rain or fluctuating water levels. Taking a few minutes to ensure that the coast is clear can make a huge difference in your day. You'll also want to wear proper footwear, as bare feet are next to useless in rescue situations. Other good habits to get into are carrying a throw bag at all times and keeping all your safety equipment secured on your body. Murphy's Law definitely applies to kayaking, and odds are that if you aren't carrying your throw bag then you're going to need it. The reality is that everything doesn't always go as smoothly as we'd like on the river, so you need to keep yourself as prepared as possible for whatever situations might arise.

Swimming

Swimming in creeks is never really fun. The water is often snowmelt, and consequently nearly freezing in temperature. On the upside, this does manage to numb your body so that the rocks don't hurt quite so much! As I was saying . . . swimming in creeks is never fun, but there are a few things to understand about the topic that could spare you some real grief.

When swimming in whitewater, you can either take a defensive position, or an aggressive position, and you avoid standing at all times. Standing up in current is the best way to become a victim of the dreaded foot entrapment, where your foot gets caught between rocks while the current knocks you off balance and traps you underwater. This hazard is much more of

Even if you know a river like the back of your hand, if you can't see the bottom and there's the slightest chance of new wood appearing, it's always worth scouting.

The defensive swimming position gets used when you are swimming over drops, or other times when you need to protect yourself.

a reality on creeks. Aggressive swimming involves actively swimming yourself to shore or away from a hazard as quickly as possible. You generally only swim aggressively in deeper water, as you are more exposed to serious injury from rocks. The defensive position comes into play when we are swimming over drops, or when there are rocks around that you need to protect yourself from. This "body surfing" position involves floating on your back, feet first, with the rest of your body as close to the surface as possible.

Pins

Fortunately, pins are not overly common, but they do happen, and have proved fatal in far too many instances. If a pin is going to happen, there's a very good chance it will be on a creek. There are two main types of pins. There are vertical pins (stern or bow), and lateral pins, commonly referred to as "broaches." Both pins represent very dangerous situations that have the potential of becoming lethal. Pins need to be dealt with quickly and efficiently. We're going to look at a few methods for dealing with pins in the "Rescue" chapter of this book, but you also need to know how to avoid pins in the first place.

Why do pins happen? Pins can happen for two reasons. Either you don't recognize the risks, or you miss your line and are paying the price. Recognizing potential pinning spots comes with practice, but there's also a major element of common sense. Unless you see a drop when it's dry as a bone, you'll never really know what kind of rock is beneath the water line. With experience, you learn to predict what is under the surface by assessing the reaction of the water. With or without this river reading experience, you can learn lots from the surrounding environment, since there's a good chance that the character of the riverbed closely resembles the character of the riverbank.

For example, are there lots of boulders lying around that would create big gaps for pinning the end of a kayak, or is the rock quite flat and smooth? It's also a really good idea to make some inquiries before running a river for the first time. The paddling world is a tightly knit community with a common lingo, so if a river has some hazards to be aware of you can be sure that people will happily share that info with you. On-line chat boards can provide great information on rivers if you don't have anyone in particular to ask. It's not a bad idea to ask the chat groups even if you do get some information beforehand. You can never be too well informed.

PLAYBOATING

Playboating, competitively known as freestyle kayaking, is about surfing, spinning, and having the most fun possible by playing with various river features. Playboating has had an enormous impact on the growth and development of the sport of whitewater kayaking. It has made the river appealing and accessible to more than just the hard-core outdoors enthusiasts looking to challenge the extremes of Mother Nature. There are now more paddlers than ever addicted to

the sensation of surfing waves and to the challenge of learning new moves. Thanks to this flood of new paddlers into the sport, manufacturers have been working overtime to bring out the latest and greatest kayaks and gear. This has driven the sport forward even further and has made moves possible that never would have been considered in the past.

The first freestyle kayaking competitions took place in the late '80s and early '90s and were very casual in nature. Surfing, spinning, enders, and paddle twirls were the big tricks in those days. These fun and playful events rapidly grew in popularity. Boat manufacturers took notice and new kayaks began appearing on rivers. In 1993, the first-ever Freestyle Kayaking World Championships took place at Hell Hole on Tennessee's Ocoee River, with such legendary paddlers as Scott Shipley, Corran Addison, Bob McDonough and Eric Jackson taking part. Since then, the World Championships have taken place every two years, with warm-up "Pre-World" Championships being held in the between years. In 1995, Germany hosted the World Championships on the Eiskenal River in Augsburg and it set a new standard for Freestyle Competitions with a very professional organization. The World's then moved from Canada's Ottawa River in 1997, to the Waikato River in New Zealand in 1999, to Spain in 2001, Austria in 2003, Australia in 2005, and most recently took place back on the Ottawa River.

Each World Championship has marked a significant stage in the evolution of the sport, as it provides the best opportunity for paddlers from around the globe to meet and learn from each other and to showcase the latest moves.

Freestyle kayaking is now a very competitive sport that requires an athlete's complete dedication. The limits of what human and kayak can do together have been pushed to unbelievable levels, thanks to the creativity of paddlers along with innovative developments in equipment design.

Playboating continues to grow in popularity and all the new equipment is allowing recreational paddlers to reach their goals far more quickly than ever before. However, even with the best equipment, you need to have a foundation of skills and an understanding of the concepts in order to learn playboating moves. This book has already provided a very solid foundation of skills and techniques, so now we're going to look at some specific playboating moves and how you'll use these skills to perform them. We'll start with a look at some specific playboating equipment, and then we'll get into some flatwater moves, followed by wave moves, holes moves, and finally a few river-running moves. Please understand that we're just taking a look at some of the more popular playboating moves and that there are countless others to learn. Many of the following are actually segments from *The Playboater's Handbook 2*, which thoroughly covers all freestyle kayaking technique.

PLAYBOATING EQUIPMENT

The equipment you use for playboating will have a huge impact on the speed at which you will learn new moves and even on your ability to perform some of them. Your boat selection will have the largest impact on these things, but there are some other important pieces of equipment that you need to consider.

The short length and low-volume ends of playboats turn flatwater into a playground.

Playboat Selection

If you're interested in buying yourself a playboat, then we have some good news and some bad news for you. The good news is that we guarantee there's a boat that will be perfect for your body type and paddling style. The bad news is that you can expect it to take some real investigative work to find, because a plethora of new designs is introduced each year. We're going to do our best to make this sorting process as easy as possible for you.

Your body type is one of the biggest factors when picking a boat, but you also need to make some personal decisions. You need to decide whether you can afford to get a kayak that will be used almost exclusively for play, or whether you are looking for more of an all-round playboat that you can confidently run rivers in. Regardless, you want to choose a boat that meets your needs as you continue to improve. This means choosing a boat that is short (typically less than eight feet), has a planing hull, and is a reasonable width so that rolling and holding an edge are easy.

Exclusive Playboats vs All-Round Playboats

To make this as simple as possible, we'll just say that the smaller the playboat you choose, the more responsive it will be for aggressive, freestyle moves. The larger the playboat, the more forgiving and comfortable it will be, so the better it will be for other types of paddling. An unfortunate reality of freestyle kayaking is that if you have long legs, you can expect to be slightly uncomfortable in a playboat that is the ultimate size for you. This is because the less volume a playboat has in its ends, the less air you need to force underwater for vertical moves, but the less space you have for your feet. A kayak with more volume in the ends will be more comfortable and more forgiving, but harder to throw around. Of course you can go too far in both directions. You don't want to get a boat that's too small for you or too big for you.

Width

As a playboat gets wider, its planing surface grows. A large planing surface will let you flat spin very well, and it will be more stable to sit in. On the downside, as a boat gets wider it also gets more difficult to move from edge to edge and more difficult to roll. You can get away with using a wider boat by padding your seat so that you sit higher and have more leverage, but be sure not to raise your centre of gravity too much or you're going to be flipping all the time. As a general rule, the taller and heavier you are, the wider the kayak you can get away with.

Volume

Your weight will have a major impact on the volume of the boat you choose. As a rule, a kayak becomes easier to throw around as it shrinks in volume, but it also becomes less forgiving. Smaller boats are edgier and sit lower in the water, so they'll flush off waves and out of holes more easily. However, they can be a godsend when you're practising moves on flatwater. Ideally, look for a boat that you can throw around on flatwater, but that provides enough volume to be slightly forgiving.

Length

The effect of a playboat's length is simple. As a kayak gets shorter, it gets slower, but it becomes more manoeuvrable. In general, the shortest boats make the most moves possible, although this doesn't necessarily mean that the shortest boats make all moves easy to perform.

Paddles

Paddles have a smaller impact on your playboating performance than the kayak you use, but it's important to have one that you are comfortable with. Because it can be tricky to move from one paddle style to another, we suggest that you choose one paddle that

OTHER USEFUL GEAR

Thanks to the popularity of playboating, there are a number of pieces of gear that have been introduced specifically for the playboater.

Playboating Shoes: These flexible, padded playboating shoes are smaller than the traditional booties and let you squeeze your feet into small places.

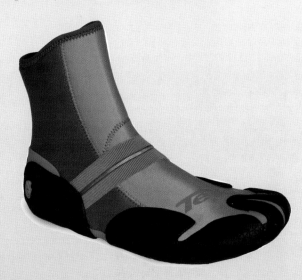

Drydeck: The drydeck is a combined skirt and dry top that allows playboaters incredible freedom to rotate because there is nothing tight around the waist.

Implosion Protection: There are a number of different pieces of gear that fit underneath your skirt to prevent water from pressing your skirt inward. This lets your kayak maintain a consistent volume of air and also helps prevent skirt implosions when

surfing big waves.

Paddle Wax or Tape: A small amount of wax or tape on your paddle shaft can dramatically improve your grip and therefore increase the amount of power that you can apply.

Playboating PFDs: Playboating requires lots of dynamic body movement, and these low-profile life jackets minimize the interference with your movements without removing any flotation. The flotation is simply moved away from the most active areas (shoulders, chest, and sides) and repositioned in the least active areas (stomach, mid-back).

Taping the shaft can dramatically improve your grip, but know that it can also give you blisters if your hands aren't used to it.

will accommodate all the different types of paddling you'll do. If you plan on spending a large part of your time playboating, then you should consider using a paddle with minimal offset. In fact, many playboaters use paddles without any offset, which can come in handy when both blades are in the water at the same time.

FLATWATER MOVES

Stern Squirting

The stern squirt involves slicing the stern of your kayak underwater and pivoting around with your bow in the air: basically a stern pivot turn initiated with a back sweep. It's often done when crossing an eddy line so that the main current can help pull your stern underwater and pivot around, but you can also squirt on flatwater. Stern squirting is a great way to practise the skills that are essential for more advanced playboating moves, while at the same time making you more comfortable with being on end. Keep in mind that playboats are designed to get vertical easily, so if you're getting vertical on a powerful eddy line, it doesn't necessarily mean that you're using proper technique. In order to focus on using the proper technique, you should practise your stern squirts on flatwater, or on weak eddy lines that make it a bit harder to get vertical.

Wherever you practise the squirt, your ultimate goal should be to do a full 360-degree turn with a single stroke. Contrary to popular belief, the ideal squirt is not a vertical move! Your bow should be lifted anywhere from thirty to eighty degrees. Keeping it under vertical allows you to stay balanced while pivoting around on your stern. The size of your kayak relative to your body weight will certainly have a bearing on how easily you can get it up, so not everyone can expect to be able to lift their bow high into the air right away.

One of the keys to stern squirting is keeping your weight over your kayak at all times. This is going to require a real separation of your upper and lower bodies. On flatwater, you'll start with some forward speed, and then establish spin momentum in one direction with a light sweep stroke, while keeping your boat flat so that your stern will slide out rather than carve. As your stern slides out, start winding up your body so that once you've slid out to ninety degrees (about a quarter turn), you're fully wound up and ready to initiate the squirt. When squirting on an eddy line, your goal is to initiate the squirt after your hip has crossed the eddy line, and with your boat perpendicular to the main current. This lets you take most advantage of the power of the current.

Winding up for a squirt means turning your head and body aggressively to the inside of the spin.

Plant the paddle deeply in the water and edge your kayak to the outside of the turn.

With your paddle planted deeply, you can sweep it out and upwards to help drive your stern underwater.

Level off the boat tilt before your sweep is finished to avoid "hitting the wall."

Continue to lead the way with your head and body.

A good stern squirt should turn your kayak a full 360 degrees.

Winding up for a squirt means turning your head and body aggressively to the inside of the spin. As you do this, lean back, reach and plant a powerful reverse sweep as far back as you can. Both your hands should be reaching over the side of the kayak and your back arm should be straight. You also need to edge your kayak to the outside of the turn so that your back sweep will push your stern underwater. Start with a relatively small boat tilt, which you can increase as your balance improves. Ultimately, you'll initiate your squirt with your boat tilted at a fifteen- to thirty-degree angle. It's also very important that you plant your back sweep deeply enough in the water so that you can push upwards while at the same time pushing away from the kayak. Pushing upwards with your blade helps to force your stern underwater. As you push on your paddle, you'll receive the support needed for your stomach muscles to pull the bow of the kayak up and around. This effectively unwinds your body. Your back sweep should be reaching its end once you've turned about 180 degrees from your initial position. At this point, your stern should be underwater and your body should have returned to an upright sitting position. This upright position is much more stable and is absolutely essential for the more advanced moves.

The success of your stern squirt now relies on your ability to avoid "hitting the wall." From the "Pivot Turn" segment, you'll remember that this means levelling off the tilt on your kayak before your stroke has finished. By levelling off your tilt, your kayak will continue to spin around as the stern floats its way to the surface. This is the only way you'll be able to perform a full 360 spin from your initial back sweep.

To make the most out of your stern squirt practice, focus on these three elements: winding up and unwinding your body using your stomach muscles, finishing your back sweep with your body in an upright position, and levelling the tilt on your kayak before the back sweep is finished so that buoyancy energy keeps you spinning. Once you can routinely put these elements together, not only will you have a great stern squirt, but you'll have opened the doors to virtually every other advanced playboating move. Finally, practise these squirts on both sides from the beginning so you don't end up with lopsided skills like most boaters!

Getting Vertical

Practising any move in a controlled environment is the best way to develop good technique. Since playboats have shrunk to a point where vertical moves can be performed on flatwater, more and more paddlers are reaching their "vertical goals." Does this mean that you should squeeze yourself into the smallest boat possible to practise vertical moves on the flat-water? Absolutely! The smaller the boat that you use on flatwater, the easier vertical moves will be to learn. Of course, when you're cramming yourself into a small playboat, there comes a point when the pain factor exceeds the fun and learning factors.

Whether you've got a tiny playboat to practise with or not, you need to accept that vertical moves require a combination of technique and power. Neither one on its own will do the trick! We'll start by looking at one of the most basic advanced skills called the "double pump." The double pump is a technique you use to throw your bow underwater, which is necessary in one form or another for the initiation of many advanced moves.

The Double Pump / Bow Wind Up

The idea behind the double pump is to pull your bow into the air so that you have more energy to then force it underwater. To pull your bow into the air (often referred to as "winding up the bow"), there are three things that you need to do at the same time: tilt your kayak on edge, shift your weight back, and take a forward sweep stroke. Once your bow is in the air,

Double pumping the bow into the air requires good balance on edge, and upper and lower body separation.

DOUBLE PUMP DRILL

Here's a drill that helps get your legs and stomach muscles involved with the move: It involves alternately sinking your bow and stern, and is commonly referred to as the "bobbing drill." It starts with a double pump, but once your bow is in the air, you don't commit as aggressively to smashing it underwater. As your forward sweep transitions into a back stroke, shift your weight into a neutral position instead of throwing it hard forward. Your body should remain in the neutral position from this point on. Now, use your knees and stomach muscles to pull your bow (feet) downwards. Once it's underwater, turn your back stroke into a forward stroke and pull the bow back upwards. Continue to bob your bow in and out of the water a total of ten times.

The key to this drill is taking very short and powerful strokes with your blade completely in the water. You also need to have the balance to hold a steady tilt on your kayak while your stomach muscles work overtime to pull your legs up and down. Since your body stays in a neutral position, your stomach muscles will be doing virtually ALL the work. It shouldn't take too many of these bobs to get your abs burning!

A common problem is getting the paddle caught under your boat after a few bobs, which tends to pull you upside down. To prevent your paddle from diving, use a sculling technique for each stroke to maintain a climbing angle with your blade. This means curling your wrists slightly forward as you take a back stroke and cocking your wrists slightly back as you take a forward stroke. This technique keeps your paddle near the surface, about a foot or two out to the side from your hip and knee.

Keep in mind that the goal of this drill is not to sink your bow and stern as deeply as possible! The goal is to feel your knees and stomach muscles actively involved in pulling your bow up and down.

don't hesitate before throwing it down. The power you need to throw your bow underwater can be gained only through torso rotation. Plant a back stroke just behind your hip and turn your whole upper body so that your chest faces the water. Now as you push off the paddle, throw your weight aggressively forward and unwind your body by pulling your feet down with your knees and stomach muscles.

Bow Stall

Bow stalling involves balancing on the bow of your kayak with your stern in the air. This takes some awesome balance and a lot of practice, but it's a great move to learn because it teaches you about the vertical balance points of your kayak, and it's really fun.

Like any other vertical move, bow stalling is easiest with the lowest-volume kayaks. So, the smaller the boat you practise with, the more quickly you'll see results.

Before you can even contemplate bow stalling, you need to be comfortable with double pumping and pulling your bow completely underwater. If you're not there yet, then keep working on both.

The ideal bow stall position has your kayak at around a seventy- to eighty-degree angle from a side view, with your body in a moderately aggressive position that keeps your centre of gravity low. Your paddle should be completely in the water and as far out from your kayak as is comfortable in a low brace position. Imagine that your kayak and paddle blades form a tripod. The farther these points are from each other, the more stable your tripod will be.

With this ideal stall position as your goal, you'll

1. The ideal bow stall has your kayak on around a 70-degree angle, your body in a moderately aggressive position, and your paddle in the water, out from your kayak.
2. Leaning forward while bow stalling will flatten out your kayak.
3. Leaning back while in a bow stall will pull your kayak more vertical.

couple of the most frequently misunderstood concepts in playboating. When balanced on your bow, leaning back will actually pull your kayak more vertical. This can be confusing, because the natural thing to do when you feel yourself falling forward is to lean back. Leaning forward, on the other hand, will help flatten out your kayak if you're starting to fall over vertical.

Ultra Cleans

The ultra clean is the most effective way for playboaters to develop the fine edge control that is needed for any freestyle move.

The ultra clean is a complete spin on flatwater that is accomplished without the use of a paddle stroke. This seemingly impossible task is done through a combination of body weight and edge transitions that alternately sink the bow and stern, allowing for the use of buoyancy energy. Buoyancy energy, you'll remember, is the desire your boat has to resurface anytime it is underwater.

Getting the ultra clean started is tricky since there is no buoyancy energy to work with. You'll need to sink your stern and get things rolling using only aggressive body motions. Let's follow the case shown and consider slicing the right stern edge underwater to turn to the left. Starting from a still position you'll need to do three things at the same time to engage your stern: tilt your boat slightly to the right, snap your weight backward and onto your right hip, and turn your upper body aggressively into the turn to help pull your bow around and generate spin momentum. Even with the smallest boats, you can't expect to sink the stern very deeply. If you can get it a few inches underwater to begin with, you're doing well.

As soon as your stern begins to slice underwater, you need to make a quick edge transition. This means pulling upward with your trailing knee (the right one in this case) while dropping your leading knee. By tilting your boat into the other direction, you present your stern with an escape route in the direction of your spin. Now, as your stern slices to the surface and your

need to throw your bow down at around a seventy-degree angle, and then stop yourself when your kayak is nearly vertical. To stop your spin momentum, put on the brakes by using your paddle as a low brace. Staying stalled is now simply a matter of balance!

Using your paddle blades to brace yourself will help stop your bow from slicing out to the side. Your paddle is also helpful for stopping your kayak from falling forward or flattening out, and this is why you need to keep your blades completely in the water.

Having said that, it's your body position that plays the biggest role in keeping you balanced, and the effects of your forward and backward leans are actually a

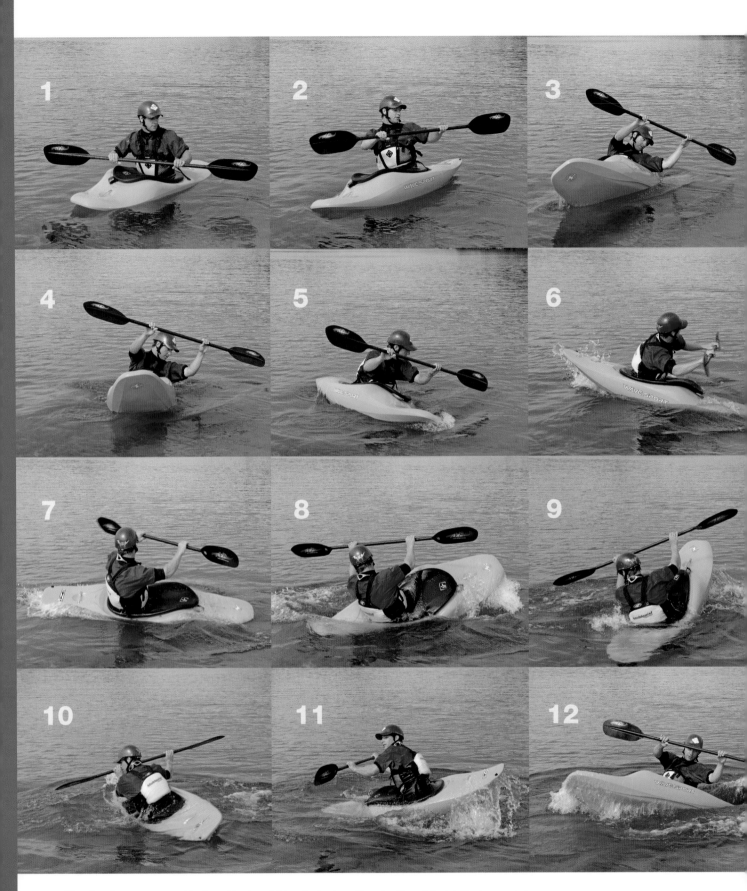

The ultra clean uses a combination of body weight and edge transitions to alternately sink the bow and stern.

bow falls downward, you'll want to encourage the bow underwater by throwing your weight forward. As soon as your bow enters the water, you'll once again need to make a quick edge transition, which means pulling up your leading knee and dropping your trailing knee. Once you've presented your bow with its escape path, then you'll again help your stern underwater by throwing your weight back and turning your body aggressively to lead the way.

Using this seesaw action, you can generate an amazing amount of spin momentum without even using your paddle. Without even knowing it, you've entered the world of clean cartwheels!

WAVE MOVES

Front Surfing

Front surfing is a skill at which most paddlers become proficient quite quickly, thanks in large part to great boat designs. Back surfing, on the other hand, is one of the most under-practised skills. By practising back surfing, you not only develop an important playboating skill, you enhance your backward awareness—which will do wonders for all aspects of your paddling! The best way to prepare yourself for back surfing is to spend time on your reverse eddy turns and ferries. You need to reach a comfort level where your strokes and boat tilts become instinctive, because you won't have time to think them through while surfing a wave!

We're going to look at wave surfing skills from a front surfing perspective to keep things as clear as possible, but it's important to realize that you use these same techniques for back surfing. The only thing that really changes for back surfing is the direction that your kayak points and the back strokes that you use instead of forward strokes.

DROPPING ONTO A WAVE

Dropping onto a wave (or "catching it on the fly") requires a bit more finesse and power. The toughest part about dropping in is lining yourself up to catch the steepest part of the wave. It's a bit easier to line yourself up by approaching from just off to one side with a slight ferry angle so that you can keep track of your position by looking over one shoulder. When you get close to the wave, slow yourself down as much as possible with powerful forward strokes. When you hit the trough of the wave, lean back to help keep your bow from diving, but as soon as your bow is clear, throw your weight forward and take a few quick strokes so you don't float right past the wave. The steeper the wave, the more important this weight shift will be to keep your bow from diving.

Catching Waves

Catching a wave is often the toughest part of surfing. You have two options. You can catch a wave on the fly, or you can ferry onto a wave from a nearby eddy. Ferrying from an abutting eddy is easiest because you have little or no downstream momentum to stop. The challenge is to set your ferry up so you slide right onto the face of the wave. Staying on the face of the wave means you won't have to worry as much about having your bow dive underwater. If you enter the current too far upstream of the wave, you risk being carried all the way up and over it by the fast-moving water as you drop back down. You also risk catching your bow underwater as you drop back through the trough of the wave.

In order to successfully ferry onto the wave's face, you need to consider your kayak's angle, speed, and its point of entry into the current. Because every wave is different, and the speed of the main current can be very different, there's no single way to catch a wave, but there are a few key points to keep in mind. First, you need to aim your bow at or slightly downstream of the wave's trough. Second, the faster the water is moving, the more upstream angle you need to enter the current with. Whether the wave is right beside the eddy or a short ferry away, you must remember your ferrying technique. As you break through the eddy line, you need to establish some spin momentum into the main current, and then follow up with a forward stroke on the downstream side that pulls you right across the eddy line and momentarily holds your ferry angle. Once you're on the face of the wave, you can start using a rudder to control your surf. If in doubt, you're better off having too much upstream angle, because it's easier to let your angle go than to recover from losing it.

The toughest part about dropping onto a wave is lining yourself up to catch the steepest part of the wave.

Surfing

Nice work, you've caught the wave! Whitewater kayaks have become incredibly forgiving for surfing waves. The short, low-volume ends allow you to blast in the trough of holes or breaking waves, and their considerable rocker lets you surf on any part of all but the steepest waves without having to worry about your upstream end purling. We're going to start by looking at the fundamentals of surfing, and then we'll move quickly onto more advanced surfing techniques, which will help you surf waves of all shapes and sizes.

First of all, you have to understand that most of your surf time should be spent on the face of a wave. Because whitewater kayaks have been designed to surf so effectively, you can sometimes get away with surfing passively down in the trough. Unfortunately, this won't work on all waves and it won't be useful for setting up other play moves. On mellow waves, you can often surf on the face without any effort whatsoever. In these cases, all you need to do is maintain control of your boat with rudders. On steeper waves, or when a wave is breaking, you need to get more aggressive with your surfing in order to stay on the face. This involves carving back and forth from one ferry angle to the next. The steeper the wave is, the more aggressively you have to do this. Let's look at how the body, paddle and boat are involved in making this happen.

Body Position: First and foremost, you need to keep your weight centred as much as possible when you're surfing. Sitting upright puts you in the most stable position and affords you the most control over your boat. This doesn't mean that you can't lean back if you need to. Feel free to be active with your forward and backward leans. If you're sliding into the trough of the wave and your bow is diving, it's alright to lean back if it helps you recover. If you're falling off the backside of the wave, then lean aggressively forward to slide back down the face. Just return to your default body position as quickly as possible.

The Paddle: Your paddle should be acting as a rudder at all possible times, because the rudder is the steering

The best rudders are positioned at the back of the boat with your paddle parallel to your kayak, and your upper body rotated towards it.

wheel for your kayak. If it's not in the water, you're not really in control. Your rudder gets planted with your paddle parallel to your kayak, and with your front hand held between shoulder and eye level. Keeping this front hand high buries your active blade deeply in the water. Having your paddle parallel to the kayak ensures that your rudder is not acting as a brake. Though braking rudders can be useful in aggressive surfing situations, they can easily pull you off the smaller waves. Your chest and belly button should be turned to face your paddle. This winds up your body so that your rudder can act as a pivot from which your stomach muscles can help pull the bow around. Turning your chest towards your paddle shaft also keeps your hands in front of your body, which, as you already know, helps keep your shoulders safe. Keeping your elbows down will also keep your shoulders in the

safest position.

From this ruddering position, you can turn your boat in either direction by simply rolling your wrists. By rotating your wrists upwards, you'll catch water with the power face of your blade and draw your stern towards your paddle. By curling your wrists slightly downwards, you'll engage the back face of your blade and will pry your stern away from your paddle.

The Boat: Your boat will be in one of two positions when front surfing. It will either face directly upstream (12 o'clock), or it will be on a ferry angle to one side. When pointed to 12 o'clock, your kayak will want to shoot down into the trough of a wave, so unless you're on a fairly flat wave, you're going to want to spend all of your time alternating from one ferry angle to the other.

By curling your wrists slightly downwards, you'll engage the back face of your ruddering blade and pry your stern away from your paddle.

By rotating your wrists upwards, you'll catch water with the power face of your rudddering blade and draw your stern towards your paddle.

The next big question is how to edge your kayak. Most paddlers' instincts tell them that they should tilt their boats into each turn when they plant the rudder. On flatter, smooth waves this does work quite well, and you can carve some great turns like this just as a surfer does. However, on steeper waves that are breaking, it becomes more important to keep your kayak tilted downstream to prevent your upstream edge from getting caught, which is what we're going to look at next.

Aggressive Surfing

You already know that the key to surfing steep waves is staying on the face, and the best way to stay there is to carve back and forth across the wave. When waves get really steep, cutting back becomes more difficult, and so the shoulders of the wave are the best place to do so. The shoulders are the sides of a wave that are less steep than the rest of the wave. Some waves may not have clearly defined shoulders, but there will always be mellower sections of a wave that you can use in lieu of a perfect shoulder. Once you reach the shoulder, cut back and ferry in the other direction. How far out on the shoulder you should carve depends on the character of each wave and will take some experimenting to figure out. In the case where you're setting up some other play move, then you'll want to cut back a bit harder than normal so that you end up right on top of the wave.

Regardless, you need an active and committed rudder for each successful cut-back. There are two

Aggressive surfing involves carving back and forth across the face of a wave, with a rudder engaged deeply in the water.

BOW RECOVERIES

No matter how good you get at surfing, your upstream end will dive underwater or "purl" every once in a while. To recover from this, quickly and briefly tilt your kayak on edge. This temporarily relieves the water pressure on your bow, allowing it to resurface. You can also recover by spinning out when your upstream end begins to purl. This means that as soon as one of your ends starts diving underwater, you can initiate a flat spin. Instead of your bow being taken directly down, you're providing it with an escape route off to one side. This spin-out recovery only works with a very quick reaction and, of course, only if you're a competent flat spinner. We'll get there!

If your bow purls while front surfing, by quickly and briefly tilting your kayak on edge, you'll temporarily relieve the water pressure on your bow and allow it to resurface.

types of rudders that you can use. There's a slicing rudder and a braking rudder. A slicing rudder causes the least amount of resistance in the water. This rudder is planted near the back of your kayak, with your body turned to keep your hands in the power position and with your top hand kept between shoulder and eye level. This is a great rudder to use when you want to keep your speed up. The braking rudder does just the opposite, and gets planted out to the side of your body. It guides or turns your boat, while at the same time acting as a big brake. This is a helpful rudder when you need to pull yourself quickly up a wave or stop yourself from shooting further down. Depending on your situation, use one or a combination of these rudders to cut back at the shoulder of the wave.

Back Surfing

As we already mentioned, back surfing is one of the most under-practised skills among both recreational and professional paddlers. Aggressive back surfing is also one of the most difficult moves, because you really need to feel your way around the wave instinctively as you don't have the same visuals. The only way to develop this sixth sense is through practice and the development of your backward awareness.

We're not going to look at back surfing in depth, because it follows all the same rules as front surfing. The only thing that changes is your rudder technique. The back surfing rudder is very similar to the front surf rudder, except that you plant the rudder at the bow of your kayak rather than at the stern. Your top hand should be held between shoulder and eye level to ensure the blade is engaged deeply in the water and your wrist rotated forward so that this rudder blade is parallel to the boat. You need to resist the temptation to roll your wrists back, which allows your rudder

to become a brace! You really need to be aggressive and dig your rudder in to grab water if you want to maintain control of your boat. This is the most common problem people display. They are timid with their rudders, which means they don't carve well and inevitably they end up down in the trough where their stern catches and things go downhill.

There's no doubt about it: back surfing is a tricky skill that will require more practice than any other move. At the same time, it has real and significant spin-off benefits and is well worth the time and effort required to learn it. When learning, we highly recommend getting to know a wave by front surfing it first. Learn where the wave's sweet spots and weak spots are and then spin to a back surf or back ferry onto the wave and plug away. Be aggressive and persistent.

Flat Spinning

Flat spinning is the motion of rotating 180 degrees or more while on a wave. Now that playboats are designed to be as "loose" (easy to spin) as possible, it really doesn't take much to get them spinning on big, fast waves. It's on the smaller, more finicky waves where proper flat spinning technique makes a big difference. Let's look at the set-up, the initiation, and the recovery of the flat spin.

The best place to set up for a flat spin is at the peak of a wave. The best way to get up onto the peak is to carve out to the shoulder of the wave and then cut back and ferry your way up top. Once you're there, you then need to establish some upstream momentum, which you'll do by pointing your kayak to 12 o'clock, leaning forward and letting yourself slide down towards the trough. You should practise doing this successfully several times on a wave to master it before actually going for the move. When you're ready to go for it, then just as you feel yourself beginning to drop down the face of the wave, it's time to initiate your flat spin!

Similar to front surfing, the back surfing rudder is planted deeply in the water with your paddle parallel to your kayak and your upper body rotated so as to maintain your power position.

To initiate a flat spin, you need to release the stern edges of your kayak by using a back sweep, a slight downstream boat tilt, and throwing your weight forward.

To initiate the flat spin, you need to pop the entire stern of your kayak out of the water, or "release it." Until you pop these stern edges out of the water, your boat will want to carve a turn. To release the stern and initiate the flat spin, use a back sweep with a slight downstream tilt on your boat, and throw your weight forward. You should recognize this from the basic bow pivot turn that we covered in the "Essentials" segment, where we used a back sweep to pull our bow underwater and throw our stern into the air. Though you're not necessarily looking to pull your bow far underwater when initiating the flat spin, you definitely need to pop your stern out of the water. The amount of boat tilt to use depends on the situation and on how much your stern needs to get popped out of the water. On faster waves, your boat planes very high on the water and it doesn't take much tilt, if any, to release your stern. As waves get slower and smaller, your stern edges sink deeper into the face, so it takes

more pop to release them, which means incorporating a stronger downstream tilt into your initiation. On these smaller waves, it is also helpful to push down on your back sweep to help pop your stern up.

As soon as your stern is released, then just like the bow pivot turn, you need to level off your boat tilt in order to keep your spin momentum going. Let's look at this move from the beginning . . .

Make your way to the top of the wave, and just as you start sliding down the face, initiate the flat spin with a back sweep. While pushing down and away with your paddle, throw your weight forward and tilt your boat slightly downstream for an instant to release your stern from the water.

Once your boat is spinning, you have two choices: you can stop in a back surf, or continue with a full 360-degree spin. On the smallest waves, you can only expect to spin 180 degrees at a time because a full 360-degree spin will usually pull you off the wave. On these waves, a "recovery stroke" is necessary after each 180-degree rotation. A recovery stroke is

When spinning from a back surf to front surf, you'll need to release your bow edges by using a forward sweep stroke, a slight downstream boat tilt, and throwing your weight towards the stern.

a back stroke taken on the opposite side of the kayak from your initiating back sweep. This back stroke helps keep you on the wave and establish control in a back surf. To spin back to a front surf, things get a bit trickier. Ideally, your recovery stroke has set you up perfectly at the peak of the wave where you can quickly establish some upstream momentum by pointing your stern to 12 o'clock and sliding down the face. If not, then you need to get set up while back surfing. Obviously, you need to be pretty confident at back surfing before having this type of control. If you are set up, then spinning back to a front surf is similar to the first part of your spin.

Once you start moving down the face, lead the spin with your head and body and use a forward sweep to pull your bow around. This time you'll need to release your bow edges, which you do by throwing your weight back and tilting your boat slightly downstream. Do you recognize this stern pivot turn from the "Essentials" segment? The amount of downstream tilt you use will depend on how aggressively you need to pop your bow edges out of the water. On the smallest waves, you again need to finish with a recovery stroke, which is a forward stroke on the opposite side of the kayak as your initiating sweep.

On faster, steeper waves, you can do full 360-degree spins, which is actually easier than stopping halfway, because you never have to back surf. The key to the full "360" is keeping your spin momentum going once you've established it. You must make smooth and precise edge transitions, lead with your head, and get your second sweep stroke in the water as quickly as possible. For the smoothest edge transitions, you need to tilt your boat downstream just enough to be able to release your ends, but no more. Any extra tilt will just catch more water and slow you down.

You also need to level off your boat as soon as you've released an end, as a level boat will plane out

Pat Camblin flies on the renowned Buseater wave.

Co-author, Ken Whiting, in mid-helix.

more effectively on the water. To get your second stroke (the front sweep) in quickly, drop your blade into the water at your knees and don't worry about taking the extra second to reach to your toes. By getting this second stroke into the water quickly, you don't give your boat a chance to stall out and you can continue to pull it around with your stomach muscles.

As your set-up improves and your edging transitions become smoother, you'll soon find that you don't even need a second stroke to get yourself around. Full, 360-degree flat spins that are accomplished with a single stroke are called "clean spins."

Advanced Moves

One of the greatest things about waves is the awesome potential that they provide us with. On big, fast waves, there's an enormous amount of energy just waiting to be harnessed, and the newer playboats are designed to do just this. With aggressive carving edges and hulls

that like to be bounced out of the water, a world of aerial acrobatics has opened up to paddlers. Here are a couple of the hottest aerial moves that you'll see on the river today:

Aerial Blunt and Backstab: The aerial blunt is a radical move that involves rotating from front surf to back surf by bouncing your boat into the air and throwing your stern up and over your head. The aerial backstab is the same thing, but done in reverse so that you are moving from back surf to front surf and throwing your bow up and over your head.

Air Screw: The air screw is a horizontal aerial pirouette that doesn't use a single paddle stroke!

The Helix: The helix is an inverted, aerial 360, and is without a doubt one of the most sensational moves out there.

HOLE MOVES

Side Surfing

Side surfing is the act of balancing sideways in the trough of a hole. This can be one of the most intimidating skills to learn, but once you've developed the technique, then even the biggest holes can be relatively easy to surf. It's getting out or moving around that causes the most problems! That's why we're going to take a quick look at each of these things on its own.

The ideal side surf position involves balancing on your downstream butt cheek and lifting your upstream edge with your knees just enough so that it doesn't catch the downstream flowing water. Any extra boat tilt makes for a bouncier ride as you expose more of your hull for the incoming water to hit. Though it's tempting to lean your body downstream and use your paddle like a crutch, you need to focus on keeping your head and weight balanced over your downstream edge. This way, your paddle is free to move you around in the hole. It's also very important to sit in the moderately aggressive position when side surfing. This position gives you the most edge control and prevents your stern edges from catching water, which is quite common. As a final note, you should spend the majority of your time looking upstream. It doesn't matter if your kayak is facing upstream, downstream or sideways, the best way to keep track of your position in a hole is to keep your eyes on what's happening on your upstream side.

Side surfing is a balancing act, not a fight against the water.

Moving Around and Escaping Holes

Once you're comfortable balancing in a side surf, it's time to start moving yourself around. The first rule for moving around in a hole is that all of your strokes are to be taken on the downstream side of your kayak, in the foam pile. Because the foam pile itself is aerated and doesn't provide much substance, you actually need to reach under the foam pile to the hard, green water below.

To escape from a hole, or to set up any freestyle hole move, you need to move from the trough of the hole up onto the foam pile. The most ideal places to do this are at the weak spots, such as the tongues or the corners of a hole. There are a couple of good ways of getting yourself to these spots. The easiest way is to simply take forward or backward strokes on the downstream side and pull yourself to the tongue or out to a corner.

A more powerful, but slightly more difficult, way of getting on top of the foam pile or escaping a hole is to "blast" your way from the trough of the hole out to the side. Blasting means front surfing in a hole or breaking wave. To pull yourself into a blast, take a powerful sweep stroke while keeping your boat as flat on the surface of the water as possible. In the blasting position, one end of your boat is underneath the foam pile while the other is pointing directly upstream. With a rudder in the water, you can then ferry out to the corner of the wave. This blasting technique requires you to be very aggressive, but it's definitely the quickest and most powerful way to move around in a hole.

Spinning in a Hole

Spinning in a hole is the foundation of many of the advanced hole moves and the ultimate test of your ability to work with, and not against, the power of the river. You need to have a good awareness of your position in a hole and quick and stable weight and edging transitions. Thanks to flat hulls and

When sitting passively in a side surf, you should keep your paddle ready as a brace. The type of brace you use will depend on your situation, but whether you're using a high brace or a low brace, you've got to keep your paddle below your chin and keep your arms in close. It's when you overreach with braces that your shoulders are put at risk. If you happen to catch your upstream edge, you're gonna flip, so don't fight it! Trying to save yourself with an upstream brace will only jam your paddle into rocks or tweak your shoulders. If you're comfortable with the back deck roll, this is the perfect time to use it. You'll throw your body back and into the flip and roll back up on the downstream side.

Blasting is the most powerful means of moving around in a hole. A powerful sweep stroke will pull your boat into a blast.

slicey ends, flat spinning techniques can also be incorporated to make your spins quicker and more controlled. But let's start by looking at the most basic spin.

Hole spins are easiest when a hole has a spin corner to work with. A spin corner is a corner that feeds water (and paddlers) back into to the hole. To do a spin, you'll need to stay balanced over your kayak, leaving your paddle free to move you around the hole. As discussed in the "Side Surfing" segment, this means keeping your weight on your downstream butt cheek. Looking over your upstream shoulder, work your way to the corner of the hole and let your bow get taken downstream until your kayak is parallel to the main current. Without pulling yourself right out, you need to reach a point far enough out of the hole where your stern won't catch when you switch edges. As each hole is different, it may take a few tries to find this point, so approach the corner slowly to begin with. If you feel yourself being drawn back into the hole and aren't sure that you can complete the spin, don't fight the water. Keep your boat on edge and let yourself slide back in, then try again. Eventually, with your weight forward, you will reach a point where your stern is clear of the green water and your bow points to 6 o'clock. Now keep the spin going by planting a forward sweep/high brace on the other side, looking upstream over your other shoulder, and tilting your kayak in the other direction by shifting your weight from one butt cheek to the other. In general you won't need very aggressive boat tilts. Not only is it harder to balance when your boat is right up on edge, but you can end up carving yourself right out of a hole. On the other hand, if your boat is too flat, your stern can easily catch the green water.

The second half of a hole spin tends to be easier since your back won't ever be turned to the hole. This time, back paddle to reach that same balance point up on the corner of the hole. Once there, plant a brake/ low brace on the other side, and swap boat tilts while

Spinning in a hole requires a combination of balance, edge control, and hole awareness. The key to spinning in a hole is using the shoulder or tongue of the hole to get yourself out of the trough and onto the foam pile, where you can manoeuvre. It's also critical that you keep your eyes upstream as much as possible, as this is where the action is, and it gives you the best understanding of your boat position relative to the hole.

leaning back slightly to keep your bow from diving.

Spinning in a hole isn't an easy move to maser because you need to be comfortable being backwards in a hole. Reaching this comfort level will take plenty of practice. This is just another great reason to work on your back eddy turns, ferries and surfing. The more comfortable you are with being backward, the easier spinning in a hole, or any other advanced hole move, will be.

Cartwheels

A cartwheel is a smooth combination of elevated bow and stern pivot turns that can be done both on flatwater and in a hole. If done properly, the boat should be revolving around a fixed point at a fairly consistent rate. The cartwheel provides the foundation for virtually every vertical move, both on waves and in holes. Since every hole is different, there is no one method of cartwheeling, but there are some key concepts and techniques that can be slightly modified to fit any situation. We're going to take a look at the set-up, the initiation, and the "linking of ends."

The Set-up

Without a good set-up, your cartwheel is doomed from the beginning. Your ultimate goal is to initiate the cartwheel at the seam of the hole, with as little upstream speed as possible and with some spin momentum already established. Though the best paddlers have learned to initiate carthwheels from the trough of a hole, it's much easier to start on top of the foam pile. The easiest way to get set up is to ferry onto the foam pile when you enter the hole. If you're trying to get set up from a side surf, then you have to work yourself to a tongue or corner to get on top of the foam pile. Once there, it isn't easy to remain in place, as the hole's recirculating water will want to pull you right into the trough. This is where your braking strokes come in handy. Braking strokes are powerful back strokes that get planted deeply out to the side of your hip. Using alternating braking strokes, you

can stop yourself from being sucked into the trough of most holes. These strokes also help you set up the right initiation angle on your kayak, which is what we're going to look at next.

The Initiation

As we just learned, your ultimate goal is to initiate the cartwheel:

1. With as little upstream momentum as possible.
2. With your bow at the seam of the hole.
3. With spin momentum already established.

You need to initiate with as little upstream

Initiate the cartwheel at the seam of the hole with as little upstream momentum as possible.

momentum as possible because extra upstream momentum will simply drive your kayak deeper into the green water, which in turn will pop you into the air (ender style) or push you downstream and out of the hole.

Initiating your bow at the seam of a hole is a good guideline, because it forces you to use a combination of your own power and the power of the river. If you initiate in too much of the green water, you'll get pushed downstream and out of the hole, whereas if you initiate too high in the foam pile, you'll tend to tumble down into the trough of the hole.

When we say to initiate with spin momentum, we mean that you should already be pulling your bow around and downwards before it enters the water at the seam. This forces you to use your own power instead of relying on the current to take your bow downstream. To establish this spin momentum, use braking strokes to set yourself up on an angle slightly off of 12 o'clock. Then, use a small double pump right there on the foam pile to smash your bow down at the seam of the hole. It's important to understand that you aren't looking to pull your bow directly downward, but that you need to slice it down and around, underneath your body just like a bow pivot turn.

As a general rule, if you are intending to initiate a cartwheel to the left, you should set up with a slight right angle (around 1 o'clock), and if you intend to initiate a cartwheel to the right, you want to set up with a slight left angle (around 11 o'clock). Whichever way you are cartwheeling, the goal is for your bow to initiate at 12 o'clock. You set up slightly off of this mark to account for the small amount that your bow will come around between the set-up and initiation. For more vertical ends, your kayak will be tilted more aggressively on edge and your spin momentum needs to be directed more vertically than laterally. For lower-angle cartwheels, your kayak should be initiated with a tilt between twenty and forty-five degrees, and your spin momentum should be directed more laterally.

Now that you understand where to initiate your cartwheel, let's take a closer look at how your body and paddle are involved.

The paddle is responsible for three things:

1. It provides the braking power that will stop your kayak from diving too deeply into the green water.
2. It provides a pivot from which you can pull your bow down and around using your knees and stomach muscles.
3. It acts as a brace, although it isn't a crutch for you to lean on, as your weight needs to stay over your kayak.

To do all these things, you need to plant your initiation stroke firmly in the green water under the foam pile, with your arms in the power position and with your whole body turned to lead the way. This power position allows you to use the power of your whole torso for the initiation and keeps your shoulders safe. With your body wound up, pull your bow down and around with your stomach muscles and legs, and by shifting your weight forward. As you do so, focus your eyes on the seam of the hole so that you can keep track of your position in the hole. The length of time that you remain looking upstream will depend on the power of the hole and the speed of your cartwheel, because staying ahead of your kayak is the top priority. If you're initiating a cartwheel in a slow hole or pourover, you can look upstream right up until your initiation stroke has finished its job. However, in a powerful hole, you'll have to turn and lead the way with your head right away to keep ahead of your kayak.

Linking Ends

Once you've initiated your cartwheel, keeping it going involves staying ahead of your kayak, keeping your weight forward, making smooth edge transitions, and moving quickly from one stroke to the next. To demonstrate this, we'll take a quick look at the actions of your boat, body and paddle.

A little bow wind-up will help you initiate your end.

Watching the seam of the hole lets you keep track of your position in the hole.

Move quickly from one stroke to the next.

The head leads the way when going to the next stroke.

Try to keep your body forward and quiet through the cartwheel.

Get your next stroke in the water before your next end.

to make your edge transition before your initiation stroke has finished. When practising pivot turns, you were levelling your kayak off; but for cartwheels, you need to make a complete edge transition so that the submerged end slices back to the surface. The amount you tilt your kayak onto its next edge dictates how vertical your cartwheels are. If you're slow in making this transition, your cartwheel will usually stall out or you'll get turned downstream in a pirouette.

The Paddle: Your paddle has three main functions when you're cartwheeling. It acts as a pivot point from which your stomach and knees can pull your bow around; it acts as a brake to prevent you from catching too much green water in the trough; and it acts as a brace with which you can make small corrections. It's important to note that all these things require that your paddle be planted as early as possible for each rotation, so that you have the maximum time to control your kayak. In small holes, you need power from your paddle to pull each of your ends through. In big holes, where your cartwheels are quicker and you have less time to reach for your strokes, it's okay, because the water provides most of the power. In this case, your strokes are in close to your body and your focus is more on making smooth edge transitions and staying ahead of your cartwheels with your upper body.

Your paddle acts as a brake to prevent a powerful hole's recirculating water from dragging you down into the trough. In weaker holes, the recirculating water may not be powerful enough to hold you on its own while linking cartwheels. In these holes, you may need to take small recovery strokes after each end. Recovery strokes are quick, short strokes that move you back upstream to keep you in the hole. For example, after initiating your bow to the left, your recovery stroke would be a small back stroke on the right, which is taken immediately before the forward sweep on the right that pulls your stern through.

The key to linking ends is getting your next stroke firmly planted before the next end reaches the water.

The Body: There's no one position for your body when cartwheeling. You need to make constant adjustments as each end comes around. As a general rule, though, you want to stay forward and keep your upper body as quiet as possible.

Let's look at your ideal body position in more depth. When your bow is down, your body is best off in a relatively neutral position, or leaning slightly back as you stand up a bit on your foot pegs. If you find yourself falling on your face, then it usually means that you're leaning back too much. Remember the effects of your forward and backward leans when bow stalling? Leaning back actually pulled your kayak more vertical! When your stern is submerged, your weight should be in a more aggressive, forward position. Though these forward and backward leans play a major role in cartwheeling, the most important job for your upper body is staying "wound up" and leading your kayak through each end. As long as your body leads the way and you get your strokes planted early, your stomach and knees can continue to pull the bow around and you can make any small corrections

Kevin Varette in mid-loop.

that are needed.

Cartwheeling is one of the most difficult freestyle moves to master, because it isn't a single move. It requires constant control in a hole and the ability to make quick and effective corrections. But as we mentioned at the beginning, cartwheeling provides the foundation for most other playboating moves, so once you've developed the control for cartwheels, then there's no reason you can't perform any of the more advanced moves!

Advanced Hole Moves

There are a number of more advanced hole moves that you can learn, but most require a cartwheeling foundation. The best place to practise most of these moves initially is on flatwater, where there are fewer variables. This will require a small playboat and the use of more of your own power as there is no current to help with the moves.

Splitwheel: The splitwheel is a two-ended cartwheel with a 180-degree pirouette between ends.

Clean and Super-Clean Cartwheels: The clean cartwheel is a two-ended cartwheel that is done with only a single stroke. The super-clean cartwheel is a three-ended cartwheel with only a single stroke. Though these are the only named "clean" cartwheels, there is really no limit to how many "clean" ends you can do. Clean ends are accomplished by leading aggressively with your head and torso, pulling hard with your stomach muscles, and switching your edges with precise timing.

Loop: The loop is a complete front flip that is done by popping ender-style out of the hole and into the air. The best loops are actually completely airborne and are one of the most dynamic moves that you'll see on the river. An ender is done by ploughing your boat deeply into the green water of a hole with your boat pointed firmly at 12 o'clock. Your boat is rejected by the water once it hits the wall and you get shot straight back up into the air.

Tricky Whu: The tricky whu is a funky move that involves linking a splitwheel with a stern pirouette.

Brendan Mark taking off during a kick flip.

The move uses a single paddle blade and requires great balance and edge control.

RIVER RUNNING MOVES

The Wave Wheel

The wave wheel is an airborne cartwheel that is done with a well-timed launch downstream off the peak of a wave. Freestyle paddlers sometimes use it as an entry move into a hole, but more often than not, the wave wheel is a way of spicing up a simple wave train. The bigger the wave you use, the more dynamic your wave wheel will be. With a big enough wave, you can even get your entire kayak out of the water! Learning to fly this way is remarkably easy once you're comfortable with the flatwater cartwheeling technique. The trickiest part of the move is actually lining up your approach and timing your initiation stroke.

So what's the best type of wave for wave wheels? The most ideal waves are relatively steep (but not breaking, as this will stall you out) and deep on their downstream side.

On the approach to your wave wheel, it's important to have some forward speed, but your focus should be on timing a powerful launching stroke on the face of the wave, just before you reach the wave's peak. This launching stroke is used to do two things: pull your

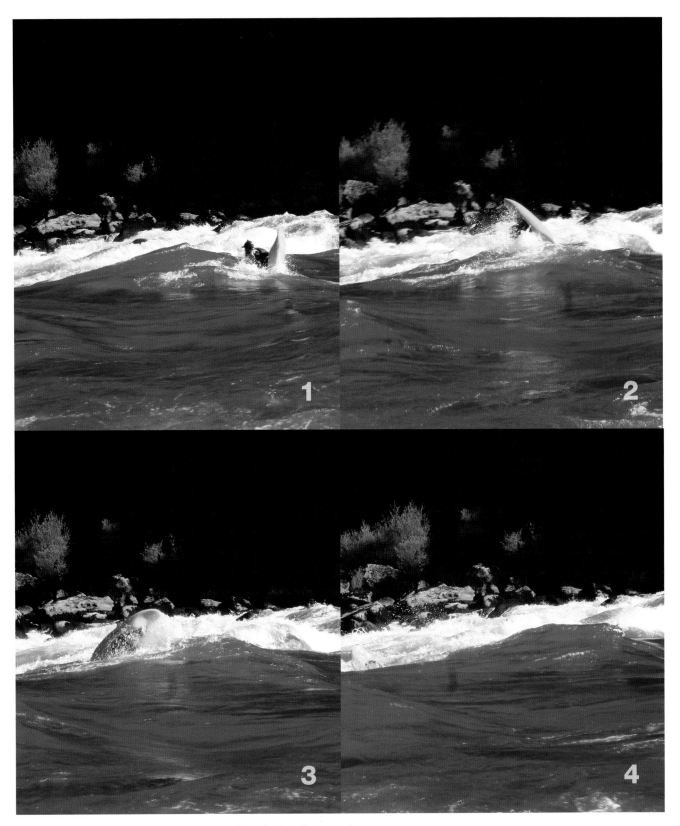

Tyler Curtis nailing a macho move.

the wave, just before you reach the wave's peak. This launching stroke is used to do two things: pull your bow into the air, and pull your hip past the wave's peak. This stroke is a cross between the "power stroke" we covered in the "Essentials" segment and the "double pump" we covered in the "Flatwater Playboating Moves" chapter.

Here's how it works. As you climb the face of the wave, tilt your kayak right on edge and plant the launching stroke at your toes with your top hand at shoulder level. Pull down on this stroke to lift your bow, and pull forward to launch yourself downstream off the wave. As soon as you've taken this stroke, continue with your double pump motions. This means rotating your head and upper body aggressively downwards and turning your launching stroke into a back stroke that gets planted behind the cockpit and at the peak of the wave. With your body wound up and your back stroke planted, throw your weight forward, push your stern into the air and pull your bow down aggressively with your stomach and knees. After hitting your first end, you can keep the wave wheel going with your standard flatwater cartwheeling technique. In a wave train, you can even keep using wave after wave to do several wave wheels in a row. Wave wheels aren't limited to standing waves, either. They can be done on virtually any kind of wave. For instance, a small roller above a hole or a reactionary at the top of a rapid both make great wave wheeling ramps.

Advanced River Running Moves

Any river running move requires a good launching platform, which is ideally a consistent standing wave with minimal break. The steeper waves will usually work best. Although speed is nearly always an asset, the timing of your last stroke will always be more important, so take your time and be precise in setting up. It may even take a few trial runs to get your stroke rhythm worked out. We have spent hours doing laps at a good wave just trying to get some techniques nailed down. Here are some of the more impressive moves that you can then consider trying.

Kick Flip: The kick flip is an airborne, horizontal pirouette that is done while launching off a wave. Landing a big kick flip is an awesome feeling. This has always been one of our favourite moves!

Macho Move: The macho move is a downstream loop done while launching off the peak of a wave and is one of the trickiest moves to learn.

Freewheel: The freewheel is a wave wheel done off the lip of a waterfall, which results in an airborne cartwheel. Yee haw!

WHITEWATER RACING

11

SLALOM

Slalom is the oldest and most established form of whitewater competition, as well as the only whitewater sport to have a presence in the Olympic Games. In slalom racing, paddlers negotiate their way through eighteen to twenty-five "gates" that are hung over a 250- to 400-metre-long section of rapids. The objective of slalom competition is very simple: navigate, without fault, through all the gates in the shortest amount of time. Paddlers are required to go through some of the gates in an upstream direction (which are coloured red) and others in a downstream direction (which are coloured green). Faults result in time penalties and are incurred for touching (two seconds) or missing gates (fifty seconds). Touching faults are given for any contact with the gate by boat, paddle or body. Missing a gate means not completely manoeuvring the head and at least part of the boat through the gate. Decisions on these faults are made by judges positioned along the riverbank. A full-length slalom course will usually take around two minutes for an experienced racer to complete.

In a standard race, competitors are given two runs through a course and the times are combined to give a final score.

Slalom boats are quite different from other whitewater kayaks, as they're designed to be as quick and responsive as possible, yet they must meet certain dimensional requirements. They're extremely light and rigid, being made of composite materials such as Kevlar, carbon fibre, and fibreglass, and are not designed to withstand the same abuse that their plastic cousins do.

Slalom racing is an incredible test of strength, endurance, precision and planning. For some, the adrenaline rush of racing and physically pushing oneself is a lure to the sport, while many recreational paddlers spend time running through slalom gates to improve their overall paddling. Racing through gates, either casually or competitively, will develop your boat control, timing, and stroke efficiency. In the end, it can have a fantastic impact on your paddling and can make those tight, must-make eddies a lot easier to hit when you're pushing your limits in more adventurous whitewater.

Extreme races are the ultimate test of stamina, skill, and nerve

EXTREME RACES

Extreme races are the latest craze in whitewater competition, both for paddlers and for the media. These races take competitors down a short and intense section of Class 5 whitewater that usually involves at least one major waterfall. Unlike slalom, there is no set of strict rules for extreme races, as each location has its own challenging variables that competitors need to negotiate. Sometimes small groups, or "heats," of paddlers will race "head-to-head," fighting their way through the mob in a mad dash to the finish line. In some races, the winners from each heat will keep moving on to the next round, and time is not a concern. This is a form of round robin that leaves one winner at the end of the final heat. In other races, competitors will have to race one at a time against the clock. Those with the top times move on to the proceeding rounds, which may either be timed or head-to-head, until a final winner emerges.

Make no mistake; extreme races are just as they suggest: extreme! These are races designed exclusively for the expert whitewater paddler who is willing to take an already challenging piece of whitewater and make it more difficult by racing his or her way down it. Needless to say, these races are amazing to watch and absolutely exhilarating to take part in. They're the ultimate test of nerve, technique, precision, and power.

SURF KAYAKING

12

Photo by Wayne Barson

Surf kayaking is an amazing spin-off sport from whitewater kayaking. There really are few feelings that can compare with shooting down the face of an ocean wave and carving a hard turn. If you've ever been kayaking in the ocean surf then you know what we're talking about. You'll also be able to appreciate it when we say that playing out in the ocean can be very intimidating. This is probably a good thing, because although the ocean is a wonderful natural playground, it can be very dangerous and should be treated with the utmost respect.

Surf kayaking began in the 1950s, but the first true surf kayak wasn't built until 1968, which caused the sport to boom in popularity. Equipment continued to evolve through the '70s, but it wasn't until the '80s that competitions really began to take form, and the first World Surf Kayaking Contest was held. Since that time, equipment has been constantly improving, and the limits of what can be done in the surf have been pushed to awe-inspiring levels.

THE FORMATION OF WAVES

To make the most of your time on the water, you need to understand how surf waves are formed. It all starts when the winds from offshore storms churn up waves. These waves can be huge, but very choppy, erratic, and not great for surfing. As these waves move through the water, friction causes them to lose some of their energy. If the storm didn't give them enough energy to begin with, then the waves will flatten out before reaching our beaches. If the storm was strong enough, the erratic waves will hit each other and their energy will combine. If this happens enough, swells will be created and make their way to beaches on opposite sides of the ocean. Along the way, friction will work out the small and choppy elements of the wave, leaving a smooth, glassy face that is ideal for surfers.

Photo by: Wayne Barson

WAVE SIZE

Waves are measured differently in different surfing communities. Most surfers refer to the size of the wave's face, from crest to trough, but some use the backside of a wave as their measure, resulting in smaller perceived sizes of the same waves. Make sure you know what system is being used in the area that you'll be surfing. The difference between five feet on the front side and five feet on the backside is substantial! There's nothing more frightening than being caught in surf that is beyond your ability to deal with.

Tides also play a major role in the development of surf waves, although there is no general rule to follow. Each beach has a "break zone" where waves crest and surfers surf. The depth of the water at the break zone varies with the tide, and the unique characteristics of each beach dictate what part of the tide cycle provides the best surfing. Local knowledge is of utmost importance.

TYPES OF BREAK

Break is formed when ocean swells reach shallower water, which causes them to slow down and pile up on themselves. This is why waves grow in height and steepness when they hit break zones. The type of waves that we get at break zones depends on the speed, power and direction of the swell, along with the tide height and configuration of the ocean floor. The more quickly the ocean floor becomes shallow, the more quickly the waves crest and break, and the steeper they become. An ocean floor that becomes shallow more gradually will create less steep waves that build and crash more slowly. There are three common break zones.

Beach Break

Beach break is the most common type of surf. Waves build as the ocean floor becomes shallower closer to the beach. You find a wide variety of waves at a beach break and so you may spend some time finding the areas that offer the best surf on a particular day. Shore break more accurately describes the zone where waves crest a final time and roll into the beach, providing minimal surfing potential. At a beach, you often have an initial break further out and then a shore break as the waves hit the shallowest water. In big swells, the shore break can be a very challenging barrier to paddle through as you try to get out to the smoother break for a surf.

Point Break

Point breaks often provide surfers with the best surfing, and of course will usually be the busiest surf spots. Point break waves are caused as swells refract (or bend) around a point and into shallower water. This has the tendency of creating waves that steadily break outward as opposed to just dumping. As such,

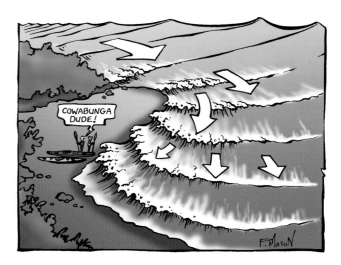

Point break waves are caused as swells refract around a point.

they can provide sustained, high quality surf zones. To the outside of the point break you can usually find a calm zone for paddling back out, which makes life much easier and saves your energy for the surf.

Reef Break

Reefs are shallow spots in the ocean and reef break is caused when swells hit this shallow zone. The great thing about reef break is that it is usually surrounded by calm water, which makes paddling out to the drop-in zones very easy. On the flip side, reefs are composed of sharp rocks and coral, which can spell disaster for the out-of-control surfer. Depending on the site, a reef may form a dumping break or a sweeter point break.

CURRENTS

Rip Tide / Current

Rip tides are the primary cause in over 80% of swimmer rescues at surf beaches, because they can be tricky to detect and are surprisingly powerful. These rip currents are formed when water that has been pushed up on a beach by breaking waves is pulled back out by gravity. Because waves may continually push more water up the slope of the beach, there can be a lot of water searching for the quickest way back to fill this void. Under certain conditions, this outflowing water can be concentrated into a channel, which becomes a strong underwater current moving away from the beach. When in control, you can use these rip currents to help you paddle out past shore break, but if you find yourself swimming, these rip currents can be very dangerous. A rip can be recognized in a few ways. It may create especially rough or choppy waves, be a darker colour because of the deeper water, or may leave a foam trail. To escape from a rip current, you must swim perpendicular to that current until you're free. Again, local knowledge is very important.

Longshore Currents

The same forces that cause rip currents also cause longshore currents. These currents are most obvious when waves hit the shore at an angle. This causes water to be pushed laterally along the beach away from the oncoming waves. You've probably found yourself swimming at a beach and after a short time wondering how you ended up so far away from your stuff! Longshore currents are generally less dangerous than rips because they don't pull directly out to the open sea, but it should be noted that they can feed water and swimmers into rip currents. Longshore currents can be a pain for surfers, as you now need to fight against them on top of fighting your way through the shore break.

EQUIPMENT

One nice thing about surf kayaking is that you can use your whitewater equipment for it. Of course, it's not ideal, so if you were going to spend a lot of time on the ocean, you'd probably want to look at buying a

Pulling through a wave that has just crested involves planting your paddle deeply in the water and leaning forward, while shielding your face with your forearm.

surf kayak or wave ski. The difference between a surf kayak, wave ski and a whitewater playboat is largely in the hull design and length. Surf kayaks and wave skiis are longer and designed for speed and carving ability, whereas whitewater boats are designed to turn quickly, to be easy to get vertical, and to be forgiving. Wave skiis are different to surf kayaks in that they have no deck. They more closely resemble surfboards with seats and hooks for your feet. The effect of the different hull designs is that whitewater boats are typically slower and can lack the speed to stay ahead of the break on big dumping ocean waves. As such, they will often get caught in the break and side surf into shore; or in bigger surf, can get thrown bow over stern! Most of the time however, whitewater boats let you have a super fun day at the beach.

Other pieces of gear to consider when surfing in the ocean are a good paddle and a good skirt. The power of the ocean can only be compared to the power of a big volume river. Big ocean waves have the ability to break your paddle in your hands or to pop your skirt right off your cockpit rim. You can dramatically reduce the chances of either of these things happening by using a good quality paddle and skirt. You don't need to look at the top of the line by any means, but you also don't want to rely on an entry-level paddle that might break much more easily.

Swimming in ocean surf can be a terrifying and dangerous game, and you should do your best to avoid it. On that note, an implosion bar or some type of device that will help prevent your skirt from popping is a very good idea at the beach.

PADDLING OUT

One of the very first challenges of surf kayaking is getting on the water and paddling out past the shore break to the surf break. The best place to get into your kayak is somewhere where one of the bigger waves will wash enough water up the slope of the beach to lift you off the sand and let you paddle out. This means you should take a minute and watch the shore break before picking your spot. When you decide the time has come, set your boat down, climb in, and get your skirt on before the next wave takes you away. You can expect to have to push yourself further into the surf using your hands after getting into your boat. You can also expect that waves often appear erratically and grab you before your skirt is on!

Paddling out past the shore break requires a combination of aggressive paddling and wave reading. Look ahead, watch the waves roll in, and try to pick out where the weak spots will be. The weak spots are parts of waves that haven't yet broken, or that have broken far enough ahead that most of their energy has dissipated by the time you encounter them. You can also use rip currents to help pull you out.

The best way to get through waves that have broken or that are breaking is to use the boofing technique that we covered in the "Managing Holes" segment of the "River Running" chapter. This means approaching the wave with a slight angle, then taking a powerful last stroke that pulls your bow to 12 o'clock and on top of the foam pile. Using this boofing technique, you can bounce over some amazingly large breaking waves, but you had better have some forward speed and an aggressive body position to do so.

The worst-case scenario involves hitting a wave just after it has crested and has begun to break. In this case, there's not much you can do to avoid taking a hit from the ocean gods. By leaning forward and placing one of your arms in front of your face and body you can sometimes split the wave and deflect some of its impact. Leaning forward will also protect your skirt. A large wave can easily blow your skirt if it's allowed to dump directly down on it.

CATCHING WAVES

The secret to catching waves is choosing the right wave and positioning yourself correctly for it. Both these things require that you learn where the best break zones are by watching earlier sets, and that you read the waves as they come in. Before the next set arrives, you should have a good idea of where the sweet spots are, how many waves to expect, and which waves are likely to be the best. When you've chosen a wave, turn your boat toward shore and accelerate with some quick and powerful forward strokes. As the wave picks you up, you need to lean forward to help establish your position on its face. If you've timed it correctly, the wave should just be steepening up and about to peak. Gravity will then take over and send you screaming down the face of the wave.

SURFING

You surf ocean waves just as you would big river waves. Most importantly, this means that your time should be spent carving on the face, where gravity is

Effective surf kayaking involves staying on the face of the wave.

working on your side. The higher on the face of the wave you carve, the more room you have to accelerate. If you let yourself shoot down into the trough, you'll lose all your speed and therefore your ability to move around on the wave. If the wave is breaking and you're in the trough, it is very probable that you're going to get creamed.

The rudders you use to carve on ocean waves are no different than those you use on river waves, although you're not going to need braking rudders very often. Your focus should be on using rudders at the back of your boat that don't slow you down at all. Something else to consider is how to get the most performance out of your kayak. Whether you're using a surf kayak or a whitewater kayak, it's important that you use the forward edges of your kayak to carve on a wave, which means keeping your weight forward as much as possible.

SURF KAYAKING ETIQUETTE

Wherever there's surf, you'll find surfers; so you need to follow some surfing "road rules" to avoid collisions and confrontations on the water. Unfortunately, there's a high rate of "road rage" in surf zones. For some reason a lot of this tension exists between board surfers and kayak surfers, and much of it comes from our lack of understanding of surfing etiquette and a lack of appreciation for the board surfers' feelings toward us kayakers. We're going to take a quick look at some issues that will help you avoid conflict in the surf.

Due to the speed and power involved with surfing ocean waves, collisions can be catastrophic; so the single most important rule in the surf has to do with

the surfing "right of way." It must first be understood that this rule dictates the right of way on unbroken waves only. A surfer has no right of way on broken waves. Two factors determine who has the right of way on ocean waves.

First and foremost, the surfer who catches an unbroken wave first has the right of way. If it's questionable as to who caught the wave first, then the right of way goes to the surfer closest to the break. A surfer is considered to have caught the wave once he or she has stopped paddling, kicking, or stroking, and is moving down the face of the wave due to the force of gravity alone.

It also must be understood that it's a surfer's responsibility to avoid all swimmers, surfers, or paddlers encountered while surfing a wave. Having said this, those paddling out should do their very best not to interfere with surfers. This might mean taking the long route out and paddling around the surf, or it could mean paddling directly into the broken sections. Something we need to consider is that we kayakers don't have the same ability to carve free from a wave once it is breaking. This means we have less control than the surfers at this point, and have become a risk in their eyes.

Another thing to consider is the advantage that kayakers have over other surfers. We can catch waves earlier than board surfers, and it's easier for us to paddle back out after each surf. What this means is that surfers will often consider their rides more valuable than those of kayakers and will easily get frustrated by a kayaker who repeatedly takes the right of way by catching waves first. If you're aware of this issue, then common courtesy should dictate when you sit back and let other surfers grab a few waves.

On a final note, surfing has a territorial issue that isn't as prevalent in river communities. Local surfers often believe that they have more right to "their waves" than others. Though we may have trouble understanding this logic, it's not something that you should fight. You need to respect these territorial feelings, consider yourself a "guest" at their surf spots, and provide the local paddlers with a wide berth. It goes without saying that a friendly greeting and an "after you" mentality will go a long way to making your time in the surf more enjoyable, even if you do end up getting a few less surfs than you'd like.

The right of way goes to the surfer who caught the wave first, or the surfer closest to the break.

SQUIRT BOATING 13

BY WORLD CHAMPION BRENDAN MARK

The first squirt boats popped up in the late 1970s, thanks to the creativity and the "out of the box" thinking of the now legendary Snyder brothers and Jesse Whittemore. Since then, squirt boating has developed a cult-like following of die hard whitewater enthusiasts enchanted by a slightly different aspect of paddling than the general kayaker.

Squirt boats are kayaks designed specifically for playing with the currents below the waterline. This is accomplished by having the kayaks made as small as possible while still allowing them to float, albeit just barely. To do this, squirt boats are custom-built to suit a paddler's body weight, leg length, foot size, and paddling style, in order to get rid of any unnecessary volume. This makes for a very tight and often uncomfortable fit, but it's deemed a worthy sacrifice by the squirt boater as it allows them to ride low in the water and tap into currents that other paddlers wouldn't even notice. This intimate connection that is developed with the water is one of the reasons that squirt boaters are some of the most devoted and obsessed whitewater paddlers.

WHY SQUIRT BOAT?

THE SUBCULTURE

One aspect that draws people to squirt boating is the subculture, the desire to stand out among the crowd. Whitewater kayaking in itself is a niche sport, so to stand out and be niche within a niche, you can begin to understand the uniqueness of squirt boating. It's not uncommon to see squirt boaters with customized designs on their boats, playing in eddy lines or pourovers that no other plastic paddlers care to frequent. It's a truly close group of paddlers that are ultra-dedicated to the sport.

Squirt boating is incredible practice for all other types of whitewater kayaking.

THE CHALLENGE

Squirt boating is another means to enjoy the river, and it poses a whole new set of challenges. With a kayak that is virtually neutral in buoyancy, a simple run down a river can pose problems and challenges that a typical plastic boater would never face. The kayak floats through waves as opposed to over them,

and every little current wants to grab your stern and pivot you around. Surfing a glassy wave can keep you mesmerized for an entire day and going for downtime is a balancing and coordination act that takes a lot of time to master.

LEARNING

Aside from being really fun, there's also the concept of how squirt boats can benefit absolutely any kayaker. The average paddler is not fortunate enough to have a world-class learning river at his or her doorstep and even if they are, that river becomes way too cold to paddle during the off-season. Squirt boats are very versatile and can be used almost anywhere—from eddy lines and waves to winter pool sessions, or on the lake at your cottage.

With the streamlined design and minimal volume, learning new freestyle moves is much easier with a squirt boat. Whether it be your first cartwheel or a more advanced move, such as a super clean or a tricky whu, a squirt boat can help you master it. By minimizing the force necessary to submerge the ends, squirt boats allow you to concentrate solely on your technique and not so much on power. Once the technique is mastered, adding power is much easier.

CHOOSING A BOAT

Squirt boats are custom-made kayaks and are very labour intensive to build. It takes a minimum of twenty-four man-hours of precise craftsmanship to build one of these boats, and considerably more time when intricate graphics are requested. A base model squirt boat is made from six to seven layers of fibreglass. It increases in value and decreases in weight as fibreglass is substituted with carbon and/or Kevlar. The entry level squirt will start at $1,400 USD.

To appeal to a growing number of paddlers, squirt boat designs have changed radically over the past few years. They are shorter and easier to use; and there are numerous designs to choose from.

A paddler's inseam initially determines what boats are appropriate for him to use. From this assortment of models, the paddler must then consider what his most common use of the boat will be. Similar to choosing a plastic boat, if you wish to run rivers you would purchase a more river-running-friendly design, and if you want to play you would purchase a playboat.

In the world of squirt boating there are two main disciplines—downtime and freestyle. Briefly, downtime is the use of eddy lines and specific currents to work yourself below the surface of the water and then resurface further downstream. Longer squirt boats, those eight feet or more, are better suited for performing downtime, as they have more surface area for the currents to work on. A proper-fitting downtime squirt boat should be snug and float so that the cockpit is almost even with the surface of the water and the stern is approximately one or two inches below the surface. In general, shorter squirt boats are better suited for performing all the latest freestyle manoeuvres. They'll be a bit more comfortable, have a flatter hull, and possibly edges.

Choosing the squirt boat ultimately depends on how you plan on using it. If it's downtime you are interested in, the longer your boat will be, and you'll be sacrificing play-ability. If it's learning freestyle moves that motivates you, your kayak will be much shorter but unstable underwater for downtime. If you're looking to take advantage of both aspects of squirt boating then a hybrid boat in between the two lengths would suit you best.

GEAR

Squirt boaters pick up a few more pieces of equipment that can be useful.

Spray Deck: Skirts are generally smaller and require a larger "lip" to create a tighter seal around the cockpit. A limited number of manufacturers make squirt-specific decks. By far the most popular are those made by Mountain Surf.

An alternative to the traditional wooden paddle is one made from composite. You will still want a shorter paddle in length (190 cm or below) with smaller blades, but you should also consider a zero-degree offset. I have found that when underwater, a zero-degree paddle can offer more stability and control.

Hand Paddles: Many squirt boaters love to use hand paddles.

These can be webbed gloves or plastic circles such as Power Paws strapped to your hands. They're a lot of fun and many squirt boaters find them easier to use when going for downtime as a paddle can often get in the way.

Booties: The design of the squirt boat does not allow for regular footwear; there simply isn't room. Although it is tempting to go barefoot, the textured fibreglass rubbing on your feet will quickly change your mind. Neoprene socks or even an old pair of wool socks will keep your feet happy.

Brendan Mark on his way to some downtime on an eddy line.

An old pair of wool socks is enough to protect your feet from the textured fibreglass boat.

Paddle: Traditional squirt paddles are made of wood, have smaller blades, and are shorter in length. These features allow for increased manoeuvrability when performing both freestyle moves and downtime. Jimistyx are the traditional blades used by squirt boaters; they are beautiful hand-crafted wooden paddles by artisan Jim Snyder.

The Extras: A diving mask, swimming goggles, nose plugs, lifejacket with removable foam, and an altimeter watch to gauge depth are just some of the extras you'll see squirt boaters using.

TRICKS

The low volume of the squirt boat is what makes tricks different for this type of kayaking. Many of the moves are very similar to how you would perform them in a plastic kayak; the main differentiator is your technique. In a plastic kayak you contend with excess volume in your bow and stern, requiring a lot more muscle to push the kayak around. The low volume of the squirt boat eliminates the need to power your moves and gets you thinking about technique, focusing on what knee you should lift to tilt the kayak and where your body position should be.

When getting in a squirt boat for the first time it will seem very tippy. Take the time to get comfortable and semi-stable before attempting any moves. On the positive side, squirt boats are the easiest boats on the market to roll, so if the elusive hand roll has been a challenge, a squirt boat could be your solution.

The following is a brief look at some of the techniques you can perform in squirt boats.

Bow Stall

One of the easiest moves you can perform in a squirt boat is the bow stall. To do this, extend your hands straight in front of your torso, lean forward, and voila! Your bow will slowly sink and you will be in a perfect bow stall. Maintain your balance by adjusting your body weight: counterintuitively, you should lean back if you are losing verticality and lean forward if you are falling over vertical. Keep your paddle in the water to control side-to-side movement by pushing on the blade you are falling over on.

Bow stalling.

Bow Screw

A true bow screw is a pirouette when the stern of your kayak is over your head, or simply, when the kayak is over vertical. Once in a bow stall position, use a forward sweep to pivot yourself around. Keep sculling that blade back and forth to maintain the screwing motion; make sure your blade does not leave the water. Keep your weight forward and look in the direction you want to turn.

Advanced Element: Do it underwater! Once you've figured out the regular bow screw, try leaning all the way forward. With your body completely submerged, you'll need to combine pulling on your blade and feathering it in the water. Tip: a zero-degree paddle will help a lot.

Flatwater Cartwheel

Begin with a reverse sweep followed by a forward sweep. Continue doing this until you are comfortably spinning in a circle. The next step is to edge your boat by lifting the opposite knee from the blade you are sweeping with. With a back sweep, you will be knifing the bow of your boat underwater, and with a forward sweep, you will be pulling the stern of your boat underwater. It's really important to wind your body up before each sweep in order to then harness the power of unwinding your torso. Take a moment to visualize this. At first, you will be doing low-angle cartwheels. However, the more you really concentrate on lifting your knees, the more vertical your ends will be. Advanced squirt boaters can even perform past-vertical flatwater cartwheels by aggressively lifting their knees.

Advanced Element: Super Clean Flatwater Cartwheel

Super cleans are complete cartwheels without using a paddle. To do this, you need a shorter squirt boat (eight feet and under) and good balance. Begin as you would a bow stall: lean forward and let the bow of your boat sink approximately a foot underwater. Next, edge the boat on the side on which you are most comfortable cartwheeling—if you prefer left, then you will lift your left knee. Aggressively turn your torso to the left, and the bow of the boat will then shoot out of the water. Now you want to dive the bow back under by lifting the right knee (for a left cartwheel), cranking your torso around to the left again and leaning forward. As you repeat these steps, you can rock your body forward and back to help sink each end. The more aggressively you lift your knee, the higher your ends will be out of the water.

Stern Screw

A proper stern screw will pirouette the boat over a vertical 360 degrees on its stern. Wind up your body and plant your blade deep in the water at the back of your boat. Unwind your body while doing a powerful back sweep. As you begin unwinding, aggressively lift, and pull towards your chest, the knee on the same side as your back sweep. Just to be sure, with a left back sweep, you would lift the left knee and vice versa for the right side. One stroke should be sufficient to bring the boat vertical. If you are still not vertical, repeat the steps above with another big back sweep. As your kayak passes vertical, continue to lead with your head by looking in the direction you are turning. To finish the move, you'll use the standard sweep roll as your bow falls toward the water.

Advanced Element: Try and keep the blade you initiated with during the back sweep in the water the whole time. As the kayak pivots around on its stern, keep feathering the blade back to your body and pushing it away to keep your stern screw going. With the proper balance, you should be able to link multiple stern screws in a row.

Washouts

Washouts are bow screws done without your paddle touching the water. To perform this trick, you will need to have mastered your bow screws and flatwater cartwheels. Begin with flatwater cartwheels. As you pull your stern through the water, lift your paddle out so it is at face level. Let the bow of your boat initiate without smashing it under using a back sweep. Keep your body position back and aggressively look in the direction you are spinning. If you were cartwheeling to your left, look over your left shoulder. Your boat will pirouette around on the bow, so be certain to keep the paddle in the air in front of your face. As with the bow screw, the boat should go over-vertical. When you near the end of your pirouette, reach around with your trailing blade (in this case the right blade) and recover from the spin by pulling the stern of the boat through the water, like the second end of a cartwheel.

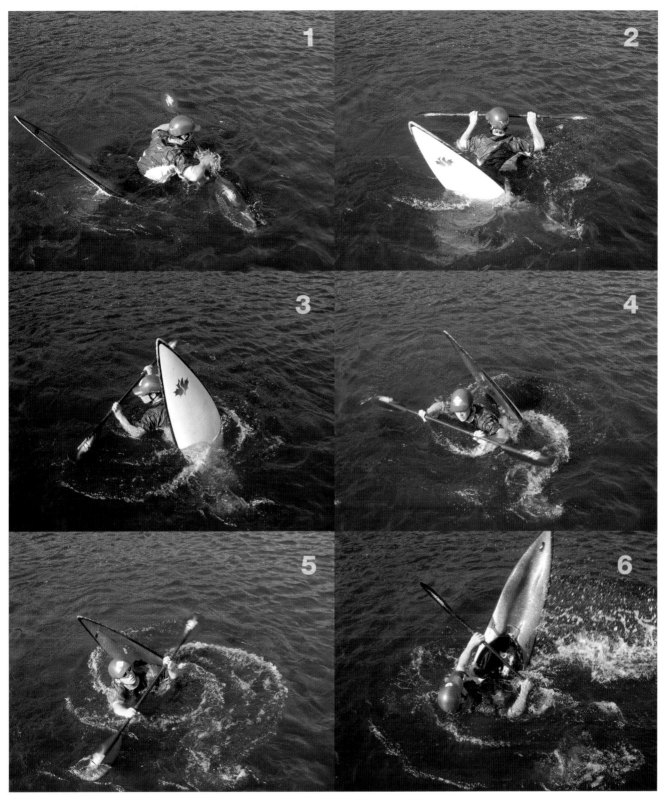

A washout.

Downtime / Mystery Move

Probably the coolest move you can perform in a squirt boat is the mystery move. You disappear underwater and resurface further downstream ten, twenty, and even thirty seconds later. The ability to do mystery moves is what really differentiates squirt boats from plastic playboats. To do them, you will need a crisp eddy line or seam line, a pourover or a steep breaking wave. The underlying idea is to purl your bow underwater (approximately one foot), slice the stern down the same distance, and then level the boat so that it's flat. At this point, the forces of the river can act on the flat deck to push it down. A reverse sweep is generally the easiest way to sink the stern and then there is a variety of strokes you can use to "screw" yourself deeper underwater, ultimately completely submerging.

Getting Underwater

On and eddy or seam line: One of the most common places to do a mystery move is on a crisp eddy line or seam line. To get down after the initial purling of your bow, it's generally easiest to follow with a sequence of forward sweeps that turn your boat in the same direction as the current. With each pull on the forward stroke you should feel that you're spiralling deeper underwater. The most common mistake is leaving your paddle at the surface of the water and hands above your head as your boat is sinking below the surface. You'll maintain better control, balance, and leverage over your kayak if you keep your paddle at chest level as you begin to disappear underwater.

On a wave: Disappearing off a wave is a fun way to get downtime. Any wave that is steep enough to purl your bow and looks deep below is a good wave for downtime. The trick is to keep your weight forward when sliding down the face of the wave. As your bow purls underwater and the kayak starts to dive, force the stern of the kayak under with a big back sweep. If all goes well you should be drifting underwater through the wave train behind the wave.

At a pourover: Pourovers can be a fast way to get under; usually the flow of the water is pushing straight down so it's just a matter of keeping your balance as you paddle into it. To get under, paddle at the pourover so you're entering it at a slight angle (not straight at it). As your bow begins to be pushed underwater, use a back sweep with the downstream

Initiating a mystery move on a wave.

Initiating a mystery move at a pourover.

paddle blade to push the rest of your kayak into the pourover. Keeping your weight forward and the blade you are using for the back sweep in the water will help you stay balanced.

Staying Underwater

There's a number of ways to stay underwater, and each of them depends on what the current is doing. The key through all of this is to keep your boat level; as soon the kayak is not flat (i.e. if you lift your knee, or your body position shifts forwards or backwards), you will quickly resurface. Advanced squirt boaters can control the speed at which they descend, level off at a certain depth, and even ascend to a desired level when too deep.

There are a few common strokes used to corkscrew and maintain your depth underwater. You'll often see forward sweeps or the box stroke. Forward sweeps are as they sound, a series of sweep strokes you're doing to keep yourself spinning underwater. The box stroke is done at your knee with your paddle shaft vertical. You're essentially pulling water towards your knee from the side of your kayak, then feathering your paddle blade back out to start the stroke over. It's like a series of repetitive draw strokes towards your bow that will keep your boat spinning underwater.

The wing method of staying underwater is a way I've developed with a zero-degree offset paddle (essential to do this method). Holding the paddle at chest level with your paddle blades parallel to your kayak is the neutral position; you're essentially maintaining the depth you are at. To sink underwater faster, you

Brendan scouts the bottom of the river.

can feather your lead hand forward and then pull the water (while pushing with your other hand) to get your boat corkscrewing faster. If you are spinning to the left, lower your left hand so that it's closer to your knee and roll your wrists forward so that your paddle blades are angled down. Now hold this position. Your paddle blade is acting like a wing and you'll quickly begin to spiral deeper underwater. Once you're deep enough, you can level off once again in the neutral position or even ascend by rolling your wrists back and tilting your paddle blade towards the surface. Throughout all of this, you always keep your paddle in front of your chest and elbows close to the body.

Hand paddles are also a very popular way to stay underwater as you don't have the problem of keeping your blades active. To stay under, there's a number of different techniques you can use including a sideways "doggy paddle," a two-handed push to keep the boat spinning, and simply upward thrusts towards the surface to push you under.

RIVER SAFETY AND RESCUE **14**

With some common sense and attention to basic safety principles, you can effectively avoid most trouble on the river. The unfortunate reality is that rivers are dynamic and somewhat unpredictable, so sometimes things that are out of your control just happen. In this chapter we take a look at some basic safety principles, some safety equipment, and a variety of rescue techniques. Hopefully this sheds some light on the options that you have in dealing with issues that arise on the river. The bottom line, though, is that no amount of reading can prepare you for dealing with the rescue situations that will pop up. You need to make informed decisions on what safety equipment to carry with you, learn how to use it all correctly, and then practise these techniques. We've said it before and we'll say it again: the best thing any paddler can do is to take a swiftwater rescue course—because on the river, knowledge is power.

GROUP DYNAMICS

Whatever type of river you're running, you've got to be comfortable with your paddling group. Too often, paddlers cruise down the river without consideration for the other members in their group, or for other groups on the river. First of all, you've got to be sure that you can count on your paddling partners to make wise decisions, because they can have a major impact on everyone in the group. Your group also has to acknowledge that they are only as strong as the weakest paddler. Don't expect to move downstream any faster than is comfortable for the weakest paddler.

Leapfrogging down a river is one of the safest river running techniques as there is always someone watching you run a rapid.

River signals: '"stop", "I'm OK", and "go ahead".

Signals

Make sure that everyone in the group understands the signals that you use on a river. Lack of communication is a very common and preventable cause of accidents. There are some universal signals that everyone needs to know, such as "stop," "go ahead," and "I'm okay," but many paddlers will have a number of other signals that they use on the river. Make sure you discuss these signals before hitting the water.

Spacing

Crowding can be a major problem on some rivers, so be careful that you aren't pulling out in front of someone who's upstream of you. Remember that upstream boats have the right of way. When heading downstream, it's nearly always best to move one at a time. This is especially important when there are holes to negotiate that can stop a paddler and cause a pileup, such as at the bottom of a waterfall. Collisions between paddlers create some of the most potentially dangerous scenarios and need to be avoided. Don't let your anxiety on the river get the better of you. Be patient; don't rush; and make sure things are clear below before setting out.

Spacing is also very important on tight rivers with small eddies. You never want to put on a river like this with a large group. If you're in a large group,

split yourselves into smaller groups. There's nothing more frustrating than finding yourself crowded into a small eddy, and there's nothing more frightening than not being able to fit in an eddy and having to run the following rapid blind.

Group Awareness

When paddling challenging whitewater, it's easy to get caught up with what's happening in front of you, so don't forget to keep your eyes on the paddlers behind you. If you're not watching them, who is? Make sure that you pull over whenever possible and set yourself up in a position of safety from which you can help the next paddler through the rapid. Keep in mind that the less-confident paddlers usually hang back. The most nervous paddler will often opt to run a rapid last, but this should never happen, because if they get into trouble, it may only be possible to help by moving to them from upstream. For this reason, the strongest paddler should always lead the group and the next strongest paddler should be last, in what is called the "sweep" position.

KAYAK RESCUE

Before we delve into rescue, it's worth emphasizing again that prevention through safety-minded paddling should always take priority. However, just like in any other sport or even some daily activities, accidents do happen on the river. When they do, it becomes all too clear to those involved that river rescue training is a worthwhile investment. The river presents unique rescue conditions that require specific knowledge and practice to deal with effectively. A basic river rescue course, particularly one tailored to meet the needs of kayakers, is one of the most useful, responsible, and enjoyable ways to prepare yourself for incidents on the river.

In a rescue course, you'll apply basic rescue principles to realistic scenarios and learn to use a variety of equipment. You learn to tie important knots, to swim effectively in whitewater, to deal with strainers and shallow water crossings, and to rescue victims from a variety of situations. We'll have a look at some basic river rescue gear for paddlers and some fundamental skills as a useful reference, but the most valuable thing about a course (which we can't provide here) is the physical and mental practice. Kayak rescue usually involves the application of some pretty basic techniques, but you don't want the real thing to be your first time applying them!

BASIC RESCUE FOR GROUP LEADERS

As a group leader or instructor, you often have a different relationship with the paddlers in your group than if you were with a bunch of similarly skilled friends. Here are a couple of basic rescue techniques that you'll likely find yourself having to perform.

Aided Re-entry

On small rivers, the best option for rescuing swimmers is to get them to shore with all their equipment so that they can comfortably get themselves ready for the next round. In the calmer areas at the bottom of rapids on big-volume rivers, or when teaching on lakes, the shoreline can be a long way off. In these cases, you may be better off getting the swimmer back into his or her boat on the water. This is what we call an aided re-entry.

The first order of business is getting the water out of the kayak and flipping it upright. To do this, use the "boat-over-boat" technique we discussed earlier. The boat-over-boat technique involves dragging the upside-down kayak over your own cockpit and then

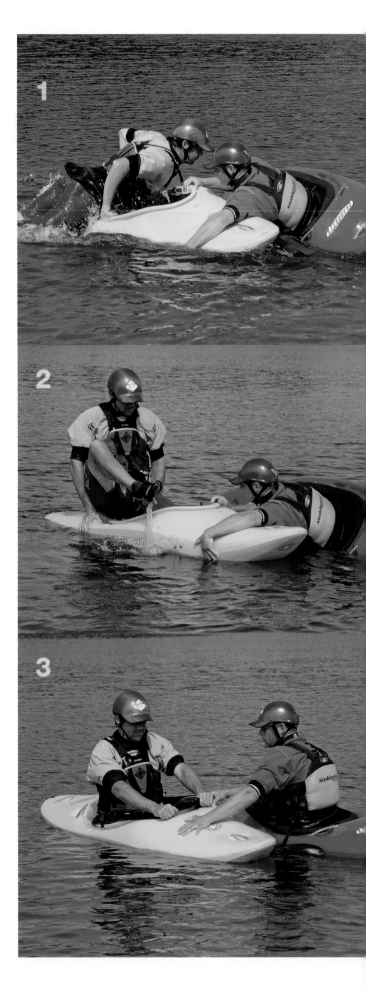

An aided re-entry is a great option when the shore is a long way off and there is little to no current.

rocking the boat back and forth to dump the majority of the water out. Ideally, there are air bags in the back of the kayak that you are emptying. If there are, then it is easiest to pull the bow of that kayak over your own cockpit. If there aren't airbags in the kayak, then it won't matter which end of the kayak you start with, but with all the water in the upside-down kayak, you may need some help from the swimmer to get the boat pulled up onto your lap. In this case, the swimmer can help by pushing from the far end. Once you've emptied most of the water out, flip the kayak upright and bring it alongside your boat.

The next step involves the rescuer holding the kayak stationary as the swimmer climbs back in. To hold the boat steady, the rescuer should lie on the front deck of the empty kayak and hug it. The swimmer can approach the kayak from the stern, grab the cockpit rim, and pull him/herself up into a sitting position just behind the cockpit. The weight of the paddler on the back deck of the kayak will sink the stern and lift the bow into the air, so one of the rescuer's biggest jobs is to keep the bow down. For playboats, this can be very tricky. If the playboat is small enough and the paddler heavy enough, then it may not even be possible. Once the swimmer has reached the sitting position on the back of the cockpit rim, he should swing his legs into the boat and slide himself back in. At this point he'll probably need to sponge out any water left in his boat before snapping on his skirt, grabbing his paddle, and heading off. Ta-dah!

The T-rescue

The T-rescue involves a rescuer offering one end of his kayak to an upside-down paddler to use for support as she hip-snaps her boat upright. The T-rescue is the most basic form of kayak rescue and will only really come into play when there is a special teacher/student relationship between the two paddlers. Otherwise, it's unreasonable for any kayaker to expect to receive a

The T-rescue is only a real option when there is a special teacher/student relationship.

T-rescue when out on the river. It's also crucial that the one getting rescued has practised and become comfortable with the skill of hip snapping, which we've looked at in depth in the "Rolling" segment of this book.

The T-rescue starts with the "victim" upside down and the rescuer close by. Because the victim knows the rescuer is there to provide a T-rescue, the victim calmly tucks his body forward while upside down to protect his face and body. He then reaches up to the surface with both hands, one on each side of his kayak. The first thing he should do is slap the bottom of his boat three times to let the rescuer know he needs help.

He will then proceed to run his arms alongside the kayak to create as large a target area as possible for the rescuer. The rescuer will then approach the victim at ninety degrees and offer her bow for support. This usually means running lightly into the side of the upside-down kayak in the area that the arms are sweeping. The victim's arm will soon bump into the rescuer's kayak and then he grabs that end with both hands. On occasion, the rescuer is dead on target and the victim gets a little jolt of pain from the impact on his hand, but in the big picture, we can't worry too much about this!

The success of the T-rescue now revolves around the victim's ability to hip snap the kayak upright. Hip snapping refers to the action of rotating the hips to right the kayak. Without a good hip-snap the victim will naturally try to push his head and body back over his kayak, which won't do anything but sink the rescuer's bow and maybe even scare the rescuer off! Once upright, the rescuer can help recover the lost paddle, and then both can continue to head downstream.

On top of being a rescue reserved for situations where there is a special student/instructor relationship and the clear understanding that the rescuer will be looking to provide a T-rescue, it is of course very important that the T-rescue be practised and used in deep, safe whitewater in which a paddler isn't subjecting himself to further danger by hanging out

upside down. If in doubt, get out!

Hand of God

The "Hand of God" is a very useful rescue technique for dealing with beginner or novice paddlers who are stuck upside down, or for any paddler that has been knocked unconscious while upside down. The Hand of God is a means of flipping a victim upright while in your kayak. Let's look at how this works.

The natural thing to do when trying to flip someone upright from your kayak is to pull her head up towards you. You can get a paddler's head out of the water like this, but it is very hard to completely turn the kayak upright. Instead, try to simulate the same motions we go through in a roll: start by rolling the boat up and finish with the head. Move in beside the victim's boat, drop your paddle in between your two boats, and reach with the closest hand across the hull of her kayak to grab the cockpit rim that's furthest from you. It's a long way to reach, so you'll need to lean on the upside-down kayak. Once you've grabbed that far cockpit rim, place your other hand on the closest edge of the upside-down boat. Now push down on the close edge, and pull the cockpit rim up and toward you aggressively. The trick is committing yourself to the move, and using the victim's kayak as a brace while you roll it up. It should be noted that smaller paddlers will have a harder time reaching across the hull to the cockpit rim, especially with the wider, flatter-hulled kayaks. It will require somewhat of a lunge over the kayak to grab the cockpit rim, which makes it even more important to practise this technique before trying it in a real rescue situation.

The Hand of God will work for beginner to intermediate paddlers who are in a situation where a swim should be avoided. In this situation, the T-rescue will usually be the first choice, as it provides the rescuer with more room to manoeuvre, and less direct contact with a potentially panicky victim. If there isn't enough room, or the victim doesn't have the awareness to do a T-rescue, then the Hand of God

will work. If you do have to use the Hand of God to pull a paddler upright, be sure to cover your face, as this rescue tends to surprise victims, and paddles can flail around uncontrollably as they roll upright. An unconscious or injured paddler will roll much more easily, and won't pose as much of a threat to the rescuer. The actual type of injury sustained will dictate the precautions that need to be taken so as not to cause further injuries, but the first priority is always making sure a victim can breathe and is out of danger's path. This means getting him upright immediately. Once he's up, you can then worry about further first aid, such as stabilization for potential neck and back injuries.

RESCUE GEAR

With today's shorter boats, the increasing variety of paddling activities, and the growing diversity of people getting into the sport, there is some lack of clarity and agreement around what gear paddlers should carry. Does it depend on the situation? Maybe, but it's probably best to always pack a basic rescue kit in your boat that you can beef up if a particular excursion calls for it. The effect of an extra two or three pounds will never extend beyond the psychological, and the gear isn't too expensive, so why not have it there just in case?

There have been times when we've felt great to be able to contribute to a rescue, and there have been others when we've felt and looked pretty unprofessional and irresponsible, not having even the basics for a rescue. The latter were situations where we either were not informed about what we should have, or we just made the decision not to bring any rescue gear because it was very unlikely that anything would happen. It's pretty simple to us now: if you always have at least the basic gear, you'll never be left wishing you had it.

So what should a basic kayaker's rescue kit look like? There's a plethora of name brand variation in rescue products, but the essentials are all very similar. The equipment you bring down will depend heavily on the type of river you're paddling. Here are some of the most important pieces of gear to choose from.

- Throw Rope
- Tow Line
- Whistle
- Pin Kit
- Tubular Webbing
- Pulley
- First Aid Kit
- Breakdown Paddle
- Duct Tape
- Carabiners
- Prussic
- Knife

A short tow line, also referred to as a cow tail, is a convenient means of rescuing a kayak.

A throw rope is one of the best pieces of rescue gear and should be kept with you at all times.

RESCUE PFD

Your PFD can also be an important piece of rescue gear. A good rescue vest will have a quick-release harness system. The chest harness is secured around the centre of your PFD and should tighten independently of the straps that secure the PFD to you (i.e. the tightness of the PFD should not rely on the chest harness). The harness should have an easy quick-release system up front. You might also have a leash or "Cow's Tail," which has its own steel O-ring attached to the back of the harness and a lightweight carabiner at its other end, which should clip into a quick-release point on the front of the PFD.

The leash is usually stretchy tubular webbing so that it hugs your body and does not interfere with normal movement. It's intended to use as a quick means of clipping into a rope. Many people use the leash for towing boats, but the use of rescue gear for this kind of thing is not highly recommended. If you're going to use your leash for towing boats regularly, it's probably best not to use it in dangerous tethered rescues.

RESCUE TECHNIQUES

Because of the dynamic nature of the river environment, the first goal of kayak rescue is to keep things as simple as possible. As a rule, you should try the easiest and lowest-risk solution first, and then move to more difficult approaches if necessary. The very worst scenario would be to add yourself as a victim in the situation, so always consider your level of training and ensure your safety before proceeding with a rescue.

The risk assessment of a particular situation will be based first and foremost on the urgency presented: the less time you have, the more risk you might accept as the rescuer. For instance, if it's an equipment retrieval or even body recovery situation, the level of risk you accept as the rescuer should be reduced significantly. The problem with making yourself a victim is that you then put other rescuers in danger who have to rescue you, not to mention that the initial victim is no better off.

The following is a list of rescue techniques in order of increasing difficulty and risk. The value of practising these techniques cannot be overemphasized.

Self-Rescue

"There are only two types of paddler: those who have swum and those who are going to swim." (Unknown)

Swimming

There are two ways of swimming through a rapid. You can swim defensively or offensively. Defensive swimming is also referred to as "body surfing" and involves floating downstream in a protected position: lying on your back, feet downstream, arms out to the side and with your whole body floating as close to the surface as possible. This is the best swimming position to assume if your goal is to ride out a rapid, or if you're in shallow water and worried about hitting rocks. You

can also back ferry from this position, but it is not an effective way of moving in whitewater.

If you need to get somewhere fast, then you'll adopt the offensive swimming technique. Offensive swimming involves getting on your stomach and swimming hard with the front crawl technique. You swim aggressively to get to shore in deep enough water, cross eddy lines and to stay afloat in boils or whirlpools.

Swimming in whitewater can be a frightening experience, especially if you're not used to doing so. The best way to prepare yourself for an unexpected swim is to practise by jumping in the river and deliberately swimming through a safe rapid.

Swimming through Holes

If you find yourself swimming into a hole, you need to understand that the only way you're going to get through the hole is to hitch a ride with the green water that flows beneath it. If you try to stay on the surface, you'll run into the foam pile and you could get stopped and stuck there momentarily or longer. This means that when you float into a hole, you want to stay low and let yourself slide under the foam pile. If the hole looks nasty enough, you may even want to give yourself a little push underwater. Of course, you

The "body surfing" position is the most protected way to swim through a rapid.

need to be careful that you don't push yourself too deeply, because holes often indicate relatively shallow areas. If you push yourself too deeply you could end up bouncing off the river bottom.

Swimming Out of Holes

Although a swimmer will get washed downstream quite quickly out of most holes, there are some holes that have the potential of holding a swimmer for extended periods of time. If you find yourself caught swimming in a nasty hole, then you again need to remember that the escape route is below you, in the green water that is flowing under the backwash and downstream. This means that you need to fight the urge to stay on the surface and should aggressively push yourself downward or tuck into a ball and let yourself sink.

Swimming over Strainers

Strainers are obstacles, or collections of obstacles, such as trees, which let water through but stop large objects, such as paddlers or swimmers. If you were ever to find yourself in a situation where you are swimming into a strainer and it can't be avoided, you need to get on your stomach and swim hard towards it. When you reach it, lunge with all of your might and crawl your way over the top. The key is being aggressive and not wavering. Once you are washed under a strainer, things are much harder to control.

The offensive swimming technique involves getting on your stomach and swimming hard.

To swim through a hole, you need to hitch a ride with the green water that flows underneath the foam pile.

Rolling

Your best means of self-rescue is the roll. The roll will save you a load of grief and an unbelievable amount of energy. You're also much safer in your kayak, as it acts like a huge life jacket to keep you afloat. If you don't have a roll yet, read the rolling segment then get yourself to a pool clinic with professional instruction and learn it. Your confidence will soar, your paddling will improve dramatically, and you'll enjoy your time on the river more than ever!

Reaching

Still a lower-risk technique, reaching involves making contact with the victim from a point of safety, most commonly using a throw rope, or perhaps a paddle or stick. Regardless of the method, the first priority for the rescuer is to make sure he is secure and ready to handle the load.

COMMUNICATING

The most preferable type of rescue is one where the rescuer communicates instructions to the victim to help him or her complete a self-rescue. From your perspective on shore or in a boat, you can shout or signal to the person, encouraging her and directing her in the best course of action. You can use your whistle to get her attention if need be. Use a minimum amount of simple words and clear signals to avoid confusion. This type of rescue avoids all physical contact with the victim, which decreases the risk factor significantly.

Throwing the Rope

There are several different ways to throw the rope, and the decision is based on your personal preference for a given situation. In general, an overhand or sidearm toss is usually best for longer distances, while an underhand throw can be effective for quick, short rescues. Regardless of which type, to become proficient with a throw line you need to practise. With its odd shape and the drag of the uncoiling rope, it's much different from throwing a ball. On top of this, you often have only one shot—so accuracy is crucial, and anticipating the river's flow makes aiming more difficult. For this reason it's best that at least some of your practice be on a river, where hitting the target is more challenging and realistic.

The first thing to do is alert the victim to your location and to the fact that you are throwing him a rope. You can do this by shouting or using your whistle. With regards to the toss, start by pulling out an arm's length or two of rope to give you the freedom to wind up. Hold the free end in one hand and the bag in your tossing hand. Ideally, you want the bag to land right in front of the victim. With that said, it's also good to keep in mind that it's better to throw the bag too far and slightly upstream of the victim than too short and downstream. The reason is that with more line out and the bag just upstream of him, the victim still has a chance to swim to the rope before it starts to pendulum into shore. Once the victim has the rope, quickly brace yourself for the tug and get rid of any slack (if you have time).

IF YOU'RE THE VICTIM

As a knowledgeable swimmer, you can make the rescue go much easier. When you are swimming, be alert and look around for the rescuer. When the rope lands, try as hard as you can to get to it, because it might be your only chance for rescue before being washed downstream. Grab the line, not the bag, as the bag may have forty more feet of cord in it! Once you have the rope, hold on tightly with both hands and get ready for a very strong pull. Roll onto your back (in the defensive swimming position) and place the rope over your outside shoulder (the one furthest from shore). In this position, it's easier to keep your head above the surface, and with the rope over your outside shoulder you're maximizing the pendulum effect.

Positioning

In the best-case scenario, you've taken the time to set up safety by positioning someone with a throw line in a good spot downstream. In other cases, you may have to act quickly by running down the bank or even throwing from a boat. On the bank, the ideal placement has the rescuer within reasonable reach of the swimmer above a relatively safe landing zone to pull him or her into (an eddy or slower water near the shore). Be sure that your footing is solid, both for the toss and the pursuant rescue. It's best to use a rock or something else to help brace you. Another technique is to crouch or sit down, brace your feet, and use a hip belay, which is achieved by bending the rope around your waist to add friction. Notice that we said bend.

Where would you set up? Answer on next page...

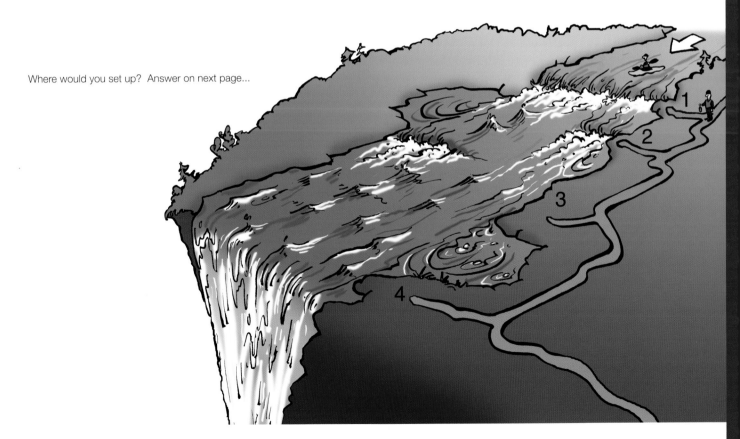

A tethered rescue: a rescuer, attached by a quick release harness to a rope, swims out to the victim, grabs hold of them, and then they both get pulled in to shore.

It's important never to wrap the rope right around any part of your body—the forces are strong! Lastly, consider the angle at which the rope will be pulling on the swimmer. The idea is to throw the bag out to her so it pendulums them back in toward you. Once the swimmer is directly downstream of you, the rope will be serving no use but to hold her stationary. In some cases, it you may need to move further in from the bank as she gets closer to shore to maintain the pendulum angle.

Towing

The next step up the risk ladder is paddling to the victim in a boat and towing him to safety. This technique comes along with obvious risks: having a potentially panicking victim clinging to anything he can with superhuman strength can be disconcerting to say the least. It is, however, probably the most common form of kayak rescue on the river.

Before rescuing someone this way, you should consider the situation and his potential reaction. Is there a bad hole or boulder garden just below that you wouldn't want to enter into with a swimmer? Will he panic and try to grab you? Will he listen to what you tell him? Will he let go when you ask him to? The

THROW BAG POSITIONING ANSWER

1) No. If the paddler were to swim out of the hole, they would likely be too far downstream to receive a rope.
2) No. By setting up near a sticky hole, you could easily pull the swimmer right into it.
3) Yes. Setting up below the nasty features gives the swimmer time to get oriented before receiving the rope. Setting up immediately upstream of an eddy allows the rescuer to swing the swimmer into the eddy.
4) No. The swimmer will grab the rope and get swung over the falls of doom.

decision of whether or not to let the victim grab hold of you is important and must be made quickly. If you feel that the risk of direct contact is too high, then you can paddle close to the swimmer and guide him with instructions.

The most common tow has the victim hanging onto the rescuer's stern grab loop. Towing a swimmer will slow you down tremendously, especially if he is holding onto his gear, so beware of this if you are in a rapid. If possible, get the swimmer to kick his feet as hard as he can. If the water is very shallow, the swimmer might be better off letting go and getting into the body surfing position. If it is not too turbulent and the swimmer is under control, you might have him slide up the stern on his belly and hang onto your waist to reduce drag and risk of injury. If a bad hole is unavoidable, the swimmer should let go and you should spread out as much as possible. You are both better off negotiating the hole alone and then regrouping below. Finally, never tie a swimmer to your boat or your body, as this could put you both at risk if something went wrong.

Going

A final rescue effort could involve going to the victim yourself and freeing her from danger because either she is unconscious or the situation is not appropriate for a rope or boat rescue. Usually this will mean swimming out to the victim on a tether and then being pulled back to shore. As we discussed in the section on rescue gear above, many PFDs are rigged for tethered rescue with a quick-release chest harness system. If you own one of these vests, make sure you're very familiar with the quick-release system before you consider using it. The bag end of a line would be securely attached to the back of the rescuer's vest as a tether. One person should use a hip belay to manage the free end of the line, which should have no knots or loops in it at all. Anyone else present could be used to help secure the belayer, communicate with the rescuer, or provide safety down below. If anything happens to the rescuer, the person on shore can pull him or her back to safety. On the other hand, if the

situation becomes too threatening, the rescuer can release from the tether at any time. It really depends on the situation.

Swimming out to the victim will be more difficult the further away she is because of the drag created by the tether. Keep this in mind when planning the rescue! The main risks to the rescuer are being injured while entering the water, or getting to the victim and becoming entangled in excess slack in the rope. The rescuer should be a very strong swimmer and the person on belay must be experienced so as not to hinder or endanger the rescuer. Finally, make sure there is nothing that the line may get hung up on and that other river users know it is there. Have a predetermined exit spot and, if possible, other rescuers downstream in case something goes wrong.

The objective is to reach the victim and get her to safety as quickly as possible. Turning the victim on her back, the rescuer can hug her from behind and under the arms while both are being pulled to shore. This will provide a secure hold, with the rescuer taking the force of the river and keeping the victim's head above water. It also makes it possible to keep the neck relatively stable if there is any suspicion of a cervical spine injury. If the rescuer must release from the line, the best technique is to swim backwards with one arm while reaching under one of the victim's arms and hugging her so her head is resting against the rescuer's PFD. This is very difficult and tiring; remember that the rescuer should always give priority to his or her own safety.

ADVANCED TECHNIQUES

When you take a good river rescue course, one of the most beneficial, challenging, and enjoyable things you will do is practise a variety of rescue scenarios. The following are some of the techniques you can use in certain situations. They are all potentially dangerous and should be learned formally and practised thoroughly before being put into use.

Using a Diagonal Line to Cross the River

Crossing the river or getting to shore from an island can be very difficult and high risk, especially with a victim. In some situations, this process can be facilitated by tensioning a line across the water at a downstream angle. The angle will depend on the situation, but in general, a slower current will require a greater downstream angle. The bag end should be anchored securely on shore and the free end is belayed by someone downstream and on the other side. This diagonal line allows rescuer and victim to more safely cross and takes advantage of the river's force to help ferry them.

Once you've tied the rope off, often the most challenging part of the process is to get it across the river. In the best-case scenario, you can throw it across. Otherwise, have a strong swimmer or paddler tow it. Remember that adding a victim to the situation will not help anyone, so keep your safety a priority. In this regard, narrow crossings are much easier to deal with than wide ones. We've had experience with both, and the rescues were indeed very different.

If you're the rescuer, clip into the rope with your cow's tail leash or another piece of webbing attached to the back of your PFD. This will keep your head up and free your hands. Depending on the situation and on the condition of the victim, you can either clip him in the same way on your downstream side, or you can grab him securely in the towing position we discussed in the section on tethered rescue. Never tie the victim to you. If you get stuck or are not moving well, the person belaying should make his or her way further downstream. Always account for this possibility when setting up the rope—there's often sag towards the end of the crossing, which means you need more room than it might first appear. Also keep in mind the length of your rope; it could all be going very well until the rope sags and there is none left for the belayer to run downstream with!

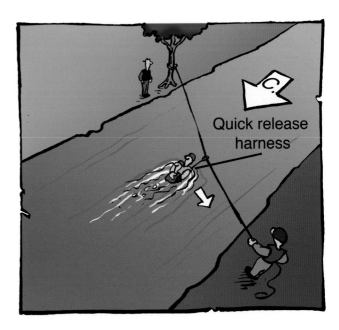

A diagonal line allows a rescuer and victim to safely cross the river while using the river's current to do the bulk of the work.

Using a Tag Line to Rescue a Victim Stuck in a Hole

Some hydraulics are strong enough to hold you even when you come out of your boat. Rescuing victims from these "keepers" can be a high-risk affair, even on a tether. The water is very aerated, so you don't float very high in it. Along with this, the turbulence and recirculating flow make it hard to both breathe and get oriented, and there is the risk of becoming entangled in the rope. If the victim is unconscious, you have no choice but to swim to him. If he is conscious, however, and the location permits, you can use a tag line to reduce the risk.

A tag line is a rope tensioned across the river or channel that has been walked upstream on both sides until it reaches the victim. It offers stability and a possible escape route. To establish it, either two people can hold it across the water and walk upstream, or it can be tied off (upstream of the victim) on one side

A tag line can be useful to extract conscious victims from sticky holes.

Using a Tag Line to Stabilize a Pinned or Entrapped Victim

A tag line can also provide crucial stabilization in some vertical pin or foot entrapment situations. For an explanation of what a tag line is, see the section above on using a tag line to rescue a victim from a hole. In a vertical bow pin, the bow of the victim's boat is lodged in an obstruction and the force of the water hitting the victim's back can make it impossible for her to get out of the boat.

Similarly in a foot entrapment situation, the victim's foot is lodged in an obstruction and the water is forcing her downstream with too much power to overcome. For either one, the idea is to get the tag line under the arms of the victim and then lift the line and stabilize her in a position that allows her to breathe and possibly free herself from the entrapment. Often just stabilizing her will give her the ability to wiggle free. If not, a decision must be made based on the circumstances about whether to go to her and help.

and walked up on the other. In a hydraulic situation, the line would be kept at water level and walked up to the victim in the hole. Once the victim has grabbed hold of the tensioned line, there are several options to get him out of the hole. Probably the most sensible is for the rescuers to pull one end towards the desired bank while line is gradually let out at the other end, allowing the victim to be pulled right into shore. With this in mind, if you're tying one end off to establish the tag line, make sure it's on the same side that you plan to pull the victim into. As with all rescues, a contingency plan should be in place in case something goes wrong. It's always a good idea to have safety set up below the rescue location.

A tag line can provide crucial stabilization in some vertical pin situations.

(A) The best way to free a pinned boat is to peel it off the rock, with a rope attached to the furthest point from you.
(B) A vector pull lets you increase the force exerted at the load, without extra equipment.

Freeing a Pinned Boat

The power of water grows exponentially with volume, so it doesn't take much to build substantial forces on a pinned or broached kayak. To free the boat in these situations, the rescuer will generally try to attach a rope to an exposed end of the boat and pull it loose. The biggest challenge is often in getting this accomplished. If the victim is still in the boat, he should get out if it is safe to do so. If he can't, he should be stabilized if possible (see the section above on using tag lines to stabilize pinned victims).

In some situations, the victim cannot be stabilized and the boat must be freed. The first choice is to throw him the rope and try to get him to attach it to the boat.

If he's unconscious or unable to move, the rescuer will have to swim or paddle to the boat to attach the rope. This can be one of the most difficult parts of any rescue, and is occasionally impossible. Which end you attach it to and which direction to pull will depend on the situation. In general, for a broached boat, you want to attach the rope to the end furthest away from where you are pulling and from a point slightly upstream. This way, you're peeling it away from the rock in a way that is deflecting water off of the boat, giving the river less and less surface area to exert force on. For vertical pins where the victim is in the boat, the situation needs to be assessed very carefully as pulling on the boat may put the person at further risk.

Using a Vector Pull and Mechanical Advantage

Quite often, the power of the river makes it impossible to free a pinned boat with just the strength of one person. In these situations, vector pulls and mechanical advantage (sometimes referred to as "Z-drag") systems can be used to substantially increase the pulling force.

A vector pull is quick and easy to set up and is great for situations where you don't have the right equipment to set up a Z-drag. Tension the rope as much as possible, and then tie it off (a tree is best). Pulling on the centre of this tensioned line at a ninety-degree angle will create a vector that multiplies the force at the load (which is the boat, since the tree isn't moving!). The best way to do this is to clip another line onto it using a carabiner and slide the carabiner out to the middle of the tensioned line. The second line is the one you pull on.

Mechanical advantage is a basic concept that can be applied to rescue systems far beyond the scope of this book. We'll keep this simple by looking only at the most basic Z-drag, a 3:1 mechanical advantage system. The general idea is that by redirecting the free end of a loaded rope through an anchored point (a pulley is the most effective) and then back again through another pulley attached to the main line, it multiplies the effect of your pulling on it. The 3:1 ratio indicates that a system such as this multiplies the pulling force by three. For example, if you can pull with a force of 100 newtons (N), this system would allow you to exert 300 N, minus some small amount due to friction.

To set up a 3:1, you'll need to draw from your rescue kit. Wherever we indicate the use of a pulley, a carabiner can be used as a replacement—it's just not as effective because it creates a sharper bend and more friction in the line. The first step is to make an anchor. This is usually as simple as wrapping a piece of webbing (or a sling) around a sturdy tree or rock and attaching a carabiner to it. For a stronger anchor,

A basic Z-drag.

you can double wrap the webbing, but make sure it's not too tight. Remember our vector pull? Well, this applies to anchors as well. If you wrap the sling too tightly, then pulling on it can act as a vector pull and unnecessarily multiply the forces being applied to the anchor. Also, position the webbing so that the knot or seam holding the ends together is away from the carabiner that will be loaded.

Once the anchor is ready, attach a pulley to the carabiner, if you have one, and feed the rope into it. Now, attach a prussic as far back down the main line

as possible. Today, you can buy pulleys that have a prussic function built into them, which is preferable because they are much faster to set up; and prussic cords can create enough friction heat to melt the sheath on a polypropylene rope. If you don't have either a prussic cord or a mechanical prussic, you can use an overhand knot to create an attachment loop. However, this is not the best set-up as you'll have to untie and retie it as you pull the rope in; and any knot in a loaded line presents a weak point. Attach a pulley at this point along the main line and feed the rope into it. You know you are on the right track if you are pulling on the end of the rope in the same direction as the main line is pulling on the load. This makes sense, since you should have made two directional changes in setting up the system. Et voilà, you've created a Z-drag, just like that!

This technique has the capacity of tensioning the line to dangerous levels. By hanging a wet skirt or PFD over the loaded line, you can reduce the potential recoil hazard if the line did ever break. One other safety consideration is that whenever you use a system such as this, the load is securely attached to the rope with no quick-release system. Always have a plan for after the victim or equipment is pulled free.

RIVER ETIQUETTE

Photo by Trevor Lush

As our rivers have become more and more crowded, the potential for conflict between paddlers has grown. Fortunately, paddlers are generally very thoughtful and courteous, which helps us all avoid a lot of problems, but it's still important that we discuss some universal river etiquette. It's also worth mentioning that this etiquette section doesn't cover all the issues that you need to consider. Rivers are like pool halls, in that every river has its own unique paddling community and its own "house rules." We must all appreciate that the rules accepted on our home river aren't always the exact same rules we'll find on other rivers.

RIVER RUNNING ETIQUETTE

The single most important rule of river etiquette is a very simple one that is too often broken. Pick up your trash! If you don't have any trash to take with you off the river, that's great! It means that you have room for trash that some lesser being has left on the ground.

The second most important issue has to do with the right of way on a river. The rule is very simple. The boater going downstream has the right of way. This has always been the case, and despite all the changes in the sport, this is still the case. Of course it's this boater's responsibility to be courteous to those paddlers downstream of him or her. For example, if someone is on a wave below you, then you should do your best to avoid that wave, or wait until he or she is done. On this same note, eddy lines are like stop signs. When you're thinking about leaving an eddy, look both ways and make sure the coast is clear before proceeding into the main current.

The way to deal with rafts on a river is also very simple. Rafts have the right of way. They're bigger than we are, less manoeuvrable and are usually on a tight commercial schedule. Often the best thing you can do is pull over and let the rafts go by. The sooner they pass by, the sooner you can continue paddling without having to worry about getting blindsided by a big, rubber, floating undercut!

Although upstream paddlers do have the right of way, dropping in on someone who has waited for their turn to surf isn't going to make you any friends.

PLAYBOATING ETIQUETTE

The growth in playboating has resulted in the formation of eddy line-ups on rivers around the world, and that's just a part of the sport we have to accept. Although each play spot has its own unique issues, we're going to look at some guidelines that will ease tensions on the river and could actually let you enjoy your time in the eddy. Personally, I think eddy line-ups provide paddlers with an amazing learning opportunity. It gives you time to think about what you did wrong on your last ride, and what you have to change for your next. It also gives you a chance to watch and learn from the other paddlers.

Dropping Onto Waves

If there's a line, be courteous and either avoid the hole altogether and get in line, or wait until the coast is clear and go for a big entry move or a very quick ride. Remember that the paddlers in line may have been waiting for their turn for quite some time and won't be ecstatic about every paddler coming down the river just dropping in ahead of them.

Multiple Eddies

If there are multiple eddies from which to enter a play feature, and lines in both, alternate back and forth between them. Sometimes there is a more difficult eddy to catch, which will then have a much smaller line. Those in the short line need to acknowledge that this doesn't give them an excuse to get more rides in than other paddlers, and they should let through a couple at a time from the longer line. Don't worry, by being in that harder eddy, you'll inevitably get more rides; but what we're saying is to maintain some form of etiquette while you're at it.

Double Features

On some rivers there are multiple play waves that can be accessed from a single eddy. In some cases, there will be separate lines for the features. Paddlers who have taken their turn on the upstream feature are not free to drop onto the second feature, but should return to the eddy and get back in line.

Time's Up

If your ride lasts much more than one minute, you can be sure there will be some ticked-off people in the eddy. The grumblings from the eddy can be held off a bit longer than normal if you're getting trashed and providing those in line with entertainment; or if you're pushing your limits and trying very cool new moves.

Line-Up Etiquette

Eddy line-ups can get messed up very easily, especially if there's any significant current to contend with. It can sometimes be very hard to keep track of whose turn it is. The best thing to do is remember who you were after. This is also a great way to approach paddlers who might be taking liberties with their position in line. Don't just sit in the eddy and grind your teeth if you think someone is butting in. Ask them who they're behind. Though they honestly might not know, there's a good chance they'll keep track of who they're behind for next time.

Many play spots have a calm eddy to the side of the river and a swirly, mid-stream eddy closer to the play spot. Paddlers will naturally want to jam themselves into the swirly eddy to assure they don't lose their spot in line, but will then spend the next few minutes bumping into each other and fighting the current. It makes a lot more sense for the line to form in the calm eddy and for the swirly eddy to be reserved for the on-deck paddlers only.

TIPS FOR WOMEN

BY ANNA LEVESQUE

GEAR FOR WOMEN

Ladies, you don't have to settle for gear that doesn't fit right or look good! Almost every manufacturer is now making gear specifically designed for women. There is a variety of women's PFDs that fit the shapes of your upper bodies, helmets with funky designs, sport tank tops and other comfy underlayers in groovy colours. So shop around and have fun picking out your gear!

OUTFITTING TIPS FOR WOMEN

Since whitewater kayaks are designed mainly by men, they are made with a man's body shape and performance potential in mind. For this reason, some female paddlers have a frustrating time in playboats that are not small and narrow enough for them to consistently perform tricks. As the industry progresses, boat manufacturers are designing more boats with women in mind, and you should now be able to find a suitable boat from most of the major companies. Each company makes boats that have their own unique shape and slightly different performance characteristics, so be sure to test drive as many as you can and don't settle for a mediocre fit.

To help create a better fit for comfort and performance, try the following outfitting tips.

1. Raise your seat. Raising your seat will counteract the sizeable depth of the kayak and give you more leverage, which translates into more power. You can achieve this by placing foam under or on top of your seat. Choose the thickness of foam depending on your height and comfort level. Usually one or two inches of additional height will be enough. The higher you raise your seat, the more leverage you will have. Remember also that the higher you raise your seat, the more unstable you will feel! If you feel too tippy after you raise your seat, take some of the foam out to lower it a little. Trial and error is the best way to find the balance point between stability and leverage for you.

2. Move your seat forward. Most production kayaks come with the seat moved all the way back. It is important for women to move their seats forward so that their body weight is centred over middle of the boat. This aggressive position makes it

much easier for women to sink the bow of the boat when performing tricks like the cartwheel. It will also make it easier for you to maintain or regain control of the boat, because less of your weight will be towards the stern.

3. Be sure to have a strong, supportive back band. Having a good back band that keeps the body in a forward position is especially important for women, because they often find themselves being thrown backwards. Be sure that your back band is snug and supportive.

THE EMOTIONAL OF KAYAKING

"Believe in yourself. Know that you can, and you will succeed!" (Ruth Gordon)

Kayaking is a relatively intense sport, and all paddlers experience emotion on the river. Sometimes it's the excitement of completing a challenging river or a new freestyle move. Other times it's frustration that comes from failing to attain a goal, fear in the face of a difficult rapid, or intimidation when sitting in an eddy full of skilled paddlers. There are many

articles and resources in the kayaking world to help paddlers improve their paddling technique, but very few have addressed how to manage the emotional side of kayaking. During the creation of *Girls at Play*, my instructional video for women, I conducted interviews with over twenty female paddlers on their approach to the emotional side of kayaking. Combining my personal experience with information collected from these interviews, I have come up with some helpful tips on how to approach and deal with the emotions we face on the river.

Fear

- Face your fear. Admit that you are afraid or nervous.

- Identify the source of your fear. It's important to separate "irrational fear" from "rational fear." Rational fear is fear that comes from a real hazard on the river: an undercut rock or a big recirculating hole. Irrational fear is fear that comes from preconceived notions we have about the dangers of the river and our own ability to successfully tackle them. An example would be someone who will not practise their roll in a pool with an instructor because they're afraid of drowning. The chance of that person really drowning in that situation is very small. Yet they may have been told that practising the roll is dangerous. Or they may have previously had a bad experience in water.

  Recognize the source of your fear to determine how best to approach the situation. If the fear you're dealing with is rational, then you might want to walk the rapid. If the fear is based on something someone else has said, or on irrational fear, then you should try to evaluate the situation objectively. Only after doing this can you determine what is best for your particular skill and confidence level.

Everyone experiences fear on a river, and everyone also deals with it in a different way.

- If a rapid makes you nervous, break it down. Focus on the Class 2, 3 and 4 moves you have to make and not on the "big, scary rapid."

- Paddle with people who will allow you to go at a pace you feel comfortable with.

- Breathe! Remember to breathe deeply, take the time to relax and assess the situation with a clear mind.

- Paddle for yourself. Don't do something because someone else wants or expects you to. If you don't feel comfortable doing something, then don't do it. Ultimately, you are the one who has to deal with the consequences of your actions.

Intimidation

- Remember that feelings of intimidation exist only in our own minds. Most paddlers are friendly people who like to see new faces on the river.

- Remember that every paddler has felt intimidated by someone at some point in his or her life. It's something that everyone experiences.

- Be kind to yourself. Focus your attention on what you are doing and what makes you happy, not on who is around you and what he or she is doing.

- Try to get to know the person that intimidates you. You will probably discover that you have a lot in common.

- Smile and be friendly to other paddlers. Chances are that some paddlers are intimidated by you.

Crying

It's okay to cry on the river. Crying is a normal emotional outlet for people, especially for women. In most cases, the person feels much better after crying. Her head will be clearer and her emotions calmer. Healthy crying usually happens in short bursts. If you give a person the space and the time to cry, he or she will feel much better and your day will go much more smoothly. If, however, a paddler is crying uncontrollably and often, it's probably a good idea to get him or her off the river.

In some paddling circles, showing emotion on the river is sometimes frowned upon. The notion that you are "hardcore" if you can "keep it together" on the river is misguided. Kayaking does not have to be hardcore. There is something for everyone in kayaking, from Class 2 to Class 5, from eddy lines to enormous waves. Accepting the emotional aspects of kayaking will help create a more comfortable and supportive environment for all paddlers.

TRAVELING AND KAYAKING

BY DUNBAR HARDY

17

STRATEGIES FOR PADDLING
BEYOND THE BACKYARD

The hazy, humid sky of Marrakesh was filled with blowing sand and dust. We waited. . . . Eventually we were the last ones in the baggage claim. Everything was in Arabic and unreadable. I went over to the non-English-speaking Moroccan airport worker and tried to explain our situation to him. I tried describing and acting out what exactly it was we were missing. It definitely amused him, but it did not help our cause in locating our kayaks. Just another reminder of the real adventure it is to try and paddle far away from home.

For some paddlers, the season never ends. With lots of curiosity, a little research, and a healthy problem-solving attitude, it is possible to paddle year-round in exotic locations all over the world. As winter approaches, it is time to bust out the map and start planning—there is so much water in the world waiting to be paddled. Chasing good weather and good levels requires extensive travelling, but they are the rewards for exploring rivers beyond your backyard.

A genuine desire to explore this world we live in is needed when undertaking a foreign paddling trip. The farther from home you go, the more the differences you will experience; this cultural diversity should be enjoyed and appreciated. A deep curiosity for the unknown is also recommended. There is suspense in not knowing, and the real excitement is in going through each experience and learning, gaining answers to new questions. True adventure lies in the unknown . . .

CHOOSING A DESTINATION

For your initial excursion abroad, it might be best to select a location that is well known. A place that has been paddled or rafted extensively will more readily provide useful information on rivers to be explored. In these places there will most likely be an in-country contact available as a resource for river levels, gear rental, shuttles, guiding, and lodging. Established local contacts can be invaluable for pre-trip planning. They know the local language and customs and may have extensive firsthand experience on the river(s) you are wishing to paddle.

The lesser-known or more out-of-the-way destinations can make for very rewarding travelling and cultural experiences, but they can also be very frustrating. The more "out there" and off the beaten paddling path a destination is, the more of a logistical challenge it will be. There are places still out there where the locals have never seen kayaks, let alone know what the whitewater is like. This "foreignness" to kayaks in these locations can make for great interactions with the local people, but it can also lead to paddlers having to create their own way. Being a true paddling explorer can lead to lots of wasted time dealing with permits, shuttles, logistics, and general transportation arrangements. These details can add up to day after day of not paddling at all, and can become the activity you spend the majority of your time doing.

Photo by Jock Bradley

DO YOUR HOMEWORK

What is that quote ... "prior planning prevents ..."? It doesn't actually matter, because things will not go exactly according to plan when foreign paddling. It is recommended to begin planning a foreign paddling trip by having some clear goals and objectives before leaving home. A simple plan of a couple of rivers that you wish to paddle, or even just one on your "must do" list can help you be organized ahead of time.

Once there is a "list" of rivers, it is a good idea to gather information about how difficult they are, where they are located, how to get there, and when is the ideal time (flow-wise and weather-wise) to be there. Getting answers to these initial questions for the specific rivers listed will give you a more solid game plan. Some of these initial answers might rule out a few rivers right away, based on your timeframe, their difficulty, and differences in goals within the group.

Asking a few more questions can further refine the "hit list." The next level of research is to look into things like what language is spoken there, what gear is available for rent, and what you must bring. What are the costs of getting there and living in this location for the duration of your trip? At this point it is also important to begin looking more closely at the budget of the trip, and see if the expenses to get to certain countries and rivers will further refine the to-do list. As for most true paddlers, we have big hearts and grand plans, but small wallets with little money!

Chile's Rio Futaleufu is a paddler's heaven, but logistically challenging without the help of an outfitter.

TRANSPORTATION PLANNING

Once you have worked out where to go and when, the next task is to figure out how to get there. A longer overland road trip to some foreign country will be perhaps the most convenient way to travel. If time is unlimited and there is a somewhat reliable vehicle available, and you are willing to risk it, then overland travel may be the preferred mode of transportation.

It is recommended to travel in a vehicle that can be serviced with parts obtainable in a foreign location. The newer and nicer the vehicle, the more difficult it will be to get it worked on and get parts for it; not to mention that it becomes more of a target for vandalism. Driving, however, allows you to transport all of your own gear and boats. It will also provide a vehicle for

shuttles and can be used for accommodations. Driving will also allow you to gain a more intimate knowledge and view of the landscape and culture as the miles pass by.

For further-to-reach places, overseas destinations, and folks with limited timeframes, air travel is an obvious mode of transportation, but it is not without some hurdles and obstacles. A plane will get you to a foreign country, but how will you then get around and transport boats and gear while there? In some locations it is possible to travel and paddle exclusively using public transportation such as buses, taxis, and hitchhiking. This can be easier on the budget, but not so time efficient when trying to paddle the rivers on your list. Most likely you will need to arrange your own transportation, either through an in-country contact that has been previously arranged, or by renting your own vehicle. It might be cheaper to land in the country then price shop around and find a vehicle in person, rather than attempting to arrange something through long distance communications before leaving home.

When getting ready to finally commit to renting a vehicle, answer a few more questions. The number of people in your team and the amount of boats and equipment will determine how big a vehicle is needed. Know ahead of time where you will be travelling and whether you need a two- or a four-wheel-drive vehicle. Does the vehicle come with roof racks or do you need to provide your own? Is it possible to rent a trailer? Does the vehicle come with a driver or do you need to know exactly where you are going and will you be doing all of the driving?

Many foreign vehicle rentals will come with a driver. This can be a good way to learn more about the country and benefit from local knowledge, as well as get help with shuttles. Be aware that these drivers can also be unwilling to rally the vehicle up dubious roads getting to that "must do" run. It is important to be as clear and patient as possible when dealing with these folks. Know that the plan can change due to the driver's caution in protecting the vehicle and themselves, or their excitement about exploring their own country with loco gringos. Just driving around can be the most hair-raising part of the trip.

AIRPORT STRATEGY

If flying with a kayak, buckle up because there can be turbulence ahead! It has become harder and harder, as well as more expensive, to fly with a kayak. It is important to show up at the airport up to two hours early and prepare to do battle. Try to pick a less stressed-out, more smiley ticket agent to help you. Don't forget to be polite, friendly and smiling—attitude goes a long way in this interaction.

When flying with a kayak, how it is packed can help get it on board the plane. It's recommended to put a boat in a bag so it becomes less obvious what it actually is. You are then able to employ a slight

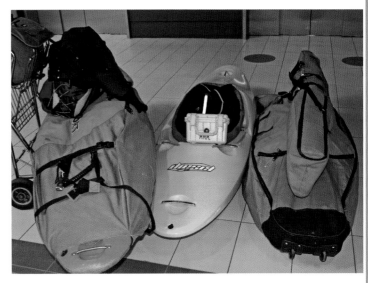

A boat bag makes moving a kayak around the airports a lot easier, and it makes them look a lot more like surfboards, which can be highly advantageous.

amount of forgivable dishonesty to your advantage. With a covered boat, you have the ability to call it a surfboard, surf ski, or windsurfer, for which all flights have a luggage category at an additional charge. Some flights will not carry a "kayak" on board, thus the need for this resourceful attitude.

Another note here when attempting to fly with a kayak. The words "air cargo" are to be feared, and you must vehemently fight against this reality. Air cargo means that your boat will not fly on the same plane as you, and this will be a much more expensive "service." There is no definite timeframe when your "cargoed" luggage will actually arrive in the country; it is usually much later than when you have arrived. Of course, it is possible to air cargo your kayak days before you get on your plane so that it is waiting for you upon your arrival. Again, a very expensive fee will be charged for this "service."

Generally, once the luggage is all classified, the added fee is paid, and all is put on board, you are on your way! My motto is to get my butt in the seat and then I can relax. An adventure awaits.

FINAL THOUGHTS

Foreign paddling trips are a great adventure. It is important to be aware that travelling can be how the majority of the time is spent, rather than paddling. I take the approach when travelling in a foreign country that if I actually wind up paddling something I will be pleased and surprised—getting on the water is a bonus. Flexibility and patience are keys to surviving the tumultuous and oftentimes inconvenient world of international travelling and paddling.

Somewhere out there in the world right now it is summer and the water levels are prime! Seeing the world from the seat of a kayak can be one of the most rewarding experiences, and it is undoubtedly worth all of the effort to get there.

OVERNIGHT WHITWATER TRIPS

BY PHIL DERIEMER

To do a self-contained trip is to experience the ultimate freedom that a kayak can offer: easing into river time where the outside world slips from your thoughts as you become focused on the moment. You challenge yourself to see how little you can do without, while experiencing the river on a much more intimate level. Group size can be small, camps out of the way, and your choice of rivers as remote as you'd like. You can make your experience a relaxing two-day flatwater cruise or an intense twenty-day exploratory suffer-fest. Regardless of the type of trip you choose, here are a few variables to consider that will help secure the outcome of your experience:

- Difficulty of the run
- Length of the run
- Remoteness
- Weather/climate
- Food

You will keep coming back to the above items as you plan your trip. It affects the boat you take, the amount and type of food you eat, the clothing and other equipment you bring, as well as your pace. Let's look at each of them and how they should be considered.

Difficulty of the Run: You want this to be a great first experience. Let your skills be your guide. If you have never run Class 5, perhaps doing it with a fully loaded kayak isn't a good starting point. Under this should also be mentioned the type of run: is it big water or creeky, pool/drop or continuous?

Length of the Run: I suggest if you are doing a self-contained trip for the first time that you ease into it with a shorter trip. This gives you a great chance to shake down your systems, fine-tune your equipment choices, and see how much you really like it. If you are doing runs of similar difficulty, terrain, and climate, but one is longer than the other, the only real difference in what you carry will be the amount of food. Your kayak, no matter how big, can only carry so much. Where possible, you can arrange for food drops or caches to stretch out the length of your journey.

Remoteness: The game gets more serious when you take it into the backcountry. You are further from everything—outside help and the nearest road—and you face a long walk out, should you bail on your trip or lose gear. Some changes I might make on a remote trip include: a beefed-up first aid kit; more than just duct tape in my repair kit; maps; good boating shoes, should I turn from boater to hiker; and the number of breakdown paddles for the group.

Weather and Climate: This is big. It not only comes into play with regards to food and shelter, but it could determine your pace. If you're doing a run where the water could come up in hours or within the time you are on the river, then you had best pay attention to the weather before and during your trip. Clothing gets tricky, too. If you are going to elevation it is easy to get fooled by hot days that could turn cold at night; so plan accordingly.

Food: I'm not a nutritionist, so I won't even attempt to tell you what to eat, but I can suggest some things to consider in choosing your foods. This is probably

the single heaviest group of items in your kit, so where possible, go for the lighter choices. At the end of a long day you are usually not too fired up about cooking. Keep it simple from that standpoint: one-pot glops and pastas. You can get by on lean rations on a shorter run, but if you are hard at work on a longer run, you need calories; and if you are in a cold climate, then you need more calories.

My earliest travels abroad to paddle not only included a mountain of gear, but one enormous duffel full of freeze-dried food. Upon our arrival in our destination country, while we didn't find freeze-dried, we did find packaged food that was more than adequate for our needs. Ask around if others have been to the area where you intend to travel; that could save you hauling unnecessary supplies with you.

Finally, you can have a lot of fun with the food on a trip. I've done runs where I went lean and mean, but others where I was fat and happy. From soup to steaks, or water to wine: Your imagination, size of kayak, and willingness to carry it are the limits.

LEARNING TO DO WITHOUT

Because of the limitations involved, self-contained trips are all about doing without. This can range from what you eat, wear, and sleep in, to what you can expect of yourself and your kayak. Obviously the Dutch oven is out, as might be the cold beers and wine at the end of the day. If you are doing a run that you know has sandy beaches, maybe you can do without a sleeping pad. A tarp may do where you were considering a tent. Try to make your equipment as multi-purpose as possible. If your paddle jacket can serve as your raincoat, or you can get by with using your river shorts in camp, you'll shed important ounces and hopefully pounds from your load. At the same time, it feels good to the body and soul to slip into something warm and dry on a cold or rainy multi-day. Treat yourself where possible. The items listed below are just suggestions to get you started.

CHOOSING YOUR BOAT

By now the topics discussed above have probably helped you narrow your choice of kayak. Unless you're willing to take a small boat and unload at every play spot (providing you can get all you need into it in the first place), you may want to set aside any thoughts of throwing intentional ends, or blunts, and bring a bigger boat. I have one boat that I do most of my self-contained trips out of. In choosing my kayak, I know that the performance will be changed because of the extra weight I will be carrying. For this reason

A loaded boat acts very differently than an empty one, so be extra conservative with your decisions until you're comfortable with how the boat is responding.

I go with a boat that is forgiving, predictable, and comfortable.

Because I don't know when or where I will be jumping out to scout, portage, or help someone in a bind, I also wear shoes in my boat. On this latter point, I do know of at least one story where a kayaker hiked barefoot eight miles out of the Grand Canyon of the Stikine after a bad swim that washed his boat away with his shoes stowed safely behind the seat.

A PACKING LIST

Besides the paddling gear you will use on your trip, here are some suggested items to consider. What you bring is based on personal wants and needs as well as climate.

Sleeping bag (synthetic is probably the better choice for the watery world, while down is lighter and more compressible)

Sleeping pad (here I often use a ¾-length ultralight Therm-a-Rest)

Tarp, bivy sack, or tent (depends on the climate)

Cook pot

Lighter

Bowl (my bowl is also my cup)

Fork or spoon

Food

Camp clothes (could be as simple as a dry shirt or as luxurious as a full set of dry clothes)

Extra insulating layers (light tops and bottoms to fine-tune your warmth; if cool at night, bottoms are nice to have)

Dry bags (There are some great ones available commercially, but if you want a cheap alternative, use trash compactor bags inside stuff sacks. The thicker plastic of the bags will last you for many trips. You simply tie them off at the top to keep water out. The stuff sacks help prevent the accidental tearing of a hole in the plastic bags as you slide them in and out of the boat.)

Breakdown paddle (number depends on difficulty of run and size of group)

Sponge (before shouldering your boat for a portage it's nice to get every last drop of water out)

Water bottle

Water purification system (chemical treatments are lighter than pumps)

First aid (What you carry is up to you. Think about where you are going and how long you'll be out. I really recommend carrying at least tincture of benzoine and steri-strips. Will you need antibiotics?)

Repair kit (this may be as simple as duct tape, but could include a sewing kit or more)

Throw rope (seventy feet ideal)

Prussics

Carabiners

Optional

Headlamp

Stove/fuel (This is weather dependent. If you can't count on dry wood, then a stove becomes essential if you plan to cook.)

Map

Camera

Leatherman-type tool

Additional clothing (This is weather dependent. If you anticipate bad and/or cold weather, then being comfortable both on and off the river is important. I will often splurge and bring a raincoat, extra layers of clothing, and perhaps a change of footwear.)

HOW TO PACK

Four of us once did a twenty-two-day trip on Baffin Island in the Arctic. While we had scheduled a food drop, we were forced to carry upwards of twelve days' worth of food and supplies in our boats at the start of each leg. Two of us had stock plastic boats that required that we cut a foot off of each end of the pillars, along with trimming an inch off the width just so we could get all of our gear in. We spent most of a day in an airplane hangar packing and sorting our gear so we could figure out how to fit it all in. Packing was like a Chinese puzzle: first one piece, then another, all in essentially the same sequence each time we loaded or unloaded. The kayaks weighed in excess of ninety pounds. Portaging was probably the most dangerous part of our journey, as stepping over and around boulders and walking on uneven ground could easily have resulted in a fall and a broken ankle.

You may never suffer a momentary lapse of judgment such as we did and venture off on a three-week-long journey. But if you've never done a self-contained trip before, you can burn up a lot of time at the put-in figuring out how to make it all fit. If you get a chance at a dry run at home, that is best.

The majority of your gear is going to end up in the back of the boat. If you have an adjustable seat, you may want to look at moving it forward so that your boat will be more balanced from front to back. When packing, I try to run the day through in my head and figure out what I am likely to need and in what order. I then combine this with the desire to keep the heaviest things, such as food, as close to the back of the seat as possible. This keeps the ends of the boat light, which translates to more control in the water.

Some items, such as food for the day, water purification, film, and perhaps an extra insulating layer, I will carry in a small "daybag" dry bag so I don't have to get into the main store of food and equipment each time to retrieve something. This adds up to time saved at each break. If you have access to the front area of your boat, whether it has it foot pegs or a bulkhead,

With so much gear in the back of your boat, it will probably be helpful to move your seat forward to keep your kayak as balanced as possible.

this can be a good place to store light, bulky items such as a cooking pot (I put it in upside down so water drains out.) or a compact sleeping pad.

Many dry bags/stow floats are conically shaped like the back end of your kayak. For this reason I rarely use stuff sacks inside a dry bag. This allows the contents to conform better to the shape of the storage system. A breakdown paddle usually goes in the back of the boat, either all of it on one side, split between the two sides, or shared amongst the participants. Either way, try to tape the pieces together so they aren't bouncing around in there when you take your bags out.

Wherever you store your throw rope, make it the last thing to be loaded, so it can be the first and fastest item to remove.

Clip it in: If you can't afford to lose it, make sure it is secured in the boat somehow; this includes your breakdown paddle. Besides swims, I have seen boats get away on scouts and portages. If they are in the water long enough, they can begin to unpack themselves on their downstream run.

PADDLING WITH A LOAD

With your boat loaded, you are going to notice a difference in how it handles. While it won't be as bad as strapping a sack of potatoes to your backside and going ice-skating, it will require an adjustment. It will spin out more readily when you don't want it to, and be more difficult to turn when you do want it to. You will learn the new handling characteristics shortly, but in the meantime, take this difference into consideration about what you do and don't run. One good thing about the extra weight is it gives you remarkable punching power, so as you're getting pushed toward that hole that you would have missed in an empty boat, take comfort in knowing you just might make it through.

ATTITUDE/DECISION MAKING

Get yourself in, get yourself out. I've always tried to follow this simple rule on all of my wilderness outings. I suppose you could throw in a cell and/or satellite phone for a little insurance, but you shouldn't use them as the reason to push things a little further. You are your own best rescue, and that begins with making good decisions.

Along those lines, another rule I've come to learn is "bad experiences make for good judgment." It's not my first choice, but I've made mistakes in many facets of my paddling, and I treat them as important learning opportunities. I file them away and draw on them in hopes that I will not repeat mistakes. The unexpected can happen, but a lot of incidents in the backcountry could be avoided with better decision-making; be it water levels, running rapids without scouting and/or carrying, or doing a run that you aren't yet ready

for. This goes for the people I paddle with as well. If someone in your group is making poor decisions and something happens as a result, everyone is affected. Chances are you will put a lot of thought into the gear you take with you—why not the folks you paddle with as well?

Enjoy the freedom and enjoy the journey. Once you do your first overnighter, it will only leave you wanting more.

IMPACT

This section isn't just for those new to the art of self-contained kayak trips, but also an appeal to those that have been doing it for some time to consider modifying their approach. The popularity of spending multiple days on a river camping out of your boat is growing each year. Runs once considered remote and unused are seeing more traffic than ever, and this increased use can have a negative impact. Each stretch of river has its own unique considerations with regards to group size, available fuels for cooking, human waste disposal, and other user groups encountered along the way. There are many rivers out there that have been run by rafters and kayakers alike for many years. These are often overseen by regulating agencies that not only control the number of people allowed on the run at any one time, but also the type of equipment that they must carry to deal with some of the issues I mentioned. While we may not agree with all of the regulations, some are in place to protect the beauty and ecosystem of the river corridor. We all love the freedom that putting on an unregulated river provides: no permit, no specified launch date, no limit to where you camp, or how long you stay and who you bring. Those freedoms could come with restrictions if we aren't good stewards. It's time we paddlers step up to the plate and take care of the resources we love so that others don't feel compelled to do it for us.

One big consideration that dictates how I approach some of the issues of impact is what the environment in which I will be traveling is like. Is it arid or lush or somewhere in between? An arid environment is much less capable of breaking down wastes and recovering from use than a lush one.

Before you put on, find out what the local restrictions and requirements might be for your planned area. If there aren't any, then think about how you might tread lightly. If this concept is new to you just type in "leave no trace" on the web to open the floodgates of available information. Here are some things to consider.

Cooking and Warmth: I have seen more changes in camps due to this than any other variable. If you choose to cook with fire, think about your wood source and the means by which you are going to use it. Driftwood should be your only source of wood, period. There is no need to start breaking branches off of trees. You don't need a massive fire ring to cook on. You are just trying to cook some food, not forge metal, so keep it really small. Try to avoid leaving permanent burn scars on rock slabs, overhangs, and vegetation. If it's fire season, don't do it. Use any existing fire rings over building another unless it is located such that it will cause scaring. Lately I have begun taking a small lightweight stove with me on some of the more popular overnight runs. You carry a little more weight, but you don't have to round up wood in camp, your meals will be ready sooner and there is no evidence of a fire when you leave.

Human Waste: Not all soils are capable of breaking down human waste. The Pacific Northwest is a lot better suited to this than an arid environment, so take that into consideration. Dealing with human

The Restop Wilderness

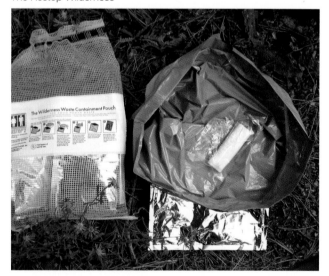

waste is not just about hiding it, it's about putting it where others don't have to smell it or step in it while it breaks down. If you're going to bury it, walk up and away from the river to find an out-of-the-way spot. If you're doing Upper Cherry Creek, camping on granite slabs with twenty of your best friends for three days while you wait for the water to come down, you're going to be hard pressed to find enough suitable places in which to answer the call. You might consider one of the many bag systems for carrying it out—Restop or Wag Bag are two good ones. I see a game of rocks paper scissors to determine who gets to pack that one out.

Other User Groups: You may not be the only ones out there and not everyone is as excited as you about the sweet line you just nailed. People out fishing and hiking are a couple of the other user groups you are likely to run into and they aren't always happy to see us. Let them enjoy their experience too—that could include piece and quiet.

Group Size: When a group is too small or too large, safety can be compromised. In addition, your impact on the environment and other groups can be felt. Give it some thought.

Camp Selection: A big group leaves a big impact at a small site, and a small group doesn't need a big site. Be sensitive to other groups that might be on the run at the same time. If there are choices, head around the corner from another group so you can all feel like you have the place to yourselves. Areas with fragile soils or archeologically sensitive areas should be avoided.

GLOSSARY

12 o'clock: An indication of the bow's position when it is pointing directly upstream. All other hours of the clock use this as a reference point.

Aerial: A move that involves getting the complete boat and body out of the water.

Aggressive swimming: Actively swimming, usually with the front crawl technique, to move from one point in the river to another.

Brake: A surfing stroke that causes maximum resistance with the main current, used to pull the surfer downstream on the wave.

Back band: A padded, adjustable lower back support attached to the seat.

Back face: The opposite side of the paddle blade from the power face, used for reverse strokes and usually convex with a spine along its centre. (also non-power face)

Backside (of a wave): The part of a wave downstream of the peak, where water flows downhill.

Blast: Front surfing in the trough of a hole, with the stern under the foam pile.

Blunt: An aggressive spin from front surf to back surf that throws the stern into the air.

Boat tilt: The balancing of your weight on a single butt cheek or hip, which leans your boat on edge.

Body surfing position: The position assumed when floating through whitewater; feet downstream, arms out to the side, and the whole body as close to the surface as possible.

Body wind-up: The rotation of your upper body in the desired turning direction.

Boil: The feature created when water is forced directly upwards to the surface.

Boil line: The point on a hole's foam pile at which the water on the upstream side flows upstream, while the water on the downstream side flows downstream.

Boofing: The technique used to prevent the bow of your kayak from diving underwater when you paddle over a drop.

Bow: The front end of a kayak.

Bow draw: A technique used to turn the boat aggressively by planting the blade near the bow and pulling the bow toward it.

Bow pivot: A pivot turn where the pivot point is forward of the centre of the boat, achieved by slicing the bow underwater, which frees the stern to come around in the air.

Bulkhead: A specific adjustable foot brace system that moves as one unit and lets you apply pressure with most of your foot.

C-stroke: A combination stroke using the bow draw and forward stroke. Turns the boat while maintaining forward momentum.

Cartwheel: A standard, advanced playboating move done on flatwater and in holes, in which the bow and stern rotate around the body, staying 45 degrees or more past horizontal.

Clean: A playboating move that involves a full 360-degree rotation with only a single stroke.

Closed face: In the context of a draw, rotating the blade so that the power face is facing toward the stern.

Cockpit: The opening at the centre of the kayak.

Corner: The side of a hole that can be used for spinning, setting up advanced moves, or exiting.

Defensive swimming: Passively swimming on your back, keeping as flat and shallow as possible with your feet downstream to fend off obstructions. (also body surfing)

Diagonal line: A rescue line that spans the river, angled downstream so that a rescuer and victim can travel from one side to the other using the current to propel them.

Displacement hull: A rounded or V-shaped hull that creates a channel in the water.

Double pump: The action of winding up the bow.

Downstream: The direction in which the water is flowing.

Downstream V: The shape formed by the main current in most cases, usually indicating the deepest and safest route.

Draw strokes: Dynamic strokes that either pull water towards or push water away from the side of the boat
at any point along its length for a variety of effects.

Dry top: A nylon top with a variety of possible water resistant coatings and latex gaskets at the wrists and neck to keep water out. A smart choice for cold water or cold days.

Duffek stroke: An open-face bow draw used to stop the forward momentum of the boat and turn aggressively toward the blade.

Eddy: A relatively calm section of water in the river, formed by the deflection of current around an obstruction.

Eddy hopping: Working your way down the river by moving from one eddy to the next.

Eddy line: The point along which the eddy current and the main current collide.

Edge: The part of a kayak where the sidewall meets the hull.

Face (of a wave): The part of a wave upstream of the peak and downstream of the trough, in which water is flowing uphill.

Ferry: The technique used to move laterally across the main current.

Flat spin: Using a flat hull's planing capabilities to change your kayak's direction on the green part of the wave.

Flatwater: Water without current.

Foam pile: The aerated, recirculating water that forms the white part of a hole.

Green water: The non-aerated water that flows into and under a hole.

Gliding draw: A draw planted at the hips while the boat is moving to act as a keel, allowing the boat to carve a smooth turn as opposed to spinning out.

Grab loop: A handle made of webbing at both the bow and stern of a kayak. Used mostly to carry with, but also in some rescue situations.

Gradient: The amount that a given section of river drops vertically over a given distance. Generally measured in feet per mile or metres per kilometre.

Hand of God: A rescue technique wherein the rescuer reaches over the upside-down boat and flips it back up.

Helical flow: The circular, spiralling or tumbling motion of water that results from one force acting on it in one direction while another force acts on it in an opposing direction.

Helmet: A plastic or composite piece of head gear designed to protect a paddler's noggin against impact from rocks, large fish or rafters. (also lid)

High brace: A technique using the front face of the blade to either recover from a moment of instability or as support to help prevent flipping over.

Hole (Hydraulic): A type of wave in which the water piles up on itself, forcing aerated water back upstream and into the trough.

Hull: The bottom of a kayak.

Hydraulic: A feature formed when water flows over a ledge and recirculates back into its own trough, becoming aerated and lighter in colour. (also hole, stopper)

Kick flip: A horizontal pirouette performed while launching from the peak of a wave.

Laminar flow: The streamline motion of water as it moves along a consistent, predictable path, such as the main flow in the centre of the river.

Loop: An airborne flip, done either forward or backward.

Low brace: A technique using the back face of the blade to either recover from a moment of instability or as support to help prevent flipping over.

Mechanical advantage: This is the added force applied to the load in a rescue situation, gained by redirecting the rescue line so that it is pulling from multiple points on the load.

Open face: In the context of a draw, rotating the blade
so that the power face is facing toward the bow.

Peak: The highest point on a wave.

Peel-out: The action of pulling out of an eddy, into current.

Peel-in: The action of pulling into an eddy, from current.

Pirouette: Spinning a kayak around on its end.

Pivot turn: An efficient change of direction that involves slicing one end of the kayak underwater, freeing the other to come around in the air.

PFD: Personal Flotation Device. Designed to float a swimmer in the water, but not necessarily with the face out of the water. (also life jacket)

Pillow: The area of still water that is piled against the upstream face of a rock.

Pin: The entrapment of a boat in current, by rocks.

Pin kit: A kit containing the basic rescue gear, including carabiners, pulleys, prussiks, and webbing. It is used to free pinned kayaks in a variety of situations.

Planing hull: A flat hull that does not displace water. When surfing, this feature allows the boat to spin on the water's surface with minimal friction. (also flat hull)

Pogies: Mitten-like attachments to a paddle shaft, used to keep cold water off the hands. Nice alternative to gloves because they allow direct contact with the shaft.

Pool-drop: A type of river that is characterized primarily by distinct rapids separated by calmer sections of water. (also ledge-drop)

Pourover: A sticky hydraulic formed by water flowing over a vertical or nearly vertical drop. Because the water pours straight down, it makes a deep depression in the river. This causes more water to recirculate from further downstream.

Power stroke: A vertical or past-vertical forward stroke that has minimal impact on spin momentum.

Power face: The side of the paddle blade that is used for forward strokes. It is generally concave and smooth. (also front face)

Reactionary: A diagonal wave formed when the water "reacts" off of an obstruction of some sort (for example, a boulder or a hole).

Recirculating: Refers to the action of the aerated water in a hole that is moving upstream.

Rescue vest: A specialized PFD with a quick release chest harness for tethered rescues and various other rescue-oriented features.

Rocker: A design feature whereby the middle of the hull is lower than the two ends. The more rocker, the greater the height difference between the middle and ends.

Roll: A technique, performed in a variety of ways, used to right an overturned kayak.

Rooster-tail: A spout of water that is being deflected into the air by an obstruction just under the surface.

Rudder: A blade that is planted in the water to control a front or back surf.

Scouting: The act of looking at a rapid, from shore or in your boat.

Scull: The action of taking strokes with paddle blades angled so that they continuously work their way to the surface.

Seam (of a hole): The point in the trough of a hole at which the foam pile meets the green water.

Seam (of a pillow): The line dividing the current that flows into the rock from upstream and the rock's pillow.

Shoulder (of a wave): The sides of a wave.

Side surfing: Establishing a balanced position on a single hip in the trough of a hole, while being held perpendicular to the main current by the hole's recirculating water.

Sidewall: The side of the kayak, between the deck and hull.

Sieve: An underwater passage that allows water through, but that often stops larger objects.

Skull cap: A neoprene or fuzzy rubber cap worn under the helmet to prevent ice cream headaches in cold water.

Splash top: A nylon top with a variety of possible water resistant coatings. May have neoprene gaskets or not, but does not keep water out completely. (also paddle jacket)

Spray skirt: A skirt made of neoprene or nylon that is worn around the paddler's waist and fits securely around the cockpit rim to prevent water from entering the boat. (also spray deck, deck, skirt)

Squirt boat: An ultra-low-volume kayak designed to work with the currents below the surface.

Stall: Balancing a kayak on end.

Stern: The back end of a kayak. (also tail)

Stern draw: A technique used to turn or steer the boat by planting the paddle near the stern and pulling the
boat toward it or prying the boat away from it.

Stern pivot: A pivot turn where the pivot point is behind the centre of the boat, achieved by slicing the stern underwater, which frees the bow to come around in the air.

Stern pry: A modification of the stern draw, used to steer the boat, primarily as a rudder while surfing.

The back face of the blade is used to pry the stern away from the paddle.

Stern squirt: A 360-degree pirouette with the bow in the air that is initiated with a back sweep.

Strainer: An obstruction in the river that allows water through, but stops larger objects.

Surfer's left: The left side of the river when looking upstream (from a surfer's perspective).

Surfer's right: The right side of the river when looking upstream (from a surfer's perspective).

Surge: A fluctuation in the size of a water feature.

T-rescue: A rescue situation in which the rescuer offers an end of their kayak to an upside-down paddler for their use to hip-snap themselves upright.

Tag line: A line spanning the section of river where a rescue situation is in progress, used to stabilize the victim by lifting them clear of the water.

Tethered rescue: A rescue situation wherein the rescuer swims out to contact and retrieve the victim while attached by a quick release system to a rope (the tether).

Thigh brace: Contoured padding attached to the sides of the seat inside boats to create a snug fit, allow better control and prevent the paddler from slipping out when upside down. (also thigh hook)

Throw rope: A coated polypropylene or Spectra cord between 50 and 150 feet long in a nylon bag, used in a variety of rescue situations.

Torso rotation: Winding up the torso to involve major muscle groups in strokes as it unwinds.

Tongue: A weak spot in a hole that water flows through freely.

Tow line: A short line attached to a rescuer by a quick release system, typically used to tow a kayak to shore.

Trough: The lowest point in a hole.

Turbulent flow: Less predictable than laminar or helical flow, this refers to disturbances in the water that last an instant or not much longer.

Undercut: A rock whose underside has been eroded over time and which water is forced to flow underneath.

Upstream: The direction from which water is flowing.

Vector pull: A basic technique for multiplying forces in a rescue situation, achieved by pulling the centre of a rescue line perpendicularly to the direction it is moving the load.

Volume: The amount of water in the river, measured in terms of how much water flows past a given point in a given period of time. Generally classified as high, medium or low and measured in cubic feet or cubic metres per second (cfs or cms).

Wave train: A series of waves.

Wave wheel: A cartwheel initiated as one launches from the peak of a wave.

Wet exit: Exiting an upside-down kayak in the water. (also swimming)

Whirlpool: A section of downward spiralling current that forms where opposing flows collide.

Z-drag: A rescue system that gains mechanical advantage by redirecting the rescue line several times. The more redirections, the higher the multiplication of forces achieved.

More Great Books from Fox Chapel Publishing

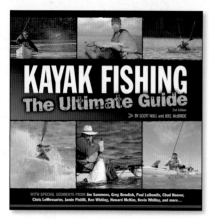

**Kayak Fishing: The Ultimate
Guide 2nd Edition**
ISBN: 978-1-56523-638-7 **$24.95**

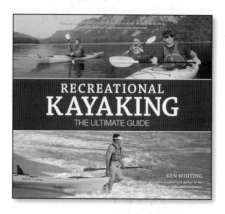

**Recreational Kayaking
The Ultimate Guide**
ISBN: 978-1-56523-640-0 **$19.95**

The Playboaters Handbook II
ISBN: 978-1-896980-74-4 **$22.95**

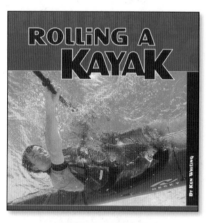

Rolling a Kayak
ISBN: 978-1-56523-645-5 **$16.95**

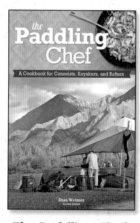

**The Paddling Chef,
Second Edition**
ISBN: 978-1-56523-714-8 **$16.95**

Camp Cooking in the Wild
ISBN: 978-1-56523-715-5 **$19.95**

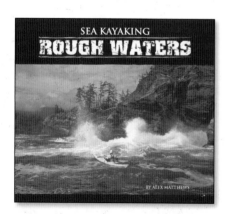

Sea Kayaking Rough Waters
ISBN: 978-1-56523-633-2 **$19.95**

**Canoeing: The Essential
Skills and Safety**
ISBN: 978-1-896980-69-0 **$19.95**

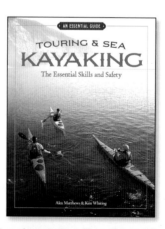

**Touring & Sea Kayaking The
Essential Skills and Safety**
ISBN: 978-1-896980-71-3 **$19.95**

Look for These Books at Your Local Bookstore or Specialty Retailer or at *www.FoxChapelPublishing.com*